CW01214130

IMPACT TO CONTACT
The Shag Harbour Incident

Chris Styles & Graham Simms — Arcadia House Publishing

Shag (2): noun – Marine birds with a distinctive crest, related to the cormorant.*(Phalacrocorax aristotelis or P. Punctatus, family Phalacrocoracidae)*

© 2013 Arcadia House Publishing.

All Rights Reserved.

This book or any portion thereof may not be reproduced or used in any manner whatsoever without the express written permission of the publisher except for the use of brief quotations in a book review.

Printed in Canada
First Printing, 2013
ISBN 978-0-9919807-0-3
Arcadia House Publishing
PO Box 36130, Spring Garden Road
Halifax, Nova Scotia,
B3J 3S9
www.arcadiahousepub.com

Contents

1   Preface

SECTION 1: IMPACT
9   Chapter 1: The Crash
19   Chapter 2: "The Night of the UFOs"
37   Chapter 3: The Quest
51   Chapter 4: Shelburne
65   Chapter 5: UFO Down Under
79   Chapter 6: The Sightings Expedition

SECTION 2: CONTACT
93   Chapter 7: Opportunity and Peril
107   Chapter 8: The Twenty Year Picnic: Making the Case for an Extended ET Presence in Nova Scotia
129   Chapter 9: UFOs and Shelburne County Folklore
147   Chapter 10: Contact
159   Chapter 11: Shag Harbour's Subtle Realm

SECTION 3: INSIGHT
195   Chapter 12: The Smith Encounter
207   Chapter 13: In Search of "Mace Coffee"
221   Chapter 14: The Master Plan
229   Chapter 15: The Cover-up?
241   Chapter 16: In The Middle of the Air
255   Reflections
265   Epilogue: The Research Continues
269   Acknowledgements
277   Appendix
279   References

Preface
Graham Simms

Chris Styles and I met in 2007 at film producer Mike MacDonald's Halloween costume party at an old Edwardian house in Halifax, Nova Scotia. Much of Mike's documentary work is of the paranormal variety, and his house was supposedly haunted. I knew Mike through filmmaker and author Paul Kimball, who was at the party dressed as Obi-Wan Kenobi. Although Mike, Paul, Chris, and I are all musicians, the thread that brought the four of us together was the common geography of the paranormal and UFOs. I immediately recognized Chris from his various media appearances.

Mike's documentary, *The Shag Harbour UFO Incident*, was aired in 2001 on CBC Television and on Space: The Imagination Station. Also that year, the Discovery Channel aired *The Shag Harbour UFO Incident: The New Roswell*, and in March 2006, the History Channel aired *UFO Files: Canada's Roswell*.[1] These documentaries all featured Chris describing his groundbreaking research unearthing the facts of the case known as the Shag Harbour Incident as well as his own experience as a twelve-year-old witnessing the UFO that glided up and down Halifax Harbour on October 4, 1967, the same night a UFO crashed into the ocean at Shag Harbour, Nova Scotia.

I sat down with Chris in Mike's dining room, unwittingly next to the fog machine, in the middle of science fiction characters walking around with drinks and intermittent blasts of thick mist that would periodically envelope our surroundings. As I had read Chris's book, *Dark Object* (co-authored with Don Ledger) and had seen the various Shag Harbour documentaries, I had questions about details of the Shag Harbour Incident and stayed next to Chris for the rest of the party. We had much to talk about. Chris had single-handedly unearthed the RCMP's UFO X-files among the archived papers of the Jesuit astronomer-priest Father M.W. Burke-Gaffney—who secretly investigated UFOs for the government at Saint Mary's University, where I had taken astronomy courses and had gone to church as a boy. So I already had respect for Chris's work and his determination and quickly felt a connection to him as a fellow searcher for truth. "If not truth," as he would say, "then at least what may be considered a valid hypothesis." I was excited to hear about his latest research.

We discussed how Chris had gained access to the classified RCMP document titled, The Master Plan: The Space Object Contingency Plan, the previously undiscovered policy document outlining how the RCMP were to respond to objects crashing from space and how they were to acquiesce to American forces. We also discussed the 1972 Smith Brothers Case, which included two documented encounters with a UFO that appeared first in Shag Harbour and then hovered above the nearby Baccaro NORAD base. There were new details about DND parapsychologist Mace Coffey who headed up the Shag Harbour UFO search. Chris had also had an enlightening conversation with Coffey's boss, Commander Rex Guy, shortly before he passed away. He also told me about a dive planned to examine the anomalies found on the bottom of Shag Harbour by the Bedford Institute of Oceanography (BIO), which ended up a success, unlike the problematic attempt to map the area for the TV show *Sightings*. These are all new leads in the Shag Harbour investigation; they form the bones of this book along with some other surprising discoveries that have been unearthed since Chris and I started working together.

During our Halloween conversation, Chris and I discovered that we both enjoyed Sherlock Holmes, and we discussed deductive and inductive reasoning, Steven King, and science fiction, including Arthur C. Clarke and Philip K. Dick. Chris admitted that he long found himself to be a lightning rod for people who have had unusual experiences, which I identified with. I found Chris to be rather grounded, perhaps not skeptical but highly discerning. He employs reason and science as filters and is not "a believer" in any dogmatic sense; he remains open-minded. This attitude mixed with natural curiosity, intuition, and a photographic memory make for a balanced UFO researcher.

Chris was curious how I had been drawn into the field and was interested to hear that I had spent time working at Dr. John Mack's Program for Extraordinary Experience Research (PEER), which was part of the Centre for Psychology and Social Change at Harvard's Cambridge Hospital in Massachusetts. This is where I became more familiar with Dr. Mack's investigation around understanding the cross-cultural, transformative, and transpersonal aspects of the UFO close encounter phenomenon. Dr. Mack was well known and probably the most respected scientist who researched people who had UFO and alien contacts. A Pulitzer Prize-winning biographer, he brought serious credentials and new intellectual vigour to the field of ufology, which Chris and I both agreed it needed.

We discussed the conclusions Mack came to, based on his years of in-depth interviews, case studies, and investigations. Mack and his colleagues at PEER were only able to take on a fraction of those who were looking for help, for answers to what was happening to them. When I worked in the office at PEER in 1996 I responded to hundreds of letters and phone calls from "experiencers," referring them to professionals in their area who were part of an international network of licensed therapists qualified and experienced in working with those affected by the UFO phenomenon. In total, Mack's centre must have received several hundred thousand inquiries over ten years. Through the centre, I would come to know several people who had these experiences and find out that some of my close friends were also holding this secret.

Chris and I became friends over the few months following the Halloween party. At our next meeting, I found out why he was interested in my experience learning about UFO contact, specifically the alien abduction phenomenon. Over coffee and tea in a downtown café, he told me that in May 2004 a letter and case-file had arrived, addressed to him, from a researcher in England asking for assistance in a case of claimed abduction, as there was a supposed connection to the Shag Harbour Incident. The information was sent by Phil Hoyle, whose organization, UFO Investigation and Research UK (UFOIRU), investigated contacts, sightings, and other unusual phenomena in England, including animal mutilations and crop circles. Hoyle included in the file background information leading up to this experiencer's ongoing interactions with "the occupants of craft" who claimed to be the same beings involved in the Shag Harbour Incident of 1967.

While Chris was familiar with the abduction aspect of the UFO contact phenomenon, he didn't know what he could do with the information from Phil. Chris had mostly focused on the nuts and bolts aspects of the Shag Harbour case, like tracking down official documents and talking to witnesses and examining and testing their testimony. But he knew there were sometimes beings associated with UFOs. Chris was obviously well-read in the literature and experienced in the field and so was familiar with the type of information associated with alien experiencers and abductees.

Ufology is not so much just the study of the behaviour of unidentified flying craft as the study of the experience of those who witness them. For me it was also about how the experience may transform the witnesses and what that means in terms of human evolution. Chris had come to notice the reality transformation (RT) aspects of various encounters, as it was often part of witnesses' observations, especially when they experienced degrees of contact with entities from UFOs. As an investigator, Chris knew he couldn't pick and choose data; he couldn't dismiss information that he didn't understand or feel comfortable with. As a UFO investigator, Chris was very familiar with the concept of human interactions with extraterrestrials (ETs). He had spoken several times with abductees and experiencers throughout North America, including a Nova Scotia couple that was startled to encounter beings on a blocked-off Government Point road in Shelburne and the navy diver and underwater photographer who filmed two exotic craft and their occupants underwater off the coast of Shelburne, Nova Scotia, in the days following the crash. These two events, which occurred between October 5 and 11, 1967, are mentioned briefly in Chris and Don's book, *Dark Object*, and the diver's story was also included in several feature documentaries. During our conversation at the Halloween party, Chris told me that DND parapsychologist Mace Coffey had suggested to the divers who had seen the aliens underwater at Shelburne that they be hypnotically regressed to see if the aliens had "tampered with them." Furthermore, on the lecture circuit Chris had became friends with famed early abductee, Betty Hill. So Chris may have found the information from the UK abductee interesting, but Paul H.'s claims that he met the aliens responsible for the Shag Harbour and Shelburne incidents would be impossible to verify.

Not knowing how to reach Chris directly, Phil Hoyle had sent his package for Chris to Mike MacDonald, the same film producer friend who had hosted the Halloween party. The file sat in Mike's office, lost behind a filing cabinet, for two years until Chris received it in 2006. Don Ledger subsequently had some limited contact with Phil via email. Chris wanted to address the material but had his hands full with the many ongoing aspects of the Shag Harbour investigation. At our coffee meeting, he asked me if I would like to take the file off his hands.

I was fairly comfortable with the patterns surrounding the phenomenon of UFO contact and abduction and was certainly interested in furthering investigations into the Shag Harbour Incident. So in March 2008, almost four years after it was sent, Chris placed the Hoyle file with me, asking me to give it some attention and to put it in some sort of perspective.

While this book reviews and furthers the relevant material covered in *Dark Object* and in that way could be seen as a sequel, it differs significantly from that book and is made up of important new material. In addition to the

PREFACE

aforementioned newly uncovered documents like The Master Plan, interviews with firsthand UFO witness Lawrence Smith and retired Maritime Commander Rex Guy, and the previously unexplored role of parapsychologist Mace Coffey, *Impact to Contact* also includes Chris's account of a newly uncovered dramatic UFO sighting by Pan Am airline pilots and crew over Shag Harbour the night before the crash, as well as new testimonies about UFO artifacts and an apparent cover-up by the Coast Guard. We also give more focus to the secret second part of the Shag Harbour UFO crash story, which occurred underwater adjacent to Canada's top secret Cold War military submarine detection base, the NORAD base at Shelburne, Nova Scotia, forty kilometres from Shag Harbour, where a flotilla of ships held station over two submerged UFOs for the week following the Shag Harbour Incident. Also included is an epilogue by David Cvet on his recent dive, following up on the anomalies found by BIO's underwater scans at Shag Harbour where the UFO touched down.

In addition to the analysis of the Paul H. abduction stories contained in the file from Phil Hoyle, my contribution to this book includes an overview of the political and military landscape in Canada surrounding the UFO phenomenon during the 1950s and 1960s; the indicators and reasons for a possible continuous UFO presence around Nova Scotia over the years; an examination of the folklore of the Shelburne County area as it relates to the paranormal; case studies of other documented UFO encounters in Nova Scotia around the time of the Shag Harbour Incident; and what these encounters are meant to convey and how the UFO phenomenon can expand our notions of reality to include more "subtle realms."

Chris and I felt it was important to add this new information to the collection of findings about Shag Harbour, as research kept revealing more facets of the phenomenon, putting it in a clearer perspective and deepening the mystery and importance of one of world's most fascinating and enduring UFO cases.

Endnote

1. My friend Paul Kimball's documentary, *Best Evidence: Top Ten UFO Cases*, which featured the Shag Harbour Incident as the sixth best international UFO case, premiered on Space later in 2007, after I met Chris at the Halloween party. It aired around the world.

SECTION 1

IMPACT

Chapter 1: The Crash
Graham Simms

"Reality is merely an illusion, albeit a very persistent one."
– Albert Einstein

"Reality is nothing but a collective hunch."
– Lily Tomlin

As long as mankind has watched the night sky we have seen strange lights and wondered if we are all alone in this universe. Since 1947, the dawn of the so called "modern UFO era," many people and even governments have asked the question, "Are we being visited?" Especially interesting are those cases where something quite tangible and real descends to crash upon the surface of the earth. Could such mishaps represent the penetration of our skies and defence systems by extraterrestrials? In the age of Stephen Spielberg and Google, clear and certain answers to such basic questions remain elusive or unsatisfying.

Anyone who is at all familiar with the field of UFO literature is well aware of the plethora of claims for UFO crash scenarios. Since 1947, UFOs have been seen to impact deserts, forests, and oceans. Many cases are easily dismissed. Some are shrouded in secrecy and cover-ups. Others become eclipsed by the ever expanding mythology that quickly grows larger than the body of evidence that supports the case in question.

The "big picture" is further clouded by the unfortunate fact that UFO research has become fractured into a dog's breakfast of competing belief systems. Beyond this, the situation is further clouded by governments, academics, and media sources that refuse to deal with the UFO phenomenon seriously. All three groups conspire to allow and even encourage a bewildered public to dismiss UFOs entirely. But some of us are not allowed to dismiss UFO reality so casually. If you are an air traffic controller or a pilot with unknown radar targets near a commercial aircraft or a police officer receiving reports of something strange crashing near people's homes, you do not have the luxury of playing "armchair skeptic." You have a duty to perform. You must investigate and grapple with the UFO problem.

At the time of publication of this book there is only one UFO crash scenario where the case is supported in that interpretation by government documents that are freely available and without any controversy as to their origin or authenticity (Randle 2000: 10). That case has become known as the Shag Harbour Incident. It remains open and unsolved and has been acknowledged by many to be Canada's most important UFO case and a compelling argument for UFO reality. This book examines the Shag Harbour Incident and its many implications with an open mind.

On the night of October 4, 1967, something profound occurred that would forever change how people think of the quaint, picturesque village of Shag Harbour on the Atlantic coast of Nova Scotia, Canada. On that moonless, clear, starry night, something that would defy explanation plunged into the ocean just off the coast. The impact of that mysterious entity would shatter the lives of the eyewitnesses and leave an indelible impression upon the tiny community. The knowledge and the lingering effects of that occurrence created ripples that moved outward to envelope the world in a Cold War incident that involved Soviet, US, Canadian, and British military forces. Following this impact and the surrounding events, the residents of Shelburne County, Nova Scotia, like the rest of the world, were left without answers to a great lingering mystery. Over time, as the Shag Harbour Incident would come to reveal itself, it has provided insight into the global and ancient UFO phenomenon. Today, we are able to make connections and gain insights into what actually happened. Observations have been made. Conclusions have been drawn. Despite government apathy and/or culpability, we have a clearer picture for the questions raised by the bewildered people of Shag Harbour and those curious people in the rest of the world who wonder about the varied nature of life itself within this vast universe.

October 4, 1967

Shag Harbour is a quiet village with a population of about four hundred. Outwardly, it is not unlike other fishing communities nestled among the coves and inlets along the South Shore of Nova Scotia. The village and its harbour, called "the Sound" locally, is at the southwestern end of the Nova Scotian peninsula and looks over the Gulf of Maine.

It was around 11:20 pm on a Wednesday night, and most of the people who were out at that hour were teenagers. Couples parked at the make-out

CHAPTER 1: THE CRASH

wharf in Shag Harbour had an unobstructed view of the water and the open sky above. They noticed an object with lights moving slowly and silently across their line of sight. Within a few minutes it was closer to them and they could see it better, only a couple hundred feet out and up.[1] The dark object behind the lights seemed to be changing its shape. It stalled on its glide path and hovered before tilting and falling into the water with a whistle, bang, and flash (Styles 1996: 27).

Moments earlier, eighteen-year-old Dave Kendricks was driving his 1962 Chevy with his friend Norm Smith, heading westward down Highway 3, the road that hugs the Atlantic coastline. They had been visiting their girlfriends, who lived on nearby Cape Sable Island. It was a school night and already past curfew. Dave and Norm were casually talking about girls, their favourite subject. They noticed lights in the sky while they were still three miles east of Shag Harbour. Norm saw them first, just over the trees. What they saw was four flashing lights. The lights were evenly spaced, low in the night sky, and descending steadily toward the harbour. Norm later said that in those first moments he thought that the pinhole lights were coming from within an aircraft's windows, but he knew there was nothing normal about the flashing lights. The object they were attached to was unlike a conventional aircraft in every way. It was too low, completely silent, and at times seemed to be almost standing still or hovering. Suddenly, the object began to descend rapidly at a forty-five degree angle and was soon lost from sight behind the treeline. The boys were puzzled and scared and drove faster hoping to regain sight of the mysterious lights (Ledger 2007: 82).

A local eighteen-year-old fisherman named Laurie Wickens was driving westbound along Highway 3 just east of Shag Harbour with his girlfriend and their three friends. As Wickens negotiated the curves and hills, he and his friends also noticed the same strange lights through the windshield. The lights sat low in the night sky and glowed with an odd yellow hue. At first the four lights were on a horizontal plane and together they appeared to be at least sixty feet across and perhaps only two hundred feet above the water. The display flashed sequentially in a coordinated way. The pattern was a simple one, two, three, four, and then all together, only to repeat over and over. It was difficult to discern the dark object's form against the moonless night sky. It was clear that the lights were losing altitude. The object then tilted downward and began to descend toward the harbour.

As Laurie's car approached Prospect Point, the lights were briefly out of sight behind the treeline. Suddenly, Wickens and the others heard a whistle and a whooshing sound followed by a loud bang. Ten seconds later, when their line of sight through the trees was restored, Wickens and company were shocked to see a pale yellow dome of light floating up the waters of the Sound (Ibid.: 78–79).

Just past make-out wharf, Laurie skidded the car to a stop in the parking lot of the Irish moss factory. All five teens jumped out and ran to the embankment overlooking the Sound for a better view. There in the water, six to seven hundred feet offshore, the object bobbed in the ebbing tide. Now only a single light illuminated the top of the dark object with at least eight to ten feet of vertical relief showing above the waterline. A crowd of locals was gathering next to the moss plant, all of them witnesses to this strange event. Suddenly Laurie realized he should report the incident to the police, and the nearest pay phone was two miles away in the village of Woods Harbour. So he got back in the car with his girlfriend and sped up the road to the pay phone at the Irving gas station to call the nearby RCMP detachment in Barrington Passage. The call was logged at 11:25 pm (Ibid.: 80).

Laurie Wickens was the first to report the crash to the RCMP. Corporal Victor Werbicki answered the phone. The thirty-seven-year-old corporal was the commanding officer of the Barrington Passage detachment and was manning his post with fellow RCMP officer Ron O'Brien. Laurie excitedly told Corporal Werbicki that he and others had just watched some kind of aircraft go down into the Sound at Shag Harbour. The constable knew Wickens and asked if he had been drinking. Werbicki went on to tell Laurie that if he had been drinking or was pulling some sort of prank, the ramifications from a false report would be serious indeed. From the urgency in Wickens's voice, Cpl. Werbicki felt that the young man's call could be in earnest. And besides, his own anxiety level began to increase just at the thought of a downed aircraft and its consequences. Wickens went on to excitedly explain that he and several others had gathered on the shore next to the Irish moss factory and had watched the strange light floating toward open sea. Werbicki asked for the number of the pay phone and told Wickens to stay put and he would call him back.

Werbicki took another call. On the incoming line was Mary Banks of Maggie Garrons Point. She had seen the event from across the Sound and reported that lights hovered in the sky and then crashed into the water. She also heard the whistling noise, followed by a bang, and was under the impression that it was an aircraft crash. As Cpl. Werbicki hung up the phone it immediately rang. Another caller, from Bear Point, just southeast of Shag

CHAPTER 1: THE CRASH

Harbour, reported the same details as Mary Banks and also felt that an aircraft was down. Corporal Werbicki radioed the only police cruiser on patrol. Constable Ron Pond was on highway patrol. He responded that he had recently driven through Shag Harbour and had seen nothing unusual but turned around and sped toward the moss plant. Once again, as soon as Werbicki hung up another call came in. This time a woman and her daughter living on Cape Sable Island, thirteen miles northeast of Shag Harbour, had seen lights, flashing in sequence, coming down from the sky.

It was at this point Corporal Werbicki called the nearby radar base of the North American Aerospace Defense Command (NORAD), CFS Barrington at Baccaro, and explained the developing situation. They reported no military air operations in the area at that time. Further checks were made with the Rescue Coordination Centre in Halifax, but once again there were no reports of downed aircraft or even overdue arrivals.

Werbicki picked up the list of local fishermen who were attached to the Coast Guard Marine Rescue Auxiliary and headed down toward the Sound in his cruiser with fellow RCMP officer Ron O'Brien. By this time Constable Pond had arrived at the Sound and joined the growing crowd on the shore that was watching the pale yellow light. Less than fifteen minutes had elapsed since Laurie first called the RCMP.

Further east on Highway 3, Dave Kendricks dropped Norm Smith off, then drove home and went to bed after telling his mother about the mysterious lights they had seen. As Norm walked up the incline to his house he noticed the same bright object, now almost on the harbour surface. He dashed into the house, brought his father Wilfred outside, and pointed out the object. Wilfred ran back into the house, woke up his brother Lawrence, and met Norm at the truck. Uncle Lawrence tried to look out the window, figured it was nothing, and went back to sleep. He had to get up in a few hours and pilot his fishing boat, but fearing the object could be an airplane that had crashed into the water, father and son Norm and Wilfred Smith decided they had better drive down to the water to get a closer look. As they attempted to turn onto Highway 3, Werbicki and O'Brien's police cruiser sped by "like a bat out of hell" with its lights flashing. Norm and his father followed the cruiser. The Smiths caught up with the RCMP constables and joined the dozen or so onlookers who were gathered on the shore next to the Irish moss factory. Everyone was watching the curious object on the water's surface less than a thousand feet away.

Constable Pond had retrieved his field glasses from the trunk of his cruiser and had watched the object for some time. He felt that the yellow light was moving under its own power and not merely adrift in the ebbing tide. Pond noted that the object was leaving a dense trail of yellow sparkling foam. When Corporal Werbicki arrived, he took over the binoculars and instructed Pond to take witness statements. One of the residents had seen the UFO without interruption descending from the sky into the harbour and described the object as plummeting at "aircraft speed." In the moment before impact someone else noticed a brief streak or flash of light, "coming from a point exactly midway between the first and third lights." Like the others, he also heard a one or two second whistling sound "like a bomb dropping."[2] Everyone near the shoreline expressed concern for the possibility of survivors. The object was now further from shore and lower in the water. It was clearly making progress toward open sea.

As Cst. Pond continued to watch the object's progress moving through the Sound, he noticed a very important detail. It caught his attention that when the UFO passed in front of the Budget buoy it completely obscured the fixed navigational aid from his line of sight. This told the observant officer that the craft exhibited at least eight feet of vertical relief above the waterline as that's the well-known dimension of the Budget buoy.

Two of the three RCMP officers, Ron O'Brien and Cpl. Victor Werbicki, commandeered an open boat to row out toward the light. Constable Pond remained on the shore at the moss plant. As the two officers began to approach the object, the light suddenly disappeared. As soon as they got back on shore Werbicki instructed O'Brien to call the Rescue Coordination Centre (RCC) in Halifax. The call was logged at 11:38 PM.[3] Corporal Werbicki left to wake Bradford (Brath) Shand and asked for his assistance in a search and rescue operation. The belief that there could be survivors made the operation one of haste and instinct. Shand's response and effort was immediate. Brath alerted Lawrence Smith, another local fisherman with good equipment and a lifetime of local experience. Their fishing boats, *Rhonda D* and *Joan Priscilla* were moored together on the outside of "the pack." Within ten minutes Lawrence and Shand met up with the mounties and volunteers, cast off from Prospect Wharf, and gunned the engines. The roar of the twin diesels made idle chatter impossible and left the men with their thoughts of dread as to what they might find—debris? bodies? Or something completely unexpected.

The two thirty-foot Cape Islander lobster boats arrived on the scene within a few minutes. Norm Smith was on Shand's boat as they worked together. Constable O'Brien went on Lawrence Smith's boat and they followed Shand to the impact site. As they approached the area, they entered a swath of glittering

CHAPTER 1: THE CRASH

yellow foam estimated to be eighty feet wide by a half mile long and three to four inches thick. They cut the engines, listening and scanning. Lawrence Smith observed one to one-and-a-half inch bubbles percolating up from below, which suggested to him that something had sunk immediately under them. He also noted the distinct smell of sulfur. Lawrence later reported that at that time there were so many bubbles that he was concerned with the *Joan Priscilla* losing buoyancy. Oddly, they found that the foam did not adhere to a net or clothing. On Shand's boat, Constable O'Brien observed one of the young men dip his arms into the foam. When he withdrew his arms his shirt sleeves were covered not in the foam itself, but only in an oily residue. The two boats navigated a rough grid pattern of the area. Eventually, four more boats joined the search. The six Cape Islanders plied the water, their powerful lights searching for anything that might yield some answers.

The Rescue Coordination Centre contacted the Coast Guard who dispatched Coast Guard Cutter (CGC) 101 from nearby Clark's Harbour. The lifeboat arrived on the scene just after midnight during the early morning of October 5. Based on what Lawrence Smith overheard coming from the RCC in Halifax on the shortwave radio, he began doubting that they were in reality searching for a crashed airplane. Norm confirmed to his uncle that he didn't know what he had seen. The RCC confirmed that according to their inquiries, which would have included checks with airports and NORAD facilities, there were no reports of unaccounted for civilian or military aircraft. Around three o'clock that morning the fishing boats and the Coast Guard Cutter temporarily halted their search to resume their effort at first light.[4]

Meanwhile, within a half hour to an hour after the UFO crash, (12:00 to 12:35 AM local time, 0300-0335 Zulu Time) there was a Strategic Air Command (SAC) bomber reconnaissance flight and a US Navy air photo mission underway directly over the Shag Harbour area. The Navy photo reconnaissance jets most likely came from the aircraft carrier group that was in the Gulf of Maine at the time, practising operations for the war in Vietnam. The carrier group was approximately one hundred miles away from Shag Harbour, ten minutes by air in the standard F-4 Phantom II carrier jets that fly up to 1,400 mph or Mach 2.2. The SAC operation consisted of a nuclear armed B-52 that came from Loring Base in Maine. From 1953 until 1994, Loring was the host base for B-52s, KC 135 Stratotankers, and air-refuelling squadrons. The 35-minute SAC operation over Shag Harbour meant the B-52, which flew up to 600 mph, would have to be repeatedly flying tight circles over the area.

By 10:20 AM, RCC was referring to the missing object as an unidentified flying object (UFO) in its communications with the Department of National Defence (DND) headquarters, as it was clear that there were no overdue commercial aircraft and none were reported missing.

Where had the object gone? Bubbles were observed near its last known surface position. There was a half mile trail of froth, foam, and oily residue leading out toward open sea. However, no debris or wreckage was ever found. A four-day Royal Canadian Navy underwater search, which started the morning after the crash, produced "nil results" (Styles 1996: 28).

The Condon Committee, a scientific group formed at the University of Colorado in 1966 to examine whether the United States Air Force should continue studying UFOs, filed a report on the Shag Harbour Incident. According to their report, when the UFO hit the water it was only two or three hundred yards offshore (Condon 1969: 352). At least sixteen named witnesses were documented as having seen the UFO in the water, including the three RCMP officers.

It seemed to be the case of the one that got away. And yet, the witnesses were all certain that a sixty-foot dark object with four bright lights had flown, hovered, and crashed into the waters of Shag Harbour. Many questions were left unanswered in the dark object's wake.

What could be both aerodynamic and hydrodynamic in the 1960s? Where was the UFO headed? What was the purpose or mission, and how much did the military really know? Rumors and speculation would abound within the tiny fishing village and throughout the UFO community. Shag Harbour would be thrust into the media "limelight" as the Canadian navy searched for a downed flying saucer. It would take decades before the whole story would surface, but once it did the Shag Harbour UFO crash would prove to be just the tip of a much larger Cold War iceberg.

CHAPTER 1: THE CRASH

Chapter 1 Endnotes

1. The imperial system of measurement is used when discussing events that predate Canada's adoption of the metric system.
2. Priority RCMP Telex 14, Oct. 4, 1967, from Barrington Passage Detachment to Halifax RCMP HQ, Burke-Gaffney Collection, Saint Mary's University Archives, Halifax, NS.
3. Ibid.
4. Coast Guard Cutter 101, ship's log entry 109, October 4–5, 1967.

Chapter 2: "The Night of the UFOs"
Graham Simms

"The beginning of knowledge is the discovery of something that we do not understand."
– Frank Herbert

"Discovery consists of what everyone has seen and thinking what no one has thought."
– Albert Szent-Gyorgyi

The UFO crash in Shag Harbour was not the only UFO event to occur in the skies of Nova Scotia on the night on October 4, 1967. In the hours before Shag Harbour's impact and well into the next morning many strange lights were seen throughout the province and over the waters of the Atlantic, the Gulf of Maine, and the Bay of Fundy. In the ufological terminology of the day, the sudden increase in reported UFO sightings was referred to as a "flap." Local investigators and Canadian researchers would come to dub the event as "the night of the UFOs."

As the media focused its attention of the Shag Harbour UFO crash and the subsequent military search for a submerged flying saucer, the myriad of other UFO sightings that occurred on the night of October 4, 1967, were quickly forgotten by the public at large but not by the authorities or the eyewitnesses. These multi-witness UFO cases added to the pressure felt by DND headquarters in Ottawa to provide some answers. They also added weight to some of the many speculations that seemed unthinkable just the day before.

Were the UFO sightings connected? Did they in fact represent some kind of penetration of our skies and defence systems by extraterrestrials? Where did they come from, and why were they here? And just what did the military know? Perhaps more important to the authorities was just who was asking these questions. The difficult questions regarding purpose of mission and point of origin were not coming from the press but from the ordinary people who had borne witness to something they did not understand. Insurance salesmen, off-duty police, and twelve-year-old children were putting pen to paper and writing to whomever they thought might provide some answers and who might make use of the curious data. People were upset with the lack of answers.

Mahone Bay, Nova Scotia
Around 8:30 pm on October 4, 1967, twelve-year-old Darrell Dorey, his sister Annette, and his mother were standing on the lawn of their historic home in the town of Mahone Bay on the South Shore of Nova Scotia, 173 kilometres from Shag Harbour. All three members of the Dorey family were watching a large yellow "blob" of light in the night sky. A smaller steady light made its way toward the larger anomalous light and eventually merged with the larger object. Suddenly the unusual display disappeared as if someone threw a switch. Mrs. Dorey invoked the call for bed and the family went inside. However, the event was not quite over.

From his bedroom window, Darrell spotted another UFO. This time it looked like a small twinkling star except for its unusual manoeuvres. This strange light darted about the night sky with impossibly fast changes of position. After several minutes the light shot silently toward the southern horizon, where it disappeared for good.

Darrel Dorey immediately put pen to paper and described his UFO sighting as best he could. Darrel wrote his report before hearing the first media coverage about the UFO crash in Shag Harbour (Ledger 2007: 73). Then, on the morning of Saturday, October 7, 1967, after he'd heard about the crash, he wrote a letter to the Base Commander at CFB Greenwood.

To the Commander of CFB Greenwood

Dear Sir,

I am writing you a short note about the shiny object (UFO) which plunged into Shelburne Harbour. I've placed a UFO report in with this note. The thing I saw was in the sky a number of nights, I've been told, but I saw it only once and I keep a pretty good track of what goes on in the night sky. The UFO I saw was in the sky the

CHAPTER 2: "THE NIGHT OF THE UFOS"

night before the morning that it plunged into the harbour and the last time that I saw it, it was headed for Shelburne.

I close for now.

Yours truly,

Darrel Dorey

PS I would be pleased if you would write back

Here is the report Darrel enclosed with his letter.

UFO Report

Time – 8:32 PM

Place – Out front of our house

Number of observers – 6 known

Place in the sky – 12 degrees above the normal horizon

Length of time sighted – 8:32 PM until 9:00 PM

October 4, 1967 report

8 PM I was called to my window. We were my mother, Annette, my sister, and myself. We went outside.

The sky visible to me was 100 % clear of all clouds. What we watched was a yellow sphere and an oval shaped cloudish thing. It went through a procedure when we first watched it. It was in two parts, sphere and oval. After about 5 minutes or so it merged to take the form of an oval. On the left was what appeared to be a red star. At first, when this object was still two separate forms, it would dim down and then flare up. It moved north to south and eventually covered up the red star. After about 10 minutes it formed one shape and rose a little higher and the star lowered to about 5 degrees above the horizon. By that time the oval shape was almost gone. One thing that puzzles me is that the star shaped object grew brighter as it went on and it showed bursts of speed from side to side until after awhile it completely disappeared. And stars just don't disappear like that. (Ibid.)

Young Darrell Dorey did get a written response from the CO of CFB Greenwood—a form thank you letter. It did not contain any answers.

The MV *Nickerson*, at sea south of Sambro, NS

On the night of October 4, 1967, at about 9:00 pm, Captain Leo Howard Mersey and eighteen crew members were fishing some thirty-two miles south of the Sambro Light. Conditions were clear and the lights of Halifax could be seen in the distance. Captain Mersey stared transfixed by an object that had three red lights that shone so intensely they were difficult to stare directly at for any amount of time. The fishing vessel's Decca Radar indicated that the object was some sixteen miles away from the ship's position. Radar also indicated that there were three other objects about six miles from the one with the bright red lights. These other three radar targets could not be seen.[1]

At 11:00 pm the object with the three red lights shot straight up into the air until it disappeared from sight. On its ascent the object only displayed a single red light. Most of the crew watched the display. Captain Mersey contacted the harbourmaster in Halifax and the Rescue Coordination Centre but they could shed no light upon the mystery. One of the crew members heard in a radio

CHAPTER 2: "THE NIGHT OF THE UFOS"

broadcast that UFOs were being sighted throughout Nova Scotia and brought the information to Captain Mersey's attention. Before the skipper could figure out what to do with his observations a request was received from RCMP headquarters in Halifax for a personal interview.

On Saturday, October 7, 1967, Leo Mersey gave a statement and signed a UFO report at the RCMP detachment in Lunenburg, NS. That signed report, witnessed by Cst. D.H. Rahn, was classified as an X-file, the designation the RCMP used for UFO files. It was forwarded to the Barrington Passage detachment that was handling the Shag Harbour investigation and to the "Air Desk" at DND headquarters in Ottawa. That report would even find its way to the University of Colorado and become part of the Condon Committee's study of UFOs that was being conducted for the United States Air Force.

The *Nickerson* sighting never received any media coverage. It would, however, provide crucial evidence that would help validate and separate the then unknown "Shelburne Story," which is dealt with in chapter 4 of this book. Leo Mersey never realized the importance of his statement to the RCMP, especially these closing sentences: "I had never seen anything like it before, but it sounds like the thing that they are looking for down off Shelburne or off of Barrington Passage. When the object left it went straight up in the air with only one red light."[2]

Halifax Harbour, NS
A woman was driving along the Halifax side of the harbour when she spotted an unusual orange sphere near the ferry wharf. She pulled over and watched as the UFO made its way up the harbour then moved toward the Dartmouth Marine Slips near Dartmouth Cove. The woman contacted a local radio station and her report became news. The radio station was soon flooded with calls. The next day the *Halifax Chronicle-Herald* carried her story explaining how the UFO continued to trace the east side of Halifax Harbour and make its way toward the harbour entrance and open sea (MacLeod 1967: 1). Strangely, no one else reported seeing the event. The large orange sphere would have passed many vessels including those docked at the Atlantic headquarters for the Canadian Coast Guard. However, it is likely that there were many other non-reporting witnesses. In fact it would appear that the orange sphere reported in the media was one and the same as the UFO seen by my co-author Chris Styles on the night of October 4, 1967, when he was twelve years old.

Chris first spotted the object from his bedroom window, which overlooked the Dartmouth Cove portion of Halifax Harbour. He ran up to the upstairs hallway and borrowed his grandfather's field glasses to get a better look. Ironically, Chris's maternal grandfather was on vacation from his job at the Dartmouth Marine Slips. He was visiting the Shag Harbour area and would be one of the many non-reporting eyewitnesses to the UFO crash in Shag Harbour, which occurred just one hour after Chris's UFO sighting.

When young Chris looked through the binoculars they revealed a large featureless sphere that glowed a dull orange similar to the colour of iron heated in a forge. It appeared to be hovering near the water's surface and moving in a leisurely course that traced the shoreline. Chris lost sight of the object as it became hidden behind several large ships moored at the Dartmouth Marine Slips. He then dropped the binoculars and ran to the nearby waterfront where Maitland Street meets the railway tracks between two warehouses.

When Chris regained sight of the UFO he suddenly realized his predicament. He was alone, on the waterfront, staring at a UFO that was steadily drawing near where he stood. Fear rooted him to the spot. He wanted to run but was overwhelmed by the size and the silence of the approaching orb that dwarfed some of the smaller vessels tied up at the nearby piers. He estimated the sphere to have an axis of sixty feet. Eventually, he found the impetus to run and made his way back up Maitland Street toward home. From over his shoulder, Chris saw the UFO continue on its shore hugging manoeuvre, as it passed the gap between the two waterfront warehouses at the foot of the street. He was relieved to see that the object made no notice of his presence or effort to flee the scene. Although Chris ceased to observe the UFO at that point, the object's course must have taken it quite near the backyards of Hazelhurst Street, which runs along the shore of Dartmouth Cove from the warehouse district and over to where the Canadian Coast Guard ships are moored.

As it turns out, one of the other witnesses to the Dartmouth Cove sighting was Dr. Maurice Coffey, better known as "Mace" to his friends and colleagues, who took in the event from his backyard at 48 Hazelhurst Street. Mace Coffey was a scientific consultant at DND's Maritime Command and would over the next few days be in charge of the search for Shag Harbour's UFO. The story of his contribution, unconventional methods, and eclectic career are dealt with in chapter 13.

CHAPTER 2: "THE NIGHT OF THE UFOS"

Digby Neck area, Bay of Fundy, NS

On the night of October 4, 1967, more than a dozen herring seiners were fishing along the north coast of Digby Neck. The *Quadra Isle* was positioned somewhere off Brier Island, Nova Scotia. Bright lights illuminated the nets that were being hauled aboard by the crew. For most of the evening things went the way that they always did under the watchful eye of Captain Walter Titus. But suddenly the skipper noticed that all work had ground to a halt. The men were distracted and transfixed by something hanging in the southwest sky.

Everyone was staring at a bright white light that appeared to be about the same size as that of the full moon, but the moon had already set earlier in the evening. The single light then went through a change and broke up into a triangle of lights. Then they flew from their position toward the western horizon and back again. The marine radio was full of chatter about the unusual aerial display.

Two of the seiners were then subjected to a dive bomb type of manoeuvre that frightened the men on board and even caught the attention of the Lent family who was watching the drama unfold from their home in Westport on Brier Island (Ledger and Styles 2001: 22–23). Thirty minutes later the UFOs broke off their "attack" and flew in a southeasterly direction until they disappeared from sight. The UFOs were the only topic of discussion on the marine radio for the rest of the night. No one who took in the spectacle has ever forgotten it, and it remains a topic of speculation whenever the local old timers tell their sea stories.

Arthur Lake, NS

Like many others who witnessed the events of "the night of the UFOs," RCMP Constable Ian Andrew was working and not simply taking in the night air. He was helping Nova Scotia Lands and Forest game wardens Bert Green, Don Brown, and Sonny Wagner who were attempting to stake out and catch deer poachers near Arthur Lake. The group of officers was in the forest just outside the village of Hassett, off Highway 340, about one hundred kilometres north of Shag Harbour.

While sitting and listening for any illegal activity, the small group of men suddenly noticed an unusual glowing object drift silently across the sky. Its track took it from the northwest to the southeast. It appeared as if the UFO was only 200 to 300 feet above the tree tops. Cst. Andrew also saw an object that looked something like an inverted candle flame. It appeared to have some kind of corona or plasma-like field around it. Small spark-like lights flew about the main object. One of the wardens pulled his compass and took a bearing as the object descended below the treeline (Ledger 2007: 77–78).

The next day the men met to discuss what they had witnessed the night before. They plotted their line of sight bearing on a map and extended the line. That bearing led to a point on the southwestern shore known as Shag Harbour. Cst. Andrew had already heard of the events and subsequent search effort underway in Shag Harbour and brought his colleagues up to speed.

These stories are but a handful of the many UFO sightings that together give the night of October 4, 1967, its unique title and status. These sightings affected the public in a different way from Shag Harbour's UFO crash. Most of these UFO cases received little to no media coverage. Their details eventually leaked and spread by word of mouth. Those that received mention in the press and on radio and television were soon forgotten once the media got its hooks into the Shag Harbour Incident. Cameras, microphones, and print space were reserved for the "meat and potatoes" case that held the possibility of physical evidence. And yet the "forgotten" cases left behind a legacy of both fear and wonder in the nearest local communities, and for the truly curious a hunger for more.

Fisherman wondered if their catches might suffer. Would there be a toxin or radiation that might precipitate or aggravate a fish kill? Could something foul or destroy their gear? Would other unknown objects come down to the earth? Might they land or crash into a home or building? There were stories in Shag Harbour of families that did not sleep for days over concerns of what might happen next. Rumours circulated throughout the southwestern shore's weekly newspapers that perhaps the navy divers had found something but were forbidden to say so. Of course this chain of logic led to the inevitable questions of what the government knew and whether they could be trusted to tell us the truth. Some media types began describing the mood on the east coast as one of "uforia." But that hardly compared to the "behind the scenes" mood in the back rooms of Ottawa's military establishment.

RCAF's "Air Desk," Ottawa

Shortly before the Shag Harbour crash of October 4, 1967, the groundwork was being laid in Ottawa to shrug off the yoke of troublesome UFO investigations. In fact, just a week before the incident a letter was sent from Brigadier N.H. Ross to Professor Greenwood at the National Research Council (NRC). It clearly stated DND's wish to transfer the responsibility for UFO

CHAPTER 2: "THE NIGHT OF THE UFOS"

investigations to the NRC, yet also emphasized its desire to coordinate and even limit the newly proposed effort. That letter appears below.

MEMORANDUM

V 2000-4 Vol. 2 (D Ops)

26 September, 1967

DSC

Attention: Mr. Greenwood

INVESTIGATION – UFO REPORTS

1. The DG OPS [Director of Operations] has recently prepared a memorandum for the MND's [Minister of National Defence] signature addressed to the National Research Council in which a recommendation was made to transfer the responsibility for investigating UFOs from DND to NRC.

2. This Directorate has been a strong proponent in advocating a single government agency being tasked with the responsibility for coordinating and carrying out an objective investigation into UFO reports. With references to the attached news item, this office is of the opinion that every effort should be made to ensure that a coordinated scientific effort is directed to the study of UFO reports in order to avoid a needless duplication of effort. Assuming that NRC will accept the responsibility for investigating UFO reports, it would be unfortunate if the University of Toronto were to undertake an

objective research study into UFO reports independent of NRC.

3. If you are in agreement with the foregoing, would it not be advisable to discuss the advantages of a coordinated scientific study of UFOs between the interested scientific agencies?

4. Your comments are invited.

Signed: N.H. Ross, Brigadier,

Director General of Operations[3]

When the Shag Harbour Incident occurred a week later, it turned up the heat in Ottawa, and the negotiations with NRC became a priority. On January 9, 1968, the T's had been crossed and the I's dotted. The National Research Council of Canada issued the following news release.

NRC News Release

National Research Council

Ottawa 7, Canada   Tel 993-9101

FOR IMMEDIATE RELEASE

If consultations between the Department of National Defence and the National Research Council of Canada are concluded, as expected, the Space Research Facilities Branch of NRC will soon be acting as a clearing house to determine whether reports of unidentified flying objects should be investigated, the Council said today.

CHAPTER 2: "THE NIGHT OF THE UFOS"

> When the Branch receives information on a specific case, this information will be examined to determine whether there are any scientific reasons which [sic] would warrant further investigation. The extent of the initial examination in terms of time and expenditure will depend on the nature of the information received.
>
> If this initial examination shows that a further investigation is warranted, other agencies, such as the Department of National Defence, may be called on for assistance since NRC has no field capabilities to conduct such further investigation. Such further investigation will not be recommended unless it is also clearly evident that such further investigation will have scientific significance.

The problem with the transfer was not the design but the execution. Field units were never utilized. Professor Tennyson of the University of Toronto and Professor Rupert MacNeil of Acadia University in Wolfville, NS, gave it the "old college try." They used phone calls and letter writing to look into UFO cases that came to their attention. On-site investigations were rare and conducted more as a matter of personal interest in the UFO phenomenon. In the end, Rupert MacNeil's personal papers at Acadia were destroyed by a jealous colleague. Only a handful of his UFO correspondence is preserved in the National Archives. The National Research Council turned over the matter of UFO reports to the Herzburg Institute in 1968. It functioned only as a final repository for UFO reports, and by the mid 1990s it stopped collecting and receiving them. The Canadian government was finally out of the UFO business.

Sometimes with UFO documents and policy statements the margin notes written by staffers can be more informative than the main bodies of text that make up the documents. Such is the case with the NRC news release of January 9, 1968. In the margin of the copy preserved within the microfilm reel at the National Archives is this little gem written by Squadron Leader William Bain of DND's Air Desk.

> D Ops [Colonel Turner]
> You may find this interesting. I have kept a copy for a book that I plan to write after I retire—"The Power of Negative Thinking."
> Jan 9, 1968
> William Bain [initialed][4]

The truth was that officers like William Bain and others of the Air Desk took their responsibilities quite seriously. They did actual investigations and did the best with the resources at their disposal. But with shrinking budgets and the unification of the Canadian Armed Forces well underway there was no possibility of dedicating resources to the sole purpose of UFO investigations. Yet someone, somewhere in Ottawa, had the manpower to keep a close eye on what was being said by "those out of uniform" about UFO reports in Canada. Press clippings were being archived at DND headquarters.

The significance of the Air Desk as the official, active military agency doing on-site investigation of UFOs in 1967, and the fact that responsibility was moved to a non-military agency shortly after the Shag Harbour Incident, suggest that the government felt the Air Desk legitimized the UFO phenomenon and that having the military officially involved to such a degree brought too much attention to it. Nor did the government want the University of Toronto to bring academic impartiality to the investigations; hence, the responsibility ended up with the NRC, under military guidance.

It is significant that the Canadian military refers to "any other known objects" in relation to what was behind the sightings and search at Shag Harbour. In effect the document says more than it says. It demonstrates that the military had reached a conclusion that was not on the pages—that the object in question was unconventional. Highly unconventional. It was a UFO. It was a flying saucer. The Canadian military at the time was characterized as "cool-headed" and not prone to rash judgments. They were cautious and not "trigger-happy." If they came to the conclusion that the craft was a highly unconventional UFO, there was good reason.

CHAPTER 2: "THE NIGHT OF THE UFOS"

History of Canadian UFO Investigations

The Canadian government has been interested in and investigating UFOs since at least 1947, when a marked increase in sightings caught the attention of the public, the media, and the military. The government's scientific, military, and intelligence arms were convinced and concerned enough to take on several active investigations of the mystery—the first ones in 1947, 1950, and 1952—despite the fact that the US had officially declared that there was nothing to the phenomenon. Between 1947 and 1967 there was a steady increase in undeniable UFO activity resulting in pressure on the military to both act on and ignore the phenomenon. It is clear that there has been a deeper level of military and government involvement and knowledge of UFOs than has been acknowledged publicly.

The reactions of the government and military to the UFO phenomenon has been characterized by continually changing attitudes and policies, a schizophrenic push and pull between genuine investigations and denial by politicians and agencies. Investigating UFO sightings and reports was like a political hot potato that was tossed to different departments as the issue of UFO reality heated up on the public stage and in military offices.

The initial impetus to address the issue of UFOs in Canada was a marked increase in sightings, beginning with one over Ottawa on June 26, 1947, just days after the famous Kenneth Arnold sighting in Washington. Documents show that in April 1950, the Minister of Defence, Brooke Claxton, called for the Chair of the Defence Research Board (DRB) and members of the Joint Intelligence Council (JIC) to organize investigations of flying saucers using the field intelligence officers of the three military services and the RCMP. In fact they had been doing so since June 1947.

Between 1948 and 1952 there had been recurring UFO incidents over the American air force base in Goose Bay, Labrador. On April 12, 1952, UFOs were observed outside the Canadian air force base in North Bay, Ontario, which caused a sensation. This was followed five days later, on April 17, 1952, by a front page story in the *Ottawa Journal* on UFOs, revealing that DND had been investigating UFOs since 1947. The article stated that beginning at that time, the Intelligence Branch of the Royal Canadian Air Force had assessed the increasing number of reported UFO encounters, collaborating with the scientific research arm of the army, the Defence Research Board (DRB). Within a few weeks following the excitement over the North Bay UFOs in April 1952, Dr. O.M. Solandt, Chair of the DRB, organized an interdepartmental committee to deal with the mysterious issue. Solandt, originally a physician, had a lifelong association with the American Research and Development Board (RDB) and was the Canadian government's "go-to man" in scientific matters. He later became the vice-president of research and development at De Havilland Aircraft.

Solandt's committee, called Project Second Story, coordinated and advised the government and military groups involved with UFO investigations and came up with the first UFO sighting questionnaire. The group included Department of Transport scientist Wilbert B. Smith and astrophysicist Dr. Peter M. Millman from the Dominion Observatory, both of whom gained some notoriety. Summarizing the 1952 sightings report, Smith noted common characteristics of the UFOs:

> They are a hundred feet or more in diameter; they can travel at speeds of several thousand miles per hour; they can reach altitudes well above those which should support conventional air craft or balloons; and ample power and force seem to be available for all required maneuvers ... Taking these factors into account, it is difficult to reconcile this performance with the capabilities of our technology, and unless the technology of some terrestrial nation is much more advanced than is generally known, we are forced to the conclusion that the vehicles are probably extra-terrestrial, in spite of our prejudices to the contrary.[5]

Dr. Millman, who did not share Smith's belief in the reality of extraterrestrials, became the chair of the meetings and would go on to be involved in the non-meteoric National Research Council UFO investigations in 1968, which followed the Air Desk UFO investigations.

It was decided that the findings of Project Second Story were not to be released publicly; the military strategists consequently began a policy of secrecy, which was the trend with the American military establishment. While the Canadian authorities may have been influenced by the American policy of UFO secrecy, little was clear at that point except that of the thirty plus cases that had been rigorously analyzed, only a few could have been misidentified natural phenomena, and the rest left the experts bewildered. The fear of possibly inciting mass public panic by attempting to explain the essentially unknown extraterrestrial UFO phenomenon probably contributed to the position of secrecy.

CHAPTER 2: "THE NIGHT OF THE UFOS"

This position of secrecy continues into the present day. According to CBC News and Chris Rutkowski's research, reported UFO sightings in Canada doubled in 2012 (1,981 sightings) compared to 2011 (986 sightings) (*CBC News online* 2013). Yet, according to documents CBC obtained under Access to Information in 2013, as of late 2012 federal governmental agencies no longer collect UFO reports, leaving that job up to civilian agencies. So despite or perhaps because of a record number of UFO sighting reports, the government no longer receives them. However, 9,500 UFO reports collected in the past are now available online. Entitled "Canada's UFOs: The Search for the Unknown," the Library and Archives Canada collection of government records on UFOs contains digitized documents from DND, DOT, NRC, and the RCMP dating from 1947 to the early 1980s. They can be viewed at collectionscanada.gc.ca/databases/ufo/index-e.html.

Wilbert Smith
Wilbert Smith was an engineer in the Canadian Department of Transport whose interest in the subject of UFOs was heightened when he made inquiries at the US Embassy in Ottawa about the subject. According to a memo Smith sent to the Controller of Telecommunications at the Canadian Department of Transport, dated November 21, 1950, the Embassy directed him to Dr. Robert Sarbacher, a consultant to the US Research and Development Board (RDB), with whom Smith had detailed discussions on the topic of UFOs. (The RDB was headed by Dr. Vannevar Bush, who was also head of the Manhattan Project, a founder of what later became Raytheon Corporation, and President Roosevelt's wartime science advisor.) In his memo, Smith notes that Sarbacher told him that the Americans had recovered crashed alien flying saucers; that the matter was classified two points higher than the hydrogen bomb; and that a group had been formed to manage and control their study. Smith's 1950 memo was classified "top secret." (It was downgraded to "confidential" on September 15, 1969, and subsequently released. UFO researcher Arthur Bray brought the memo to light, along with Smith's original notes.)

Following his conversations with Sarbacher, Smith then had discussions with Dr. Solandt about geomagnetic studies and psychic phenomenon as related to the UFO phenomenon, topics with which Smith became heavily involved. Solandt and Smith decided that they should focus on geomagnetic energy; they suspected that UFOs operated by manipulating gravity. Smith's interest in geomagnetics and UFOs resulted in Project Magnet, with Smith at the helm. The goal of Project Magnet was to use Earth's magnetic field as a propulsion method for vehicles. Smith conducted tests, reported in November 1951, that stated that enough energy was taken from Earth's magnetic field to operate a voltmeter at 50 milliwatts. He wrote that he was on the "track of something that may prove to be the introduction of a new technology" (Smith 1950). In 1952 Smith would build a UFO detection station at Shirley Bay, ten miles outside of Ottawa. The detection station recorded at least one anomalous gravity field passing overhead, on August 8, 1954, which Smith believed was caused by a UFO. Official results were again declared secret.

Around the same time, Smith claimed that he began to be in telepathic contact with a group of extraterrestrials, which he called "the boys from topside."

According to Smith's wife, he approached the DRB, RCMP, and Prime Minister Louis St. Laurent himself with the suggestion that UFOs would land in Canada if they were guaranteed a safe place, as opposed to being chased and shot at by defence interceptors as they had been in the past. All three agreed, and the DRB established a 1,000 square mile landing area at their experimental aircraft station in Suffield, Alberta. According to Minister of Defence, Paul Hellyer, who spoke with *Ottawa Journal* reporter Victor Mackie for a story published on July 20, 1967, the area was equipped with searchlights and radio transmitters to signal UFOs, and television cameras and microphones to record any potential landing. Regular military and commercial flights were banned from the area.

With the Cold War tensions of the late 1950s to early 1960s and the monitoring of the North American perimeter by NORAD radar systems, UFO reports increased and were subject to a higher level of secrecy. On April 12, 1959, a glowing red UFO was tracked and observed by eye witnesses over Air Defence Command headquarters east of Montreal at the St. Hubert Air Force Base.

In the early 1960s Air Defence Command decided to retire from taking UFO reports. Canadian Forces Headquarters (CFHQ) in Ottawa took over that duty until March 1966 when it was again transferred, this time to the Directorate of Operations (DOPS). In the 1960s military and government officials began a campaign to attempt to explain the UFO phenomenon publically as natural phenomena or man-made objects.

In October 1966 DND issued a new reporting procedure, Canadian Forces Administration Order 71-6 (CFAO 71-6), which funnelled UFO reports from Canadian Forces bases and stations, police and RCMP, military and commercial pilots, and the public to the Department of National Defence

CHAPTER 2: "THE NIGHT OF THE UFOS"

(DND) headquarters. However this reporting order applied only to UFO reports that were "unclassified." More sensitive aerial encounters were protected from public scrutiny via the Joint Army-Navy Publication JANAP 146 (D and E) that governed the reporting of "vital intelligence sightings" in the US and Canada. Designed to keep significant UFO sightings under wraps, this provision made it illegal for members of the military or civilians to report on "classified" sightings.

Despite the attempts to diffuse the UFO issue publicly, within DND the Chief of Staff, Director of Intelligence, and Scientific Deputy Chief of Technical Services were all actively dealing with the UFO issue, as is evident in a November 1967 brief to the Chief of Defence Staff.[6]

The two years from March 1966 to March 1968 were the busiest in Canada for UFO activity up to that time. Under pressure, the Canadian military increased its attempts to grapple with the enigma. Southern Ontario and the Maritime provinces experienced an especially significant UFO flap during that time (which includes the Shag Harbour Incident), and the public demanded answers from the government and the military. Shag Harbour and other cases received significant national and international press coverage. There were questions in newspaper editorials and questions in Parliament.[7]

The military was in a Catch-22, unable to disprove the existence of UFOs but officially unwilling to admit their existence. Some felt the fact that the military (at that time, the Air Desk) investigated UFOs gave undue credence to the issue. The military also complained that UFO investigations created a "disruptive" and "detrimental" workload on DND personnel. In 1968 the Canadian military, like the USAF-sponsored Condon Committee (the UFO project at the University of Colorado), decided to transfer responsibility for UFO investigations to a scientific agency, the National Research Council (NRC).

Eventually, the government got its way. It got out of the UFO business gradually, quietly. Difficult cases such as the Shag Harbour Incident and the Michalak Case (discussed in chapter 7) slipped to the back pages of broadsheets and periodicals and eventually into the "dustbin of history." There would be an interim of decades before the public and the media spoke of the Shag Harbour UFO crash again, but what a comeback it would make.

Chapter 2 Endnotes

1. RCMP UFO File 67-400-23X, the Burke-Gaffney Collection, Saint Mary's University archives.
2. Ibid.
3. DND Memo V 2000-4 Vol. 2 (D Ops.), Sept. 26, 1967, RG 77 collection, Library and Archives Canada.
4. NRC press release dated January 9, 1968, RG 77.
5. Wilbert Smith, Project Magnet Report, 1952, page 6.
6. Chief of Defence Briefing on Unidentified Flying Objects, November 15, 1967, page 3. Directorate of Operations, Department of National Defence. From the Non-Meteoric Sightings files, DND 222, Herzberg Institute of Astrophysics, Planetary Sciences Section, National Research Council.
7. Canada, *House of Commons Debates* (November 6, 1967), p. 3718.

Chapter 3: The Quest
Chris Styles

"No pessimist ever discovered the secrets of the stars or sailed waters to uncharted lands or opened a new doorway for the human spirit."
– Helen Keller

"The cure for boredom is curiosity; there is no cure for curiosity."
– Dorothy Parker

One evening in the spring of 1992 I was helping a friend prepare a late evening meal that we were about to share. My contribution to that collective effort faltered as I was increasingly distracted by a television program vying for my attention from the adjacent room. The program was a rebroadcast of the episode of *Unsolved Mysteries* that dealt with the purported Roswell UFO crash. I didn't know it at the time but it would serve as a catalyst that would change the focus of my life.

The evening meal was good, but the conversation was even better. My friend, a science major, posed the question, "Do you really think that such things are even possible?"

"Yes. I know such things can happen, because it happened here too." My answer came without hesitation. I had memories of a similar incident that had somehow slipped into obscurity, and I had always been puzzled as to why that was so. The other UFO crash scenario I was recalling was of course the Shag Harbour Incident. Though I was uncertain of the date, I knew that I wasn't quite a teenager at the time of the occurrence, therefore it had happened sometime in the late sixties.

My friend continued to pose a series of perfectly reasonable and logical questions such as, "Why have I never heard of it? Wouldn't we all have heard of it? How could you keep such a thing secret?" At the time I had few answers but lots of fuzzy memories and some strong impressions. I remembered that there had been considerable press and television coverage. I remembered my maternal grandfather's many recollections and retelling of the story. He had been one of many eyewitnesses in the Shag Harbour area at the time of the crash. I had recollections of my father and his former navy buddies sitting around our kitchen table in the evening, playing cards and "talking shop" about their involvement with the underwater search for debris from the UFO in Shag Harbour. But my strongest memory was a very personal one.

The same night that a UFO crashed into the waters of Shag Harbour I had a UFO sighting in the Dartmouth Cove area. I had first seen the sixty-foot. sphere from the safety of my bedroom window. Wanting a closer view I ran out the door and down to the waterfront where I got a closer view than I had hoped for, especially since I was alone, twelve years old, and unprepared. That brief, terrifying encounter never left me. Seeing proved to be more than just simply believing. It was a life altering experience. And it was one I wasn't ready to share that spring night in 1992.

While drying dishes my friend said, "You know that Friedman fellow, who was in the documentary, he lives in Fredericton, New Brunswick."

"Stanton Friedman lives in Fredericton?" My rising inflection made it a probing question.

"Yes, and he did a book signing at a local bookstore just last week. You should have gone and told him your story about Shag Harbour. You should call him. See if he knows anything about it."

"I will. I'll wait a few days and try to come up with the date first."

"I know you. You'll put it off and never get around to it."

With that challenge I literally threw down the towel and grabbed the telephone. I dialed the long distance operator for New Brunswick and asked if there was a listing for a Stanton Friedman in Fredericton. To my surprise there was, and I was soon dialing the number and arguably committing my first act of ufology.

That call was answered by a human answering service that informed me that Mr. Friedman was out of town, but there was a contact number if it was a matter of importance. Not wanting to lose the momentum of the moment, I told the operator that it was indeed important and took down the number, which I dialed without hesitation. I never asked where the number was located. My only concern at the time was taking that first leap before procrastination and apathy could set in.

Stanton Friedman, a nuclear physicist and lecturer who has provided written testimony to congressional hearings, appeared twice at the United Nations, and been a pioneer in many aspects of ufology including Roswell, the

CHAPTER 3: THE QUEST

analysis of crashed saucers, and flying saucer technology, was staying at a motel in Austin, Texas, and was preparing to leave for a lecture date when he took my call. I explained who I was and asked if he had ever heard of the Shag Harbour UFO crash. Friedman had no initial recollection and asked me to tell him what I remembered of it. For the most part he listened, only interrupting from time to time with the occasional, "For how long?" or "What colour?" By the end of my synopsis, Stanton did have a recollection of several people approaching him over the years when he spoke in southwestern Nova Scotia and telling him about something going into the water and turning the harbor yellow with thick foam. Stanton also told me that I had enough detail that led him to feel that there must be something to the case. He encouraged me to look into it and gave some very straightforward practical advice. "Find the date. There must be archival press material. Find the witnesses. Should be relatively easy; fisherman don't move. Check with National Archives and DND. Check with the RCMP; they always do good paperwork." Furthermore he promised to keep in touch and to ask some of the other veteran UFO researchers like Richard Hall about it. Before the conversation ended I promised to take the advice given and get back in touch with the results, if any.

After I hung up, my friend, who had goaded me into calling, remarked that the phone call seemed to go well. I agreed and quipped that I may have found a new hobby. She said it sounded more like a quest. The weeks, months, and eventually years ahead would prove us both wrong. The Shag Harbour Incident would soon draw me fully toward the state of obsession.

Both Stanton and I proved true to our word. Less than a week after our initial conversation I received a tightly packed envelope with a letter that held more suggestions and helpful tips. I had already spent several days in the reference room of the Halifax Main Branch Library and had discovered the actual date of the UFO crash and so much more. The date appeared within the pages of a reference room copy of John Robert Columbo's classic work, "Mysterious Canada." The article contained a few paragraphs about the events of the night of October 4, 1967, and the subsequent search effort. A few other works held some mention of the case, but the vast majority of UFO reference works, encyclopedias, and source books contained absolutely nothing.

However, I remember being encouraged by the page and a half found within Ivan Sanderson's seminal work, "Invisible Residents." I was especially stimulated by Sanderson's assessment of the case, which comes in the opening sentence: "But perhaps the best documented and most publicized case of all is the UFO that dived into Shag Harbour, Nova Scotia, on the 4th of October,

1967" (Sanderson 1970:38–39). But the real juicy details of the day would be found within the archived microfilm reels of the Nova Scotia dailies and weeklies.

Within the newspaper accounts were the names of many of the local eyewitnesses, including the names of three RCMP officers who had actually seen the UFO on the water. True to Stanton's prediction, the fishermen had not moved in the twenty plus years since the incident and were relatively easy to track down and interview by phone. The RCMP officers proved more difficult to locate. Their careers and numerous postings had scattered them across Canada.

The common thread that emerged among all the eyewitness accounts was that all would stand by their original observations. No one would recant or withdraw any of the details of their testimony. That fact was very reassuring to a green UFO investigator who felt that such an important case should not be left in the hands of a novice who was new to the field. But no one else seemed to be in any rush to get at it. I resolved to continue as best I could and draw on the expertise and advice of the veterans in the field. Luckily, I found that many were willing to give freely of their time and advice to help.

A year later, the investigation would become much more complicated. There would be puzzling press clippings to ponder, bulk releases of key government policy documents, military telexes, and titillating margin notes. But before I got to gloat too much over the heap of documents piling up on my desk, an unexpected surprise thrust itself upon me. That surprise would become an ongoing torment that would become known as "The Shelburne Story."

In the spring of 1993 I was quite pleased with the early progress of my efforts to investigate the Shag Harbour Incident. It had become quite clear that this forgotten UFO case had depth and staying power. And I felt that it still had much more to offer the field than had been discerned from the original military investigation, back in the 1960s. I believed that the case would become a compelling argument for UFO reality. And, there was no weather balloon. Unlike the Roswell incident, there was no ridiculous cover story, simply a termination of the DND search effort and a claim of "nil results." In the end, DND simply seemed to give up. Shag Harbour seemed to be a case of the one that got away. Of course, my understanding of the case would not remain that neat or simple; however, at the time, in early 1993, the Shag Harbour Incident seemed to be an intriguing, genuine mystery without the usual "fly in the

CHAPTER 3: THE QUEST

ointment" facts. There were no arguments about crash site location, conflicting testimony, cover-ups, or wild-eyed reports of dead alien bodies.

Ideally, an investigator likes to find an ample amount of both high strangeness and high credibility in a UFO case. The Shag Harbour Incident may not have been the best example of a UFO case exhibiting high strangeness, but it certainly featured high credibility in the form of multiple witnesses and a large accessible paper trail. But then the Shelburne Story reared its unwanted head and made a mess of my nice, neat, and all too idealistic UFO investigation.

In 1993, I remembered that the father of a high school friend just happened to be the man who trained the divers of the navy's Fleet Diving Unit. Among the many navy divers to benefit from the expertise of CPO Guy Fenn were those of HMCS *Granby*, who in 1967 had been given the task of searching for Shag Harbour's mysterious "dark object." It took little effort to track down Mr. Fenn and learn who was involved and where to find them. Fenn gave me a good "head's up" on who would likely talk and who to trust.

Seven divers were eventually assigned to the task of searching for a UFO believed to have crashed in the waters of the Sound. All whom I interviewed agreed as to which fellow divers were involved. A few of the seven were involved in other nearby UFO searches. No one disagreed with the story told by those who gave specific details. The less forthcoming of the seven divers insist that what the others offered was accurate and true. However, I suspect that their aggregate account is less than complete.

The divers spoke to me on condition of anonymity. They are among the very few for whom I have offered and honoured that promise. I typically resist using anonymous testimony in a UFO investigation. Sometimes it is unavoidable. Since 1993, and after investigating dozens of UFO cases from Newfoundland to Alberta, I have refused to grant anonymity or use anonymous testimony in all but the most rare and demanding of cases. Bear in mind that in the case of the *Granby* divers, theirs is a very limited form of anonymity. The fact that they were in Shag Harbour searching for a crashed UFO is well chronicled in archived newspaper reports and actual military telex orders of the day.[1]

The *Granby* divers' tale has become known as "the Shelburne Story." It has been told to me, both in part and whole by several others who took part in the Shelburne operation in various military support roles. For me it would become and remain the most problematic aspect of my investigation of the Shag

Harbour Incident. It will be dealt with at length and in great detail in the next chapter. The story unfolded as follows.

"You know about Shelburne? There was no doubt about what was down there. It certainly was nothing from around here. Shelburne was the real story." These were the opening words of the *Granby* diver I'll refer to as "Harry." I remember that the words came out in a rush, first on the telephone and later in a March 1993 interview in Harry's living room. It was only there, in the navy diver's home, that the full weight of the Shelburne Story first became apparent and began to reveal both its distinct connection to and its separation from the Shag Harbour Incident.

That dramatic and memorable interview was an uneven affair. At times Harry would become reluctant and even want to "pull the plug;" at other times it was a cascade of words. Sometimes the words came slowly as if with great difficulty, as if they invoked some long forgotten trauma.

"There was two UFOs on the seabed," Harry told me. "One was 'standing nines' and lending assistance to the other. We were not sure what was wrong, but we thought that one of the craft might be in trouble, might have lost an engine. And there was activity going on. There were beings down there. At that point the brass pulled us out of the water, and the whole thing became an operation of observation only. They kept us on those ships there a whole week, holding station. Then the two UFOs moved, while still submerged, out into the Gulf of Maine, broke the surface, and flew away."

Harry was reluctant to give any further details. He was, however, offended by the suggestion that perhaps he and the others might have misinterpreted or over interpreted what they saw. He and I never met again to discuss his testimony. This was his wish, and I have honoured it. Others would have much to add to the Shelburne Story and the credibility of the man who first told it. In chapter 4 you will see that while there is no "smoking gun," some credible evidence has been discovered that supports the *Granby* divers' claim that there was a second simultaneous underwater search for a UFO off of Shelburne's Government Point in 1967.

Confused, tormented, and overwhelmed by the sudden appearance of the unexpected and problematic Shelburne Story, I decided to ignore it and hope that it might leave me alone. This worked for a while, but the Shelburne Story would prove to have both staying power and many other sources. I would eventually be forced to grapple with the tenacity of the Shelburne Story and acknowledge that any complete chronicling of the Shag Harbour Incident would have to include it. A UFO researcher does not get the luxury of picking

CHAPTER 3: THE QUEST

and choosing his data. He can, however, shift his focus and employ other techniques, in the interim, until the day when more becomes known. For a few years in the 1990s I did just that and submerged myself in an archival paper chase, which would prove enlightening on the Shag Harbour Incident itself.

In July 1993 the first two batches of UFO documents arrived from Ottawa. These responses were the results of both informal telephone inquiries and formal access to information requests made to the National Archives of Canada and DND's Directorate of History. I remember that those first thick manila envelopes gave me a great sense of satisfaction as I tore them open and examined their contents at length for the tiniest detail. For me, that first pair of document packages was taken as official acknowledgement that the Shag Harbour Incident was more than just media spin and residue conjured up from a slow news week.

It may sound silly but once past the cover letter I had a favourite document right from the moment of first reading, and it maintains the status of being my favourite UFO document all these years later. It was found among the enclosures included in the DND Directorate of History response. It was a memo that had circulated throughout DND's Directorate of Operations back in October 1967. I loved the memorandum's unusual candour, strength, and clarity as DND expressed its opinion regarding the unconventional nature of whatever was responsible for the Shag Harbour UFO crash. That controversial point of view is expressed in the document's one sentence long third paragraph, which reads as follows: "The Rescue Coordination Centre conducted preliminary investigation and discounted the possibilities that the sighting was produced by an aircraft, flares, floats or any other known objects."[2] When you ponder those few words of text and consider the remaining possibilities, it leaves you with a rather short and suggestive list.

When packages of documents were not filling the mailbox and demanding my attention there were other tasks to help one make the seamless transition from mere hobby toward quest and obsession. There were seemingly endless reels of small format microfilm from the National Archives Records Group 77 collection (RG 77). The reels are composed of Canadian UFO reports featuring voluminous amounts of very poor quality text documents. The upside, however, is that many of the reports are from RCMP and other police sources and have had some preliminary investigation from their own staff. Combing through this unruly database can be both tedious and demanding. Obsession certainly helps one cope. The reels do, however, paint a picture for the investigator who can hack the tedium of the process.

Eventually you begin to see a pattern in both the mistakes and what worked for others who tried before you to figure out "what really happened." You get a feel for what types of UFO cases are worth pursuing. You learn how "two amateur astronomers" can become "two men with a telescope" and how they are not quite the same thing. One encounters the pitfalls of trying to confirm the hard details and quality of the available data in any kind of comprehensive follow-up to an earlier UFO investigation conducted by third parties disinterested in the UFO phenomenon.

A paper chase can occasionally offer up a little drama. I will give you two quite different examples of this much welcome relief. It does not happen nearly often enough within the tedium of serious UFO research. Both examples occurred during the mid nineties Shag Harbour effort.

In 1994 I made a telephone inquiry to DND's Directorate of History to ask if the annual Stroker Report for 1967 had been preserved and discovered that indeed it had been and was held by the Directorate of History. The Stroker Report is a yearly examination of major target detections picked up by NORAD radar bases that are a possible security concern for North America. It was my hope that the Shag Harbour Incident might get a mention.

The staffer who handled my call explained that she was aware of the '67 Stroker Report and that she and her CO, the chief archivist, had used the report a few days previous to my request, on other research. She seemed quite intrigued in the nature of my request and seemed genuinely surprised and interested by the fact that the Royal Canadian Navy had actually searched for a crashed UFO. Getting someone who is going to conduct a search for documents interested in what I do is a technique that has worked well for me over the years. Often you get a more complete result in a shorter response time. The enthusiastic junior archivist promised to get back to me quickly with any result.

True to her word she called me back from Ottawa in ten minutes. This remains a record in my personal experience for speedy response time from any authoritative agency that claims to have actually carried out a search and not simply refused to look. The staffer explained, "I hope that you don't read too much into this, but the Stroker Report for 1967 is missing."

"Missing?" I said.

"Yes. Missing. It is odd. It has to be signed out and only the colonel and I should have access. There will be an investigation. I believe that it will turn up, and I will get back to you. I'm sorry."

CHAPTER 3: THE QUEST

After two months there was no still call or letter, so I called back to inquire as to the fate of the missing Stroker Report. The Junior Archivist said in a nonchalant tone, "Yeah it turned up, I checked, and there was nothing on point. Goodbye." And with an abrupt click that was it. I will let readers make of that outcome as they will.

My second example of unexpected drama among my archival adventures yielded a much more satisfying result; however, it took much longer to unfold. One day I dropped into Saint Mary's University in Halifax to ask if the academic papers of the late Jesuit priest and astronomer Father Michael Burke-Gaffney had been bequeathed to the university archives and had been preserved. It was my hope that they had and would contain some Shag Harbour UFO files; after all, the former Saint Mary's prof was also a paid UFO investigator for Canada's National Research Council, which took over responsibility for UFO investigations from the Royal Canadian Air Force in January 1968. I picked up that useful tidbit combing through the reels of RG 77 at the Halifax Main Branch Library reference room thanks to an interlibrary loan that transferred the National Archives collection from Ottawa to Halifax.

Initially, I approached former Saint Mary's staffer Doug Vasey, head of information services for the university's library, with my simple request. He called university archivist Wendy Bullerwell over to his desk. I put the question about Father Gaffney's files to her and she immediately responded with, "Yes, we have them. I don't know if you can view them. You see, no one has ever asked before you."

There was a curve ball answer that I had not expected. It got stranger when I asked the young archivist who would know.

"Father Gaffney's papers were bequeathed to the university archives in his will; however, it is my understanding that they are under the supervision of two fellow Jesuits who are staff here, Father William Lonc and Father William Brezhio. I will have to consult with them and seek their permission and the terms of access. One of the fathers is quite ill. I don't know if the other will be comfortable making the decision on his own. This could take some time. Could you tell me what you are looking for?"

I explained my needs as best I could and did not expect to hear back any time soon. I knew first-hand how slow Catholic clerics could be. Six months later I got a call from Doug Vasey telling me that the two priests had granted me access. I made arrangements to view several boxes (there were twenty-six in all) on a Saturday afternoon.

When I arrived at the Saint Mary's archives, Wendy Bullerwell took me to a room that had been set aside for my viewing. Several boxes were brought in on a cart. The rules were simple and clear. Put everything back just as I found it and close the boxes when I was done. I was free to photocopy anything I wanted. No one but myself was to touch or examine the documents.

The files were mostly RCMP UFO files. Many were directly pertinent to the Shag Harbour Incident or the so-called Night of the UFOs. While I was photocopying a set of files, Wendy Bullerwell entered the little room that I was working in. She heard my sounds of delight and remarked that I must be finding what I was looking for. I offered to show her one of the documents in hand and to my surprise Ms. Bullerwell turned away to avert her gaze. She explained that the permission had only extended to me and did not include herself, even though she was the archivist. Ms. Bullerwell took her job very seriously.

Since those heady days, Father Gaffney's will was reread and his papers are now a public file at Saint Mary's and can be viewed by all without any encumbrance or special arrangements (Styles 1996: 31). Some are even available online. All off the "voodoo" surrounding the Father's files seems silly now, but that is how it was. In retrospect, though, the strangest aspect of it all was that no one bothered to look at the Father's papers before me.

Not every gain and breakthrough in my quest for all things Shag Harbour would prove as difficult or as labour intensive as those already mentioned. By the mid nineties I had become involved with MUFON, the Mutual UFO Network. At the time it was North America's largest grass roots, serious UFO group. Some of its members were involved with actual research on the UFO phenomenon. As public awareness of the Shag Harbour Incident was spreading, MUFON members and other independent UFO researchers were forwarding to me whatever they would come across regarding Shag Harbour.

Perhaps the most significant find to be unexpectedly forwarded to me was an old "APRO Preliminary Report." It was discovered by UFO researcher Jan Aldrich while researching the files of former UFO researcher John Brent Musgrave (Ibid.: 33). Aldridge directs the ambitious Project 1947, an ongoing effort to pool together anything and everything in print that has anything to do with UFO phenomena. The report had been prepared for the late James Lorenzen, who founded the Aerial Phenomenon Research Organization (APRO). In its day APRO was a large North American UFO group with a membership in the thousands. The APRO Preliminary Report provided new insight into the Shag Harbour case and featured a level of detail that went well

CHAPTER 3: THE QUEST

beyond the myriad of press clippings and even the available military telexes that had been preserved in archives. Within the densely packed seven pages were such useful "tidbits" as specific mention of United States Air Force (USAF) and US navy involvement in the search for the UFO very soon after the crash. The report was the original source for the name "Mace Coffee [*sic*];" it stated that the officer of the watch told the report's author that "if anything of extreme interest is found it will be turned over to Mr. Mace Coffee" (APRO1967: 3). Dr. Maurice Coffey was a scientific consultant to Maritime Command and the man tasked to find the missing UFO. He would prove to be a key to greater insight into the Shag Harbour Incident. His eclectic career and groundbreaking techniques are examined in chapter 13.

By now it is probably clear that my fledgling attempt to investigate the Shag Harbour Incident got out of the blocks quickly and was quite successful at garnering the attention the case deserved. In a few short years, Shag Harbour's UFO crash went from virtually forgotten and unknown to what many were suddenly calling "Canada's most important UFO case" (*Maclean's* 2001: 45–46). But I wouldn't want you to think that everything was a slam dunk. Some of my early efforts were very disappointing and others a complete misfire.

There was a trip to the National Archives of Canada in Ottawa where I hoped to locate paper only documents on Shag Harbour that could not be transferred to Halifax. The cost of that trip was underwritten by a modest grant from the Washington-based Fund for UFO Research. The effort bore little fruit, certainly no documents of high interest regarding Shag Harbour or any other UFO case. An access to information officer at the Archives revealed that perhaps 85 per cent of all RCMP UFO documents and DND UFO files have been destroyed. A terrible example of our tax dollars at work.

In the early days, before I had interviewed any witnesses or accessed any documents, I tried comparing modern charts of the seabed in the Shag Harbour area with ones from before October 1967. It was my naive hope that there might be a single discrepancy in the form of an additional circle that proved a little shallower on the seabed on charts after 1967. I have since become aware of a book's worth of reasons as to why this naive little exercise was doomed to failure. It wasn't going to be that simple. But in 1995 I did direct an underwater search, and as you will see there are still valid reasons to further examine the seabed. Those reasons are examined in detail in subsequent chapters.

These days, documents do not arrive near as often in my mailbox. Surprise breakthroughs have become less frequent, but they still occasionally happen.

Several of the chapters in the "Insight" section of this book chronicle new discoveries both of witnesses and of further documentation on the Shag Harbour Incident. None of that material has been previously published. The Shag Harbour Incident has yet to give up all of its secrets, but the quest continues.

CHAPTER 3: THE QUEST

Chapter 3 Endnotes

1. Based on several preserved DND telexes regarding Shag Harbour found within Library and Archives Canada RG 77, Vol. 310, "UFO Sightings 1965–1981."
2. DND memo dated September 6, 1967, released to the author September 27, 1993, by DND's Directorate of History.

Chapter 4: Shelburne
Graham Simms

"Security is mostly a superstition. It does not exist in nature."
– Helen Keller

"Security is a kind of death."
– Tennessee Williams

Shelburne is not just the name of a historic town on Nova Scotia's southwestern shore. From the 1950s until the mid nineties it was also the location of the high security military base, CFS (Canadian Forces Station) Shelburne, which was situated upon oceanfront property at Government Point. Throughout its operational history, CFS Shelburne was Canada's most secret military installation, and "The Shelburne Story" remains Canada's most controversial UFO claim.

The Shelburne Search Operation Story

As outlined in chapter 3, the "shell" of the Shelburne Story was first told to author Chris Styles in early 1993 by a few of the divers from DND's Fleet Diving Unit (Ledger and Styles 2001: 67–68). Basically, the story claims that while navy divers from HMCS *Granby* were scouring the seabed in Shag Harbour, another team of men were twenty-five miles away in the water off Shelburne Harbour's Government Point. According to the divers who gave testimony, two UFOs sat on the seabed at a point about halfway between Government Point and the Cape Roseway lighthouse on McNutt's Island (Styles 1996: 4). Interestingly, that position lies within sight of the former base CFS Shelburne, which at the time was a top secret NATO listening post and a coordination centre for submarine detection. The *Granby* divers claim that one of the UFOs was helping repair a damaged craft (Ibid.), which was in fact the damaged disc that had been seen to enter the water at Shag Harbour on the night of October 4, 1967. Once the divers in the water had observed this activity, they were ordered to the surface. Considerations for any attempt at a recovery action were immediately abandoned (Ibid.). The Shelburne operation was from that point on an operation of observation only. Observation was continued by dropping cameras and sensors. One of the divers served as the underwater naval photographer, and he claimed to have shot four hundred feet of film as well as still photographs.

The Shelburne operation continued for almost a week. According to the anonymous testimony of an RCAF officer and "Harry," the *Granby* diver, on October 11, 1967, a Soviet sub was detected crossing into Canada's twelve mile limit. It was on an intercept course with the position of the UFOs. The small flotilla of surface ships weighed anchor and make their way toward the approaching Soviet sub to show challenge. The two UFOs remain submerged but slowly began making their way southeast down the Nova Scotia coast toward the Gulf of Maine. Once they reached open water, just beyond the Shag Harbour area, they surfaced and flew away at high speed (Ledger and Styles 2001: 80).

The departure of the two UFOs was also witnessed by six members of the Cameron family from their home in Woods Harbour, 5.6 km away, overlooking the Gulf of Maine. At 8:30 pm on October 11, Lockland Cameron (41), Lorraine Cameron (34), Havelock Cameron (33), Brendan Cameron (28), and two children saw the first unidentified light exit the water to the southeast over Solomon's Island, one mile west of Woods Harbour, going upward at a forty-five degree angle. They estimated the light to be fifty to sixty feet wide. Up to six bright red lights flashed in sequence from back to front and then front to back. The family observed these lights for seven or eight minutes before the lights were "extinguished." Then yellow-orange lights appeared for ten minutes and disappeared over the horizon to the northwest. The RCAF at Baccaro reported no operations in the area and nothing on their radar. The Cameron family sighting provides independent confirmation of what the Shelburne diver, Harry, told Chris, that the UFOs outside Shelburne Station were there for a week. Chris found the RCMP report of the Cameron sighting within the Burke-Gaffney papers; the story appeared in the October 12, 1967 edition of the *Halifax Chronicle-Herald*.

Other than that one mention in the *Herald*, the media remained transfixed on the search effort for a crashed UFO twenty-five miles away in Shag Harbour. The Shag Harbour Incident proved to be a more than adequate cover for the events unfolding in Shelburne. The military "brass" could relax with the certain knowledge—the result of sonar data, the MAD grid search,

CHAPTER 4: SHELBURNE

and the details of the Cameron family sighting—that the UFO first sighted in Shag Harbour had long since abandoned the area.

Chris Styles was deeply troubled by the Shelburne Story right from the beginning. Although his investigation of the Shag Harbour UFO crash was only a few months old, the Shelburne Story contrasted sharply with his and others' personal knowledge, witness testimony, and the press clippings that he had gathered at that early point in his research. By the summer of 1993, the arrival of DND and RCMP documents did little to account for the navy divers' startling testimony. It had been Chris's hope to avoid the complications and pitfalls that had plagued the Roswell Incident, especially the problem of multiple, unverifiable locations and witness testimony that differed greatly from the document record itself.

UFO books and even conventional science are filled with stories of those who allow personal prejudices and practices to taint their research. Chris chose to set aside the Shelburne Story while he tied down the document trail and conducted interviews with the eyewitnesses of what was historically certain—the October 4, 1967, UFO crash in Shag Harbour. He also hoped to serendipitously catch a lucky break in the form of new evidence that might make sense of the divers' startling underwater discoveries, which included details of the flying saucers and their alien occupants. Failing that, it was Chris's hope that as he learned more about UFO research techniques he would be better equipped to tackle the puzzle that is the legacy of the Shelburne Story.

The Persistence of the Shelburne Story

Chris Styles was quite successful with his efforts to document and chronicle the events in Shag Harbour of October 4, 1967. As evidence accumulated, he would find it impossible to ignore or shelve the Shelburne Story. Time and again it would come back to "rear its ugly head." And the story would pop up in strange ways, often from the most unexpected of sources.

One of the first encounters with the Shelburne Story to come from outside of the ranks of the Granby divers was that of a former employee of Halifax's defunct tabloid, *The Daily News*. In the late 1980s, "Jim" (not his real name) was a contract courier who worked a bulk delivery contract, as indeed did Chris Styles. After being out of touch for a couple of years, Chris had a chance encounter with Jim. When Jim asked Chris what he was doing these days, Chris began to tell him about his research into the Shag Harbour Incident. Jim claimed to have been aboard one of the navy ships on the surface. Though he was actually with the RCAF at the time of the incident, Jim had been sent out on one of the ships just in case there was some type of aircraft artifact to identify, as he was trained in the identification of foreign aircraft (Ledger and Styles 2001: 72–76).

Jim's account of the Shelburne operation was essentially secondhand. Nothing was ever recovered from the seabed just off the high security NATO base at Government Point, so there was no physical evidence for Jim to inspect. More than anything else, the RCAF staffer remembered being very bored. "They kept those ships in place for a week!" A good deal of time was spent in the mess or "nursing a beer." It was during one of those times, in the mess, when Jim overheard the *Granby* divers discussing the two UFOs on the seabed below them. An American protocol officer assigned to the mission was present and became quite upset about the lack of discipline aboard the Canadian vessel. He approached the table where the *Granby* divers were drinking and reminded them that they should not be talking about the "Soviet submarine" that they had seen on the seabed below. The divers became belligerent and challenged the officer's authority to "boss them around." In the exchange, one of the divers said, "I don't know what those things are down there or where they are from, but they are not any kind of sub and they are not anything from this planet." At that point the US officer left only to return with a Canadian navy officer who was able to defuse the situation and change the topic of conversation. Though Jim had never seen a thing, he would never forget what he heard. His memory of the conversation at least served to corroborate some of the details of the *Granby* divers' Shelburne story. Unfortunately, Jim did not remember which ship he had boarded; he only remembered how glad he was to get off of it and thanked God that he had not joined the navy.

Jim's recollections of the Shelburne operation stop short of the total narrative provide by the Granby divers. This is no surprise, given the compartmentalized structure and methods employed by the military. On the ships that were involved in the purported Shelburne operation, only some of the senior brass would have had anything approaching a complete overview of the mission. And that would have been granted only on a "need to know" basis. The only others who were "in the know" were the *Granby* divers who were by necessity in a hands-on position. Someone had to place the cameras and sensors. But there were others who saw things, things that they were not meant to see. And some of those witnesses did not wear any uniform.

In the fall of 1993 Chris moved to an apartment in south-end Halifax and did his laundry at a laundromat around the corner. One day while waiting for

CHAPTER 4: SHELBURNE

his laundry to dry he was studying some press clippings about Shag Harbour, and an attendant in the laundromat remarked that he remembered the incident. This surprised Chris as the attendant seemed much too young to have any personal memories from the sixties. The young man explained that he grew up in the town of Shelburne and that he knew all of the lightkeepers in the area, especially those who had worked at the Cape Roseway lighthouse that had been situated on McNutt's Island, which would have overlooked any naval operation off of Government Point. Apparently, the lightkeepers often spoke of Shag Harbour. The young man gave Chris a detailed list of those who worked at various times at the Cape Roseway lighthouse.

When Chris tracked down the phone numbers of those on the list he found that while they had indeed worked at Cape Roseway at various times, none of the people on the list were on duty at the time of the Shelburne operation. Their knowledge was secondhand. But, they did agree with the essence of the story. Those who were actually working at the time were now either deceased or uncooperative. Chris went back to the laundromat to see if he could pick up some more names or leads from the helpful attendant, but once again fate conspired against the effort to investigate the Shelburne Story further.

The young laundry attendant had been fired. The boss was working his shift. When Chris explained why he was looking for him, she said, "I wouldn't trust any information from him." Chris informed her that, in fact, the attendant's information had been accurate and a help to his investigation. She then remarked that she knew other people from the town of Shelburne and that they might be able to help. She asked what it was all about, and Chris brought her up to speed on the Shag Harbour Incident.

When he finished, the laundry boss caught him totally by surprise with a most unexpected claim. "I don't know about that UFO crash business, but when that was all going on my friend who works at the lunch counter just up the block saw the aliens right on Sandy Point Road out near the Shelburne base."

"Really?" Chris was completely stymied.

"Oh yeah. It really happened. She has always tried to forget it. It really affected her. I doubt that she will talk to you. I wish I hadn't said anything about it. She's going to be quite pissed with me if you approach her with questions."

When Chris attempted to quiz the friend, she nearly fainted and had to sit down to steady herself. She stated that she would have to discuss the matter with her husband. Apparently, he had witnessed the entities with her that strange foggy October night at dusk along Sandy Point Road.

Chris ordered a cheeseburger and awaited the arrival of the husband who was scheduled to pick up the laundry manager's friend, as her shift was about to end. When the husband arrived there was a huddle between the couple at the far end of the lunch counter. The husband then approached Chris and stated that they could not help him. The husband explained that they had tried to forget that day. He wished Chris luck with his effort and said one more time that he was sorry, but they could not deal with what happened and would not even consider therapy. One thing was certain. The couple was not seeking attention. They did not see their purported close encounter as a positive experience. It remains one of the few close encounter (CE-3) claims from the time of the Night of the UFOs in Nova Scotia (see the Appendix for the definitions of the various types of close encounters). Unfortunately, the couple, like the *Granby* divers, refused to discuss any of the entity details such as clothing, activity, or communications.

Not all of the Shelburne Story evidence is secondhand. In fact one of the strongest pieces of evidence that the incident occurred at all is found within an RCMP X-file that concerns itself with another UFO sighting from that night, the radar visual sighting by Captain Leo Mersey and his crew of eighteen men described in chapter 2.[1]

That Mersey sighting occurred the same night as that of the Shag Harbour crash, October 4, 1967. On Saturday, October 7, 1967, Captain Mersey arrived at the RCMP detachment in his home port of Lunenburg to fill out a UFO report about the observations made at sea by himself and his crew. Three days had elapsed since the *Nickerson*'s UFO sighting off Sambro. During the interim, Captain Mersey had discussed the sighting with a number of people over the ship's radio, together with several harbour pilots, including one in Shelburne who informed Mersey about an underwater naval search at the mouth of Shelburne Harbour and how he had been tasked with keeping the area free from any hazards to navigation. The fact that Mersey believed that there was a second simultaneous search for a UFO near Shelburne is stated in his witness statement found within his RCMP UFO report: "I had never seen anything like it before but it sounds like the thing that they are looking for down off Shelburne or Barrington Passage."

When Chris discovered the RCMP report that dealt with the Mersey sighting off Sambro he contacted Leo Mersey who was retired and living in Centre, NS, outside the town of Lunenburg. In a lengthy telephone interview

CHAPTER 4: SHELBURNE

Leo Mersey confirmed that he was aware of two underwater naval searches for a UFO being conducted at the same time. He clarified that when he stated Shelburne he meant specifically Government Point and that Barrington Passage meant Shag Harbour. When Chris asked why not just write Shag Harbour, Mersey told him that the UFO had actually crashed into Woods Harbour and drifted into the Shag Harbour area. He went on to explain that, "People down the shore think of that whole area near Cape Sable as Barrington Passage, especially if you don't live there yourself." If Leo Mersey had not been at sea and had had his own UFO sighting that compelled him to seek more information, he would not have known about the Shelburne search operation. And we would be lacking a crucial piece of evidence whose discovery was truly serendipitous.

Shelburne's Secret Mission

As stated earlier, CFS Shelburne was Canada's most secret base, but what does that mean? Just how "hot" could its secrets be?

CFS Shelburne was originally commissioned as HMCS Shelburne on April 1, 1955. It was the oldest and smallest establishment within Ocean Surveillance Atlantic (OCEANSYLANT). The Shelburne base was a joint operation of the Royal Canadian Navy (RCN) and the US Navy (USN). Its publicly stated mission was that of a joint Canada/US Oceanographic Research Station, but that lie was simply the base's cover story. Its real mission was as a listening post and coordination centre for submarine detection. Shelburne was specifically tasked to support antisubmarine warfare command by detecting, classifying, and providing timely information on submarines and "other contacts of interest" to Naval Ocean Processing Facilities (NOPF). This mission would include direct tactical control of associated Towed Array Sensor System Ships tasked to gather long-term acoustic information. The simple truth was that since the inception of the sound surveillance system (SOSUS) and the magnetic anomaly detection (MAD) grid in 1954, CFS Shelburne managed an undersea warfare detection system during the Cold War years. Throughout that tense period, detection of Soviet nuclear subs operating off of North America's coast was just about as "hot" a task as you could get as a mission. The only thing that would have been considered potentially "hotter" would be those pesky, aforementioned "other contacts of interest," especially those attributable to unidentified submersible objects (USOs).

Former staff members have told Chris Styles that USOs were frequently detected at CFS Shelburne. It would be considered a USO if it was a strong acoustic or magnetic target that was too big (over 700 feet in length) or too fast (greater than 100 knots) to be a conventional submarine or torpedo. Apparently, the equipment at CFS Shelburne was remarkably sensitive and discriminating. Properly trained personnel could look at the old wet paper tracings and identify a pod of right whales one hundred miles out or the prop wash of HMCS *Whatever*. At Shelburne the frequencies used were below 500 Hz. The pick-up arrays on the ocean seabed were at least twenty wavelengths long and vertically oriented to delineate ray paths, meaning they could precisely plot the exact location of the audio source. The magnetic detection data was used for post analysis of the acoustic data. Spectral analyzers were fine enough to examine 1.0 to 0.5 Hz. In real time. In brief, it was state of the art in its day.

Advances in the modern age of sonar, which dates back to the 1920s, came during the Second World War as a result of the threat from Nazi U boats. In the 1950s it was determined that low frequency passive sound was the way to go as these sounds travel great distances in water, giving more warning of enemy activity. This was the benefit and the beginning of a practical SOSUS system. Submarine warfare would never be quite the same. Stealth was the name of the game.

In the day-to-day operations at CFS Shelburne everything was treated as top secret. Perhaps one of the best insights comes from the observations of a naval architect on staff at Maritime Command in Halifax. Robert Bedford was brought in to the Shelburne base to take some measurements for a planned expansion of one of the buildings there. As he was led past some of the sensor recording equipment a couple of staffers held up a sheet to shield the equipment and data display from the architect's gaze. He chuckled and reminded them that he had a top security clearance. One of the women responded with, "Not to see this stuff, you don't!" Robert Bedford had done design work in many bases throughout Canada, including DND headquarters and the experimental air station facility in Suffield, Alberta, but he said he had never seen a place so security conscious as CFS Shelburne. What kind of data about the underwater environment off of the coast of Nova Scotia could be so sensitive and different from the other top secret bases?

CFS Shelburne was operational from April 1, 1955, until August 1, 1994. The base's official cover story, that it was primarily an oceanographic research facility, began to crumble in the mid 1980s. The worst "hit" came when five female staff members were dismissed because it was suspected that the five individual women had been involved in lesbian relationships. At that time the

CHAPTER 4: SHELBURNE

Canadian Armed Forces considered such behaviour a security risk. It was thought that such persons were more susceptible to blackmail or coercion. All five women were investigated and dismissed from active service. As the media was covering the story the true mission of the Shelburne base was revealed. However, it was not until March 15, 1991, after the fall of the Berlin Wall, that the official cover story was withdrawn. From that point on it was openly admitted that CFS Shelburne was tasked with a mission to detect threatening submarine contacts.

Interpreting the Shelburne Story

The central question is, did the Shelburne Story actually occur as described? Is it even possible? These two questions have tormented Chris Styles since he first heard the purported details back in early 1993.

The Shelburne Story has resisted repeated attempts to discover hard primary sourced documents that would support its validity. Time and again requests for former manned records of lighthouses, ships' logs, and Stroker reports were unsuccessful. This stands in sharp contrast to the readily available paper trail connected to the Shag Harbour UFO crash of October, 1967. And yet there are "teasers," such as the statement of Leo Mersey found within the RCMP UFO file (67-400-23-X) that would suggest that there indeed was a second, simultaneous underwater search for a UFO. And that fact is stated by a disinterested third party. But why is it so difficult? Couldn't persistence and the process of elimination provide what we seek?

One of the problems in dealing with verification of the Shelburne Story is a lack of specific details. What are the names of the ships purported to have held station off Government Point? The *Granby* divers never gave any indication of what ships were involved. All they required was a small launch to act as a tender. Any small boat that could hold their equipment and that was easy to board would have sufficed. However, if it was an around the clock operation and if there was serious consideration of an attempt at recovery, then a much larger work platform would have been required. All those who spoke of the operation—such as "Jim," the RCAF identification expert—said, "They held those ships there for a week." But which ships?

The problem with identifying the ships at the Shelburne operation is manifold, with the biggest obstacle being the fact that no one has supplied a name. Unlike today, Canada had a sixty ship navy in the 1960s. It was one of the largest naval fleets of its day after the superpowers. There are a lot of possibilities. A glance at the press of the day tells us some of the ships that could not be involved. HMCS *Bonaventure* was steaming down the St. Lawrence after a refit. HMCS *Granby* never moved from the Dartmouth pier where she had been tied up for years (the divers assigned to the *Granby* used CGC 101 for their dive in Shag Harbour). Several frigates were on NATO manoeuvres in the North Atlantic. When all of the ships are removed from the list, of those whose position is known, there are still a large number of possibilities remaining. Many ships of the fleet are listed as being "at sea." Requests for their logs have repeatedly failed to be fruitful. Many logs are missing or strangely incomplete. However, one of the ships that seems to have made its way to Shelburne, via a last minute course correction, was Canada's newly purchased Oberon class diesel electric sub, HMCS *Onondaga*.

Onondaga was on its way across the Atlantic Ocean. It was being delivered by a British commander and a British crew. It was not yet under direct Canadian command. Those early logs before the boat fell under Canadian command are not held at Library and Archives Canada nor at DND's Directorate of History. In fact only one newspaper mentioned that *Onondaga* was diverted toward Shelburne instead of Halifax so that it could have its sound signature recorded. Considering the technical capabilities of the Sound Surveillance System (SOSUS), that suggestion is laughable. So HMCS *Onondaga* was there at the right time. And yet none of the original sources who spoke of the Shelburne Story mention its presence. Even if it was late to join the task force, an Oberon diesel electric sub can only stay submerged for so long. Its contribution would be minimal. It only would have been potentially useful when it came time to show challenge to the purported intrusion of a Soviet sub.

Further Tidbits

As stated earlier, staff members at CFS Shelburne have admitted to tracking USOs; the Air Desk's Squadron Leader, William Bain, admitted to seeing UFOs and light anomalies while flying the North Atlantic off the coast of Nova Scotia in the fifties and sixties; and Chris Styles has also heard of two incidents that took place before the purported Shelburne operation that involved the pursuit of high speed sonar targets that exhibited bursts of speed in excess of 100 knots. Both of these USO pursuits were described firsthand by several of the men who were there. The first involved a pursuit by HMCS *Terra Nova*. The chase was abandoned after thirty-six hours of cat and mouse chases that always ended with sudden acceleration by the mysterious sonar target. The other chase was an on-again, off-again affair that dragged through the Christmas

CHAPTER 4: SHELBURNE

holidays of 1962. It involved the crew of HMCS *Chaudiere*. Both affairs played out in the Atlantic with the nearest point of land being near Shelburne. Neither incident received any media attention.

Other Considerations
The Shelburne Story lacks the documentation that has become a cornerstone of the Shag Harbour Incident. And yet the Shelburne Story remains a persistent rumour within the community. It lives in the chatter of the relatives and spouses of former servicemen, civilians who were once employed by the base in support roles, and local residents who remember "the day they tried to keep Sandy Point Road closed." And it lives in the memories of the *Granby* divers who insist, "There was no doubt about what we saw out on the bottom off of Shelburne—no doubt. It was nothing from here."

Chris Styles still feels that one of the stronger arguments supporting the validity of the Shelburne Story is how the timeline between the moment of impact in Shag Harbour, on October 4, 1967, and the Cameron family UFO sighting of October 11, 1967, fits the initial telling of the Shelburne Story like a glove. When Chris first interviewed the diver known as Harry he claimed "they held those ships there for a week off of Government Point." Of course, Harry did not know that twenty-six years later someone was going to ask him about his role in the Shag Harbour Incident. It was a story that was already startling and unique. It did not need any more "sizzle." And yet there it was. "There was no doubt off of Shelburne. The two saucers were still there. One was helping the other, standing nines over it. They held those ships there a week," said Harry.

Harry did not keep any mementos, notes, or press clippings. He did not even remember the date. He guessed the year as 1962 when asked and not 1967. The brass ordered the matter forgotten. But there was no doubt that Harry was there and part of the operation. His trainer and CO supplied his name. "Jim," the RCAF officer, said that Harry was there. And Chris Styles's father served with Harry aboard HMCS *Cape Scott* and remembers him well and his incredible story told over a card game years after it unfolded. The military telexes of RG 77 and the press clippings of the day chronicle how the *Granby* divers were dispatched to Shag Harbour to search for what was believed to be a UFO crash. Why embellish the story? Harry was there but did not remember the date. He did not remember the Cameron family sighting that occurred one week later. However, the October 4 crash and the October 11 UFO sighting of two separate sets of lights surfacing and flying away out over the Gulf of Maine fit the Shelburne Story like a set of bookends.[2] Interestingly, Lorraine Cameron forgot the date of her October 11, 1967, sighting and remembered it as being the week before the Shag Harbour crash of October 4, 1967. Luckily, the plethora of press clippings makes the correct dates certain. The confusion of the Cameron family's UFO sighting is just another example of the plasticity of memory over time.

Perhaps the lengthy interim between the time of the events and the start of Chris's initial attempts to investigate the Shag Harbour Incident is all that is necessary to account for the uncertainty of the Shelburne Story. Then again, the missing lighthouse logs of Cape Roseway and the spotty ships' logs don't help, either, and neither did the high security of CFS Shelburne. Perhaps the plasticity of memory allowed the blending of recollections of previous searches for USOs off of the coast of Shelburne. One thing is certain, for the moment —the Shelburne Story remains just that, a story.

The Shelburne Story may not have an available paper trail proving military involvement. But there is evidence that supports what the witnesses have described. It may have been a compartmentalized mission that involved both Canadian and American military personnel. This could explain why staff members as high up as William Bain were unaware of the week-long operation at Government Point.

For Chris Styles, the Shelburne Story remains "a fly in the ointment." He still seeks the kind of hard documentation for it that the Shag Harbour UFO crash of October 4, 1967, enjoys. The Shag Harbour Incident has become a compelling argument for UFO reality. Shelburne on the other hand remains a compelling story, albeit a remarkably good one that is not easily explained or explained away.

Chapter 4 Endnotes

1. RCMP File 67-400-23-X, Burke-Gaffney Collection, Saint Mary's University archives.
2. Personal notes of Fr. Michael Burke-Gaffney regarding the Cameron family UFO sighting over Shag Harbour on October 11, 1967, part of the Burke-Gaffney Collection, Saint Mary's University archive

Chapter 5: UFO Down Under
Chris Styles

"...concerning the strange disappearance of ships. How many trains have disappeared?"
– Philip Morrison, nuclear physicist, the Manhattan Project

"The important thing in science is not so much to obtain new facts as to discover new ways of thinking about them."
– Sir William Bragg, Nobel Prize-winning physicist

The original 1967 RCN search effort for physical evidence at the site of the UFO crash in Shag Harbour was by today's standards a decidedly low tech affair. There was no side-scan sonar, no magnetometers or remotely operated vehicles (ROVs). The only resource available to the Fleet Diving Unit was a handful of brave men willing to go down below and search the seabed for whatever. The days of iron men and wooden ships may be a thing of the past, but in our modern world it is the diver who survives as much by his wits of steel as the air in his tanks. It is the lot of the diver to go below and face the unknown with little more than a flashlight and a trusted partner.

The first search effort consisted of a pair of RCMP divers who scoured the sandy bottom of The Sound with hand-held lights. The first pair of men to go below—for three hours on the morning of Thursday, October 5, 1967—was from the RCMP dive unit. They carried out a quick sweep of the area of the Sound that lay between the Budget buoy and the last known surface position of the UFO. A large Zodiac inflatable acted as the diving tender. Coast Guard Cutter (CGC) 101 held station nearby. RCMP Corporal Victor Werbicki and a couple of the eyewitnesses were aboard CGC 101 to help establish position and to share with the dive master pertinent details of the previous evening's UFO sighting.

By 11:30 AM, that initial RCMP dive was terminated and a brief verbal situation report was given to H Division headquarters (HQ) back in Halifax. HQ was told that nothing was found that could account for what was seen the previous evening by the locals and the three RCMP members. Once the men and their equipment were back on dry land, CGC 101 returned to its home base at the lifesaving station in nearby Clark's Harbour.[1] For the remainder of that Thursday, CGC 101 resumed its regular role as the primary search and rescue vessel for that immediate portion of Nova Scotia's southwestern shore.

A preliminary report, prepared in the early morning hours of October 5 by the Rescue Coordination Centre (RCC) in Halifax, had already reached DND headquarters in Ottawa.[2] That initial RCC report found its way to the desk of Squadron Leader William Bain. William Bain was a major assigned to the "Air Desk," a little-known division of the Royal Canadian Air Force (RCAF) that carried out various responsibilities including the filing, screening, and subsequent investigation of UFO incidents. The Air Desk could be thought of as the rough equivalent of the United States Air Force's Project Bluebook. Unlike Project Bluebook, however, Canada's Air Desk actually carried out on-site investigations. If the evidence seemed to support the possible involvement of true unknown objects or genuine UFOs, military field units would be dispatched to investigate. This outcome was reserved for promising UFO cases that demonstrated both high strangeness and high credibility. To put that ratio in perspective, the RCAF's Air Desk cataloged 256 UFO sightings in 1967. Nine cases from that group of reported UFO sightings were deemed worthy of prolonged on-site investigations.

As soon as S/L Bain finished reading the RCC Preliminary Report on Shag Harbour, he liaised with his CO, Colonel Turner. Turner got clearance to carry out an underwater search. Clearance from the top was a necessary step whenever money was required for an extensive search effort. A priority telex was sent to Maritime Command, asking it to carry out an underwater search in the Shag Harbour area ASAP.[3]

In 1995, while carrying out UFO research in the capitol region, I conducted a face-to-face interview with William Bain, then retired. He told me that if he had had his way, back in 1967, there would have been three Sea King helicopters on standby, stationed at diverse points across Nova Scotia, ready to dispatch to investigate high grade UFO sightings, but the money and the will just weren't there for such intellectual pursuits. 1967 was a time of shrinking military budgets and the looming spectre of unification, an unpopular government program, implemented in 1968, that combined Canada's armed forces into a single service.

The RCC Preliminary Report that Halifax forwarded to the Air Desk figured prominently in Colonel Turner's pitch for the funds needed to carry out

CHAPTER 5: UFO DOWN UNDER

an underwater search. That brief report offered a compelling argument that the Shag Harbour Incident might indeed be the result of a genuine UFO mishap. Perhaps the clincher that helped secure Col. Turner's request was the following statement from a memo that had circulated throughout DND headquarters less than twenty-four hours after the crash in Shag Harbour. The memo was both bold and concise. It read as follows: "The Rescue Coordination Centre conducted preliminary investigation and discounted the possibilities that the sighting was produced by an aircraft, flares, floats or *any other known objects.*"[4]

On Thursday, October 5, 1967, Squadron Leader William Bain sent a priority message to Maritime Command at 6:12 pm (EST). It read as follows:

FROM CANFORCEHED

TO CANMARCOM

INFO RCC HALIFAX

SUBJECT: UFO. REF RCC HALIFAX RCC 076 051320Z OCT. (1) REQUEST SUBJECT UFO REPORT BE INVESTIGATED BY YOUR HQ. (2)
CONSIDERATION SHOULD BE GIVEN FOR AN UNDERWATER SEARCH OF THE AREA ASAP.

Cc DOPS 4-2

DRAFTER'S NAME (W BAIN) S/L DOPS 4-2 2 2900

RELEASING OFFICER'S SIGNATURE (J. MORRISON S/L)

(The original message form is preserved at Library and Archives Canada, formerly the National Archives of Canada. That collection of UFO reports and documents [Records Group 77, Vol 310] is available to the public. It is preserved on microfilm and can be borrowed via Canada's interlibrary loan system. The above telex document also bears the number "120" handwritten at the bottom. This was Maritime Command's active UFO case number for the Shag Harbour Incident.)

Once Maritime Command received the Air Desk's request, things began to happen rapidly. Commander Rex Guy, the CO at Maritime Command, turned the matter over to his most trusted scientific consultant and personal friend, Dr. Maurice Coffey.[5] Dr. Coffey, known to his close friends as Mace, was a highly respected search and rescue specialist and an expert on survival in the High Arctic. He developed numerous search and rescue techniques employed by DND and presented papers to prestigious think tanks such as the Rand Corporation. Much of Coffey's groundbreaking technical work and theoretical speculations were published in a series of DND technical papers that have been preserved. They remain on display to this day in the reading room at DND headquarters in Ottawa.

In 1967 Mace Coffey was the guy that Maritime Command relied upon to locate missing things. Soviet subs, missing aircraft, nuclear bombs, and UFOs were just a few of the eclectic items that demanded Dr. Coffey's special talents. Sometimes, when the good doctor was stumped, he was known to resort to techniques that could clearly be considered to lie within the realm of the paranormal. The details of Mace Coffey's personal involvement in the Shag Harbour Incident are examined in chapter 13.

On Thursday evening, October 5, 1967, Maritime Command rolled into action. Initially, four divers were dispatched from the Fleet Diving Unit. All four men were part of a group posted to HMCS *Granby*, which was tied up at a jetty on the Dartmouth side of Halifax Harbour. The *Granby* never left the pier in Dartmouth. The four men drove through the night to the Shag Harbour area in an old army "deuce-and-a-half" truck, which was known affectionately as "Old Syd." Upon arrival they quickly loaded their gear aboard CGC 101, which acted as the diving tender for the first full day of underwater searching. By 9:00 AM, Friday October 6, the first pair of divers was in the water.[6]

The *Granby* divers took turns going below. Each subsequent pair of men scoured the sandy bottom with a handheld light. Decompression was not a concern as the maximum depth within the search area was under sixty feet. The currents within The Sound were fatiguing to the divers, but not

CHAPTER 5: UFO DOWN UNDER

overwhelming. As a result good progress was made and the divers were quickly eliminating considerable portions of the search area.

On that Friday, the team spent a full nine hours searching, from 9:00 AM until 6:00 pm.[7] Periodic verbal updates were being called in to the officer of the watch at Maritime Command back in Halifax. The details were passed on to Dr. Coffey. Coffey felt that more manpower should be brought into the search area. He wanted to scour the area as quickly as possible to eliminate the possibility of debris being shifted or buried in sand by the highly energetic currents of Shag Harbour. He was also concerned with the possibility of local souvenir hunters using grappling hooks to scavenge the bottom under cover of darkness. A chat with his colleague and boss, Rex Guy, got the result that Mace wanted. Three more divers and another 400 lbs. of equipment were flown by Sea King to Barrington Passage from CFB Shearwater in Dartmouth.[8] The additional men reached Barrington Passage before first light on Saturday, October 7, and were ready to put in a full day. Permission was given to hire a local boat so that CGC 101 could resume its normal search and rescue duties at the nearby Clark's Harbour life station. This also provided the divers with more deck space for the seven men and their bulky equipment.

The Granby divers put in a second full day, from 9:00 AM until 6:00 pm. Once again their best efforts produced "nil results." They did not find any debris or wreckage. No unusual features, artifacts, or seabed trauma were noted. All the divers saw was sand, kelp, and lobsters. The divers may have discovered nothing out of the ordinary, but the people of Shag Harbour had discovered the divers and they were being watched with great interest. And the audience would soon grow to be international in scope.

Crowds of locals parked next to the moss plant to sit and watch the underwater search. A television crew from CBC Halifax filmed a segment for the supper hour news. The *Halifax Chronicle-Herald*, one of Canada's most conservative broadsheets, ran the headline, "Could be Something Concrete in Shag Harbour UFO – RCAF." The wire services distributed the story to newspapers and tabloids around the globe. Local fishing boats milled about in the water allowing those aboard a close-up view. Speculation and word of mouth served to drive the local rumour mill. Police witnesses, military involvement, and the subsequent media frenzy conspired to create a surreal atmosphere in the most unlikely of settings. Canadian navy divers were searching for a flying saucer in Shag Harbour!

Sunday morning, October 8, the decision was made to expand the search area. A rectangle measuring 1.5 by 0.5 miles had already been thoroughly searched.[9] Emphasis was then put on the area immediately to the southwest of the searched area. That position in The Sound lies beyond the last known surface position of the UFO and is situated farther along the course that the mysterious "dark object" seemed to be following until it disappeared from view.

Back in Halifax, Maritime Command had discussed the situation with the Air Desk. It was decided that if there were still nil results by last light on Sunday evening, the underwater search would be terminated. This in fact would be the final outcome of the *Granby* divers' underwater search operation.[10]

A final situation report was telexed to Maritime Command and to DND HQ in Ottawa. It claimed nil results. Monday morning, October 9, 1967, a press release announced the cancellation of the search effort and its negative outcome. A spokesman for the Rescue Coordination Centre in Halifax stated that something definitely went into the water off Shag Harbour, but there were many theories as to what it might have been; no one knew what they were searching for. He was quoted on the front page of the *Halifax Chronicle-Herald* as saying, "It could have been anything from a grasshopper to another planet."

It was a strange choice of words to sum up the final outcome of the exhaustive search effort. To those of us who have seen and read the final situation report that was telexed to Maritime Command and DND HQ, the RCC spokesman's unusual phrasing could be seen as somewhat misleading. The brief communiqué put it this way:

1. SEARCH CONTINUED 08 OCT NEGATIVE RESULTS

2. SEARCH TERMINATED 082130Z

SITREP [situation report] - UNIDENTIFIED FLYING OBJECT[11]

The words "unidentified flying object" were circled by hand as if having some special significance to the person who received and filed the brief document.

In 1993, when I read the military telexes found within RG 77, they caused me to reflect upon the possible meanings of two suggestive statements made on behalf of two different Canadian government departments regarding UFOs. The first statement was made by Squadron Leader Bain regarding the Air Desk s investigation into the Shag Harbour incident. In the Saturday, October 7, 1967 edition of the *Halifax Chronicle-Herald*, S/L Bain told reporter Ray

MacLeod that "the Shag Harbour incident may be one of those extremely rare cases where something concrete could be found." He did not explain exactly what he meant by "extremely rare cases," but the implication seems to be that some other known cases must have produced some kind of indisputable solid evidence.

The second government spokesman's statement that caused me to ponder was that of Prime Minister Trudeau's Undersecretary of State for External Affairs, who wrote a letter on behalf of the prime minister, dated April 15, 1971, in response to veteran Canadian UFO researcher Arthur Bray, in which he says, "The Canadian Government does not underestimate the seriousness of the question of UFOs and this matter is being kept under consideration and study in a number of departments and agencies." I only wish that the undersecretary had seen fit to list those various agencies. However, due to my research into the Shag Harbour case, I knew that even a partial list would have included such diverse agencies as the RCMP, DND, the Defence Research Board, the National Research Council, the Department of Transportation, and even several universities such as the University of Toronto.

Perhaps the closing sentence in that 1971 letter to Arthur Bray revealed more than any military telex possibly could as to just how great the concern was in Ottawa regarding the question of UFOs and how they should be handled. UFO researcher Arthur Bray thought that the UFO phenomenon should be studied by an international effort under UN control. In 1971 the Undersecretary of State for Foreign Affairs seemed to agree. "If and when it appears that a resolution of the kind you mention would be likely to receive approval by the General Assembly, you may rest assured that the Canadian Government would be prepared to take all appropriate steps in this connection."

Troubling cases such as the Shag Harbour Incident served as an embarrassment for government agencies with multibillion dollar budgets and few answers. Even if UFOs did not seem to be an imminent threat to our national security, they did seem to leave both "the brass" and the public with a sense of "national insecurity." The 1967 crash of Shag Harbour's "dark object" seemed to demonstrate one inescapable truth. UFOs were penetrating our skies and defence systems, and there was nothing that the authorities could do about it.

When Maritime Command announced the termination of the underwater search and its claim of "nil results," it did not mean that DND was entirely finished searching for answers or physical evidence in Shag Harbour. It simply meant that the diving operation had ended. What followed was a casual yet methodical operation that was designed to allow a much needed "cool down" period while data was still being collected. Second interviews of eyewitnesses were conducted on the spot in bowling alleys and at lunch counters. RCMP officers continued to carry out shoreline walkabouts near the moss plant.

As the days of October slipped away, the media quickly lost interest. Shag Harbour's UFO coverage moved from the headlines to the back pages. Debunking stories began to appear.

DND was not yet ready to give up the good fight. On November 2, 1967, almost a full month after the October 4 crash and a full three weeks after the termination of the DND underwater search, an appeal appeared in every weekly newspaper in Nova Scotia. It asked the public to formally and immediately report any UFO sightings to the authorities. That article contained instructions and contact information and was written by Major Victor Eldridge (Eldridge 1967a). Back in 1967, Major Eldridge served as the Executive Officer at CFS Barrington at Bacarro. In his off hours he worked as a "stringer" writing articles about military issues of local interest for several of the southwestern shore weeklies.

In the fall of 1993 I attempted to interview Vic Eldridge on the telephone. It was my hope that the retired major could shed some light on the investigation that had obviously continued on after the failed underwater search. But Vic Eldridge claimed to have no knowledge of the Shag Harbour Incident. I attempted to jog his memory by reading from his November 2, 1967 article, but again he claimed that he did not remember writing the appeal for UFO reports. I remarked that the community had never forgotten the incident. That comment elicited a response. "There were lots of crazy things going on back then. I'm sure that there was really nothing to it. Just what is it that you're hoping to accomplish by looking into this?" (I was pleased that we had moved from "I don't remember" to him being certain that it was nothing.)

"I would just like to know what really happened," I responded. "I've spoken with many others who would also like to know the truth." There was a long awkward pause that became painful. I then prompted the major by saying, "I was hoping that I would not have to resort to speculation as to your role in the matter."

"If I were you I would be very careful," came the quick retort. "Do you know what could happen if I made one phone call?" He then told me, so that I wouldn't have to guess.

CHAPTER 5: UFO DOWN UNDER

Despite his threat, I was determined to continue with my investigation. "You tell the guy who signs your pension cheque that I am too dumb to quit." And at that point of disagreement I pulled the plug.

I never took the major's idle threat seriously, chalking it all up to Cold War era training. I figured that Mr. Eldridge was someone whose life experience had left him with a totally unrestrained level of respect for authority. Perhaps that's an unfair assessment of a man who served his country and who took his duties and oaths most seriously. But I feel that as individuals we all have a personal responsibility to speak out and act when one feels that a line has been drawn in the wrong place. I believe that those kinds of ethical considerations also apply to those who serve. I should tell you that this was the only time anyone seemed offended by my efforts to investigate the Shag Harbour case. Cooperation from most of the authorities who were involved with Shag Harbour has been excellent. (In fact, one of the major's commanding officers, Rex Guy, would prove to be among those who made a significant contribution toward my understanding of NORAD's involvement; see chapter 13)

The military's November 2, 1967 appeal for UFO reports was not the only indicator that Ottawa had not ceased its close monitoring of UFO activity around the southwestern shore of Nova Scotia. The paper chase that had deluged me in archival documents and old military telexes had yielded another strong indicator of Ottawa's former obsession with UFOs. Among the many message forms and press clippings preserved among the files of the Air Desk was a clipping from the defunct newspaper, *The Province*. Someone at DND HQ had cut out an article that featured an interview with Professor Rupert MacNeil of Acadia University. The clipping bore the heading, "He Could Believe in UFOs." A handwritten note in the margin of the clipping reads, "This does not help the situation."

Professor MacNeil was a geologist with a keen interest in the UFO phenomenon. In fact, by January 8, 1968, all responsibilities regarding UFO investigations were transferred from the Air Desk to Canada's National Research Council for "serious scientific study," according to the NRC press release. The NRC reluctantly accepted the task, and it was assigned to Professor MacNeil of Acadia and Professor Tennyson of the University of Toronto. Ottawa had "felt the heat" from cases such as Shag Harbour and the Stephen Michalak close encounter case that occurred in May, 1967 near Falcon Lake, Manitoba. Both of those cases were often mentioned and included as attachments affixed to most of the UFO transfer documents preserved within that National Archives RG 77 collection. DND did not want the UFO phenomenon to be seen as an issue of national security. The "brass" in Ottawa thought that the NRC was a more appropriate venue for the UFO problem. That sentiment appears numerous times throughout various interdepartmental correspondence. However, the execution of the original concept played out a little differently in the real world.

The transfer was set up in such a way as to allow the NRC to call upon "field units" from both the RCMP and DND as was necessary. Although this arrangement appears on paper, in fact it was never implemented. Tennyson and MacNeil did do on-site investigations, but they were carried out separately as solo efforts. The two scientists would arrive at the location of a UFO case days or weeks after the incident. The two men were equipped with little more than a notebook, a compass, and a camera. Some of Professor MacNeil's reports have survived within the microfilm reels of RG 77. When the two academics reached retirement, no one was reassigned their UFO research duties. The NRC decided to let the UFO assignment die a quiet death. Investigations were no longer carried out. UFO reports continued to be forwarded to the NRC by the RCMP, the Department of Transportation, and other agencies but were simply archived at the Hertzberg Institute located on Sussex Drive in Ottawa. In the mid nineties the NRC stopped accepting UFO reports. From that point onward, UFO investigations in Canada would only be carried out by volunteer civilian groups and a few self-appointed individuals.

Not everyone who lived near or became aware of the Shag Harbour Incident was prepared to leave the responsibility of a search for a downed UFO to the government. The October 12, 1967 edition of the *Yarmouth Vanguard* chronicled some of the suspicions that were being expressed by certain local residents and witnesses.

> In the meantime, fishermen and other residents of the Shag Harbour–Woods Harbour area are suspiciously eying the area near Bon Portage Island where the object was seen and speculating as to the nature of the object seen by so many of themselves and their neighbours.
>
> Rumours Start
> A rumour has already begun to spread through the community that the navy divers came up with several pieces of metal and that this was the reason that the search ended so early. When countered with the report that Maritime Command gave saying that they had found nothing, the men say that the navy wouldn't be allowed to say anything if the object were found. Most of the

residents of the area, however, deny the rumour but still confirm that "there suremust have been something as so many of us saw it."

Fisher men in Shag Harbour say that if the object is still there it will be found when lobster season begins. At this time, almost every inch of the bottom will be touched by the lobster pots placed all over the area by the local men. The fishermen also say that they will take a good look at the mysterious spot as they pass over it on their way to the fishing grounds with their depth finders. (Eldridge 1967b)

Some locals did not wait until lobster season. They employed their depth finders but to no avail. No one laid claim to an artifact or souvenir from Shag Harbour's mysterious dark object. Others continued to beachcomb the area around the moss plant and the shores of Bon Portage Island. Again no one struck "pay dirt." There were also "armchair" investigators who waited for the publication of new oceanographic charts of the local seabed. They hoped that a new shallow circular area would be charted that displayed a discrepancy with earlier published charts. They hoped that an area approximately sixty feet in diameter would be found lacking from its previous depth. Those dreamers continued to hope as they poured over the myriad of charted sounding values with their magnifying glasses. In time those hopeful individuals, like the government agencies before them, stopped looking but probably for very different reasons.

By 1968 the media had mostly forgotten about the Shag Harbour incident. There were a few follow-up journalistic treatments in some of the monthly glossy periodicals of the day. One of the best retellings was written by former Dartmouth resident, amateur astronomer and UFO enthusiast William F. Dawson. His article, "UFO Down Off Shag Harbour," appeared in the February 1968 edition of *FATE* magazine. Dawson's concise six page treatment put forward an intriguing theory as to the whereabouts of Shag Harbour's mysterious "dark object." He offers the reader this hypothesis:

> But where it went after it submerged remains a matter of conjecture. Three possibilities seemed to exist:
> 1. Strong tides carried the object farther out to sea.
> 2. The object came to rest on the bottom of the seabed outside the area so painstakingly searched.
> 3. The object, after submerging, abandoned the area under its own power.

The first two possibilities suggest that at this very moment an unidentified flying object, fully 60 feet in length, is resting on the continental shelf off the Nova Scotia mainland. (Dawson 1968: 52–53)

I do not know how many people read the Dawson article. It first came to my attention in 1995. At the time I was being interviewed for *FATE* magazine by one of its correspondents, veteran UFO journalist and researcher Anthony Huneeus. He was writing an article for his monthly column about my efforts to investigate Shag Harbour. The 1968 Dawson article made an immediate impression upon me. I believed that Dawson's premise was still valid. I decided that I would conduct my own underwater search. I just had to figure out how to begin and how to pay for it. I had no idea what kind of eclectic and strange adventure that effort would turn out to be.

Chapter 5 Endnotes

1. Canadian Coast Guard Cutter (CGC) 101 ship's logbook entry 109.
2. DND telex, NRC Public Archives, RG 77, Vol. 310, P 051320Z, October 1967.
3. DND telex, NRC Public Archives, RG 77, Vol. 310, Message Form P 052120Z, October 1967.
4. DND memo, released to the author from DND Directorate of History in response to a July 19, 1993 telephone inquiry. Emphasis added.
5. Author's notes from his telephone interview with former Commanding Officer Rex Guy of Maritime Command in the fall of 2004.
6. CGC 101 ship's logbook entry 111 (second copy; see chapter 15).
7. Ibid.
8. DND telex, NRC Public Archives, RG 77, Vol. 310, P 070146Z, October 1967.
9. DND telex, NRC Public Archives, RG 77, Vol. 310, P 080002Z, October 1967.
10. DND telex, NRC Public Archives, RG 77, Vol. 310, P 082319Z, October 1967.
11. Ibid.

Chapter 6: The *Sightings* Expedition
Chris Styles

"Science may set limits to knowledge but should not set limits to imagination."
– Bertrand Russell

"I believe that a scientist looking at nonscientific problems is just as dumb as the next guy."
– Richard Feynman, American theoretical physicist

By the summer of 1995 I was obsessed with one key question regarding the Shag Harbour Incident. Did any evidence of the elusive "dark object" remain on the bottom of Shag Harbour? Had physical evidence escaped detection by the original RCN underwater search back in 1967? To my way of thinking it seemed unreasonable to expect that one might discover a largely intact 60 foot craft lying on the bottom. But what about lesser artifacts or perhaps some unique type of seabed trauma? The *Granby* divers said they thought the UFO had lost an engine. In fact the Seal Island lightkeeper and other eyewitnesses reported that the bottom of the craft appeared to be on fire when the UFO was seen to pass over Seal Island shortly before its plunge into the Sound. It seemed to me that at least one of the possibilities expressed in William Dawson's 1968 article for *FATE* magazine remained both valid and promising: "The object came to rest on the seabed beyond the area already painstakingly searched" (Dawson 1968: 52). Could it be that simple?

It is an historic fact that Maritime Command claimed "nil results" as the outcome of its original underwater search back in 1967.[1] But was the term "nil results" completely accurate? Were there any unconventional ET or "grey basket" findings? And could DND's press release be trusted? Press coverage of the day stated that many of the locals believed that the navy wouldn't be allowed to release their true findings. The Vic Eldridge newspaper appeal for UFO reports seemed a strong argument to at least consider the locals' speculations regarding the navy's true discoveries about the Shag Harbour Incident. I had to weigh all of the possibilities.

There was at least one very practical reason to consider carrying out a second underwater search in 1995—technology. The original search effort was a simple, low tech operation. Divers went below carrying handheld flashlights. There was no side-scan sonar, magnetometers, GPS, or video equipment. Metallic debris could have been lying in just inches of sand and escaped detection. Larger pieces could easily be hidden in areas covered by thick kelp beds. The only tools available to the *Granby* divers for probing the bottom were sixteen-foot long corrugated iron rods. The divers would push them into the soft bottom hoping to strike something anomalous or at least hard. If their probing met something substantial the men would excavate and retrieve the hard item for examination. Ironically the divers had long before nicknamed the rusty rods "UFO detectors."

The first line of business to consider was how to pay for such a mission. Once again, as I did in 1993's pursuit of archival documents, I applied to the Fund for UFO Research for support. I knew that FUFOR moved slowly and cautiously, as they must. But it was my hope that by applying in January of 1995 that I might be fortunate enough to get approval and funding in time to carry out a side-scan sonar survey and dive that very summer or fall.

Rob Swiatek was assigned as my project manager. Rob is a physicist by training and had a considerable reputation as a UFO researcher. He was also a recreational diver. My proposal included quotes from two Nova Scotian firms for the scientific contract. The winner would prove to be Canadian Seabed Research; however, there were more than a few wrinkles and hiccups along the way toward that final outcome. For more than the first half of 1995 there was the waiting for word of funding assistance. I figured that I would use what spare time I had to get an overview of survey technology and its pitfalls.

Over the years I have been a faithful listener to CBC Radio in Halifax. It offers a much needed break from Top 40 radio when driving, and I particularly enjoy the many interview driven shows. Consequently, I was aware of one local expert who was synonymous with underwater sonar surveys, Gordon Fader.

Dr. Gordon Fader is a marine geologist who had a distinguished career with the Geological Survey of Canada at the Bedford Institute of Oceanography located in north end Dartmouth. Fader has also built a career as a consultant to those in need of his expertise. He has over the years given advice to various projects for such varied clients as the military, treasure hunters, and marine archaeologists. In brief, he helps people find things that have been lost or yet to be discovered. It was my hope that the renowned geologist could spare a little time and advice to help me choose a firm for the

CHAPTER 6: THE SIGHTINGS EXPEDITION

survey contract and to give me some pointers so that I could be sure that things were being done properly in the field. I also wanted to understand a little about interpreting the raw sonar data as it was being recorded. I wanted to gain enough knowledge about side-scan sonar to asses the target value in the field. Acoustic reflections bounced off of a seabed to a tow fish—a torpedo-like device towed behind a survey vessel at some depth below the surface that emits and receives sonar sound waves—are not much like a true visual representation. I wanted to be ready to give the order to drop anchor and send a diver down to get up close and personal with any potential artifact. Time could be of the essence on a limited time frame and budget.

Not being the shy type, I phoned Fader's work number at BIO and left a lengthy message on his voice mail. He returned my call, and the two of us had a lively discussion about the Shag Harbour Incident in which I tried to bring the scientist up to speed on the history of the case and my ongoing efforts to investigate the mystery. We set up an appointment to meet at BIO on January 12, 1995.

I invited fellow UFO researcher Don Ledger to join me for the meeting. At that time I had known Don just a short while, perhaps a year. I had received a call from Mrs. Walt Andrus, whose husband was the director of the Mutual UFO Network (MUFON), of which I was a member. Mrs. Andrus called me from Texas to ask me to look up Don Ledger. He had applied to join MUFON, but his application had been lost for two years. It turned out that Don was at that very time seeking me out after having seen me on local TV talking about the Shag Harbour Incident.

Gordon Fader met me and Don at the entrance to BIO and led us to the Atlantic Geoscience Centre on one of the lower levels of the complex, where we were joined by Fader's long-time colleague, fellow geologist, Bob Miller.

The latter part of the morning was largely filled by a lengthy retelling of the events of October 4, 1967. This served the dual purpose of giving Gordon Fader additional information about the case to help him form some opinions and perhaps give some much wanted advice and to give Bob Miller an introduction to the Shag Harbour Incident. As lunchtime approached, the four of us moved the meeting to BIO's cafeteria where the discussion continued. It was there that Fader commented, "As a UFO case Shag Harbour sounds very refreshing because unlike the majority of such claims this one did not evaporate as one gets closer to the facts."

Up to this point Bob Miller had remained largely silent, listening and reading documents that I had pulled from my briefcase and that were being passed around the dining table. He set down a handful of paper and said that he thought he may have sailed over the so-called impact site while directing a side-scan sonar survey in the summer of 1988. He went on to say that he remembered some kind of a strange anomalous detection that was brought to his attention by one of the technicians. Miller's sudden announcement quickened the pace of lunch, and it was a hasty trip back to the Geoscience Centre to retrieve the data that would support Miller's recollections from the summer of 1988.

Miller found the cruise report for the 1988 summer survey carried out under his direction by the fisheries research vessel *Navicula*. That survey was part on an ongoing provincial government program to search for gravel on the seabed. Gravel is always in demand in Nova Scotia and there is increased public resistance to surface quarries. It was not the actual report that Miller was interested in but its two subsequent charts that were tucked within the book's cover pocket.

The appropriate chart was quickly unfolded and spread out on a table. We were immediately struck by two facts. The first was that the *Navicula*'s sonar survey had actually missed both the impact site and the last known surface position. However, one leg of the research vessel's random pattern course took it to within a mile of the UFO's last known surface position. On that nearest segment of the mission, the chart showed an ambiguous plotting. The position of that anomalous seabed feature lay both down current and in the last direction of the UFO's observed drift. But there was more. And it proved to be a cruel teaser for Don and me. The label on the chart for the ambiguous sonar target was "may not be boulders." The four of us laughed and groaned together.

Before the mirth and regret had completely subsided, Gordon Fader had retrieved the actual sonar rolls from one of the lab's many storage boxes. The large rolls were quickly mounted on a big hand cranked display table. Bob read coordinates aloud to Gordon who cranked furiously through the sonar rolls at high speed. Occasionally he paused to check his relative position. Before long the correct sonar roll and relevant data was at hand. What we found in the data only served to crank our mood up another notch.

When giving a lecture, I often say that margin notes left by staff usually prove far more telling than the main body of text when it comes to UFO documents. The margin notes left by the sonar techs aboard the *Navicula* did not outshine the data, but they sure served to highlight the significance of the anomalous acoustic reflection that had been recorded. The techs had scribbled

CHAPTER 6: THE SIGHTINGS EXPEDITION

circles, lines, question marks, and exclamation marks right on the sonar roll. They also left comments such as, "What the hell are these things?" Immediately Fader and Miller donned 3-D goggles and attempted to interpret the curious data. All that the two scientists could agree upon was what the sonar target could not be. That list of improbabilities included such things as shipwrecks, shell beds, dredge spoils, spud can depressions from drill rig activity, and boulders. In the end Gordon Fader shook his head and made the comment, "We are not in the business of making ambiguous chartings" (Ledger and Styles 2001: 129).

The image on the sonar roll is quite striking. It appears as four circular depressions in the seabed. They are arranged in a slightly tapered diamond-like pattern. The diameter of the various depressions is in the three to five metre range. Their vertical relief is uncertain. The symmetry of the feature alone argues for something at least anthropogenic or man-made in origin. However, the pattern suggests nothing typically seen on the seabed. It certainly fired my imagination and inspired me to push on for a new underwater search.

The spring of 1995 was a busy period. I spent a great deal of time reading up on sonar and its nuances. Many calls were made to Gordon Fader who warned me of the simple pitfalls and gave me invaluable tips such as being ready to replace exhausted rolls of thermal imaging paper on the sonar recorders as soon as they ended and making sure that the tow fish wasn't too close to the propeller and picking up too much "prop wash." And never forget the golden rule—hire a local boat.

Many other professionals gave freely of their time and advice. Glenn Gilbert of Canadian Seabed Research, Terry Dyer of Deep Star Resources, and Rob Swiatek of the Fund for UFO Research were all called upon many times and were always there with advice and encouragement.

As summer approached, a plan was slowly taking shape. It had to be frugal yet worthwhile. I proposed a four-day survey that included side-scan sonar, a magnetometer, underwater video, and a pair of divers. A bad weather day was also worked into the budget. The final estimate was that something in the order of $16,000 should cover everything needed to carry out the search. I wrote up a formal proposal and sent it off to FUFOR for their consideration. Near the end of May I received a letter from Rob Swiatek. He said that the Shag Harbour proposal had created a "buzz" and that the proposal looked good. The letter went on to explain that FUFOR had formed a coalition with the Mutual UFO Network (MUFON) and with the Center for UFO Studies. It was the hope of all three partners that the merger would allow them to support larger research ventures such as the Shag Harbour survey proposal. Things seemed to be moving along nicely.

That summer served up an interesting distraction from the pressure and worry about the upcoming survey project. *Sightings*, a US syndicated television program that dealt with paranormal phenomena, expressed an interest in doing a segment on the Shag Harbour Incident for their fall season. The two day shoot was booked for a weekend in July. The filming went well and included interviews in Halifax/Dartmouth and on-site in Shag Harbour. Several of the eyewitnesses were interviewed as was Ron Pond, one of the RCMP officers who responded to the impact scene back in '67. Cst. Pond was interviewed in Vancouver. When production wrapped up and the director flew back to Hollywood I figured that that would be the last I heard from Paramount Television. *Sightings* would busy itself with post-production on the Shag Harbour segment and dozens of other shoots that needed the polish of Hollywood's magic. And besides, I had plenty to keep me busy.

Just as the *Sightings* shoot was wrapping up, the Shag Harbour funding proposal was "going off the rails" in far away Las Vegas, unbeknownst to me. Two representatives from the three member groups of the new UFO coalition were meeting with one of their key benefactors, Robert Bigelow. Rob Swiatek and veteran UFO researcher Richard Hall were there to present the Shag Harbour proposal for possible funding, but it was all over as soon as it began.

At the onset of the meeting a major disagreement broke out between Bigelow and the other six men. In return for his financial support, Bigelow demanded veto powers. The financier's demand was unacceptable to all three UFO research groups. Business ground to a halt and none of the research proposals were examined for their worthiness for financial support. The meeting broke up and an announcement was made that the UFO research coalition would reorganize for its second year (Ibid.: 131).

A couple of days after Bigelow withdrew his support, I received a phone call from Rob Swiatek informing me of the goings on in Las Vegas. He assured me that my proposal was very much alive and that it would likely receive support; however, it would likely be held over until next summer or until the coalition secured a new financial benefactor. I thanked him for the information and told him that the situation was disappointing but not disturbing as I was in it for the long haul.

Within a week of the coalition's financial meltdown I received a call from the *Sightings* producer, Phil Davis. He called to tell me that they really liked the footage that was shot in Shag Harbour and that post-production was going

CHAPTER 6: THE SIGHTINGS EXPEDITION

well. He also asked how the funding proposal turned out. I brought him up to speed on the Las Vegas debacle, and he seemed more disappointed than I was. He said that if the survey had come to pass that they would have sent another director back to Nova Scotia and produced another segment for the program. I told Phil that I expected to get support for next summer and that I would keep in touch. He left me with some Japanese contacts that might offer support, and I promised to give it a try. However, Phil Davis proved to be quite impatient.

During the first week of August, Phil Davis called back to say that he had another idea. He asked me if I had any idea how much my proposed survey would cost. I told him that it would run somewhere in the range of $11,000 US (the equivalent of $16,000 Cdn at the time) for the scientific contract and the divers. He said that he couldn't promise anything but that he would bring it up at a pitch meeting. He asked me to write up an itemized estimate and fax it to him. It was a Friday afternoon, and I promised to do it that weekend and get it to him for Monday. Phil came back with, "Do it now. Go to Kinkos and fax it now." The following Tuesday afternoon I received a call from the executive producer of *Sightings*, David Johnson, telling me that the money was available for the survey and that Phil Davis would be in touch to work out all of the logistical details. I was stunned and unable to respond with much more than a sincere thank you. I spent the rest of that week trying to figure out what if anything had been missed in the impromptu proposal and trying to fathom the public awareness that the *Sightings* coverage would bring to Shag Harbour.

The first two weeks of September were filled with endless calls between myself and Phil Davis. The eyewitnesses were scheduled for further, in-depth interviews. Everything was to be shot on-site except for a few post-production re-enactments. Even the Halifax Library was scheduled for a shoot on a day closed to the public. Arrangements were made to hire the large Cape Island boat *Murphy's Law*, owned and piloted by Shag Harbour fisherman Bruce Addams. The most challenging task seemed to be finalizing the technical contract with Canadian Seabed Research. They were a busy firm with a large array of equipment options. There seemed to be little flexibility when it came to the possible need to reschedule due to weather or unforeseen circumstances. This made me nervous and almost proved to be our Achilles heel. Once again events far away from Nova Scotia conspired against us.

On September 2, 1995, the annual Canadian National Exhibition air show was being enjoyed by large crowds from the greater Toronto area. Tragedy struck when a British Nimrod failed to pull out of a steep dive manoeuvre over Lake Ontario. The large turbo prop plane struck hard and was smashed into tiny pieces. The crew of seven died instantly. The sonar equipment and technical support that we hoped to rent from Canadian Seabed Research (CSR) was diverted to Toronto to assist the recovery effort. CSR had standing contracts with several government agencies that had priority. This unfortunate turn of events caused an ongoing nightmare of scheduling that nearly drove both Phil Davis and me to pull the plug. Eventually, CSR was able to give a firm time window, and the survey and Hollywood's shoot were rebooked to begin on September 17.

I remember that a couple of days before the arrival of director Alec Griffith, Phil asked me what my plans were if we found something, an artifact or obvious chunk off of a UFO. I didn't know what to say. This was solely due to the bedlam of the arrangements. There was a plan in place for scientific examination and analysis of any artifacts, but at that moment that contingency plan evaded my conscious stream of thought. I remember mumbling something about being honest about the remote possibility of discovery and the considerable elapsed time and the obscuring nature of a high energy seabed. Phil just laughed and said, "You really don't know, do you? You haven't allowed yourself to consider the chance of possibly finding it!" He laughed some more and added, "Let's just say that if you find the thing that the chequebook stays open and we keep going."

The first day began at MacKenzie's Motel in Shelburne. Plans were quickly put together. I have to say that director Alec Griffith thought of everything. I brought up the fact that I understood that a balance would be struck between searching and filming. There would be retakes and re-enactments, but there would also be a complete sonar survey done of the Sound and hopefully a cursory search to find the exact location of the *Navicula* sonar target on the Shag Harbour Rip, an area of deeper water that lies about a mile beyond Shag Harbour, toward the Gulf of Maine. This second goal was important because the coordinates written on the BIO sonar rolls in 1988 were plotted with LORAN C, which was notoriously inaccurate when compared to the modern Global Positioning System (GPS). And the Shag Harbour Rip lay in deep water that presented many diving challenges, including strong currents and rough surface conditions.

After the meet and greet we drove to the Prospect Wharf in Shag Harbour to make sure that the survey equipment had arrived. Once there, everyone pitched in to help load and store everything aboard *Murphy's Law*. The two young techs from CSR appreciated the assistance and were then left to their own devices to connect, calibrate, and mount the equipment. The rest of us

CHAPTER 6: THE SIGHTINGS EXPEDITION

drove back to Shelburne for a hot meal and a good night's sleep. While we slept, the cat was crawling out of the bag.

Seven o'clock always comes early for a creature of the night like myself. This is especially true when the telephone and alarm clock compete for my attention at the same time. A quick slap handled the alarm clock, but the phone proved more troublesome.

"Good Morning, Mr. Styles, this is Don Connolly at CBC Halifax's *Information Morning*. We're live on air and I wonder if you could tell us a little about your expedition in Shag Harbour and what it's all about?"

Having been a longtime fan of both CBC Radio and the *Information Morning* show I was thrilled to speak with Don Connolly about the Shag Harbour Incident. The questions were smart and relevant. The interview stirred up a great deal of local interest and served to bring unknown witnesses forward. Perhaps the only fly in the ointment was the emphasis put on the "Hollywood Comes To Town" aspect of the story.

The first *Sightings* segment, shot in July, had gone largely unnoticed by the local media. This time things played out very differently. Before the survey was complete it would receive national media coverage.

The filming of our survey was a complicated affair compared to the brief segment shot by director Tod Mesirow in the summer. We needed a second camera and a second boat to film the action in our boat that wasn't close up. We needed lots of B-roll for post-production, and director Alec Griffith had a list of very specific ideas as to how he wanted things to look. It was clear that his first priority was the camera, which is only natural. It was my role to see that the survey work got done, but I also had to give the director what he wanted. It was only fair. *Sightings*, after all, had footed the bill.

On that first day we laid some lines on our grid pattern search. There were the inevitable adjustments and tweaking sessions. The sonar tow fish needed extra line to distance it from *Murphy's Law*'s propeller. We also made a deviation from our course to cross over a known power line to see if it was picked up readily by the Klein 500 system we were using, and it was very reassuring to see that it was. We had decent ground truth in the field. I began to relax. I felt that even if we found nothing in the Sound that we could at least be certain that there was nothing left to find. Such a finding is far more useful to a researcher than wondering if the data is sound or trustworthy.

On the second and third day of the survey we had eyewitness Laurie Wickens and fisherman Lawrence Smith aboard. Lawrence had been the skipper of one of the two local boats commandeered by the RCMP back on the night of October 4, 1967. Although Lawrence never saw the UFO, he was witness to the strange yellow foam and the aftermath of the initial search effort. His advice and recollections proved quite valuable as did Wickens's recollections. Laurie had been on CGC 101 in the days after the crash and gave us a good account of their efforts, including the limits of the expanding search area. His estimates coincided with the DND military telexes; in Laurie's case they were based on the orientation of local features such as the Budget Buoy, which was still affixed in the same location as it had been in 1967.

The three days of survey work in the Sound went well. In the end we scanned the entire area covered in the original search effort and a little beyond in each direction. Nothing unusual was found on the bottom of the Sound. There were no artifacts, no trauma, and nothing observed that could be considered out of the ordinary in any way. The shallow bottom of Shag Harbour was largely sandy with the occasional kelp bed. The bottom was strikingly clean and free of junk. Lobsters stared back at the lens of our underwater video camera. Several dives were carried out to check promising sonar targets selected by the CSR techs as particularly promising, but all proved to be natural features. The dives were easy ventures carried out in less than sixty feet of water, so there was no need or concern for decompression. However, the first dive gave our little expedition a true bit of drama that we could have all done without.

Alec Griffith, the *Sightings* director, was himself a recreational diver. He decided to go below with the two pro divers on the first dive. Unlike the two local men, Alec suited up in a dry suit. He assumed that the water in Nova Scotia would be cold in September, but the water temperature in Shag Harbour was more than 60 degrees Fahrenheit at the time. A wet suit would have provided more than enough thermal protection. As soon as Alec went over the side, one of the seals in his suit failed and water rushed into the suit. His radio shorted out and communication was lost. The other two divers surfaced immediately and shouted that Alec was in trouble and they had lost sight of him. They were unsure what went wrong. Visibility was only twenty feet at the time of the mishap. Everyone on the boat spread out to gain a greater vantage point to scan the surrounding area for any sign of bubbles or, better yet, Alec himself bobbing to the surface. Eventually we spotted him, some distance from the boat. He did not return our signals as we sped toward him. The dry suit was filled with water and it took several of us to get Alec hoisted out of the water and back aboard *Murphy's Law*. He was shaken but okay.

CHAPTER 6: THE SIGHTINGS EXPEDITION

The one real disappointment was that we failed to relocate the *Navicula* sonar anomaly. Several times *Murphy's Law* attempted to head out to the area of the Shag Harbour Rip, but each time the surface conditions were far too intense for survey work. The water was sufficiently rough that we would have in all likelihood snapped the tow fish cable. We had insurance, but there was a $5,000 deductible to consider. The sea never surrenders its secrets without a struggle. Unfortunately, the origin of the *Navicula*'s mysterious sonar anomaly remains a goal for a future expedition.

So what did our little expedition accomplish? Like the original RCN search of the Sound, our 1995 survey produced "nil results." However, due to the uniquely strong document evidence and the large pool of credible eyewitnesses, including three RCMP officers, the Shag Harbour Incident remains intact and credible as an unsolved UFO case. In fact, a finding of "nil results" actually says something positive and informative about the nature of the case. We are in the end left with the original question: How could something that was consistently described as being at least sixty feet in one dimension be both aerodynamic and hydrodynamic and manage to escape the search area? In 1967 humankind had no such craft, and at the time of publication such a device still doesn't exist. If it did exist the military would have made good use of it by now in several recent theatres of war. It would be as familiar as any operational USAF stealth aircraft such as the F-117A Nighthawk and the Stealth Bomber.

The point of origin and mission of the "dark object" seen by so many in Nova Scotia in October 1967 remains a mystery. The Shag Harbour Incident is the world's only UFO crash scenario that is supported in that interpretation by government documents that are freely available and without controversy as to their origin or authenticity. It is still an active investigation pursued by myself and a handful of other serious UFO researchers. Shag Harbour remains a strong argument for UFO reality, and William F. Dawson's theory, that a largely intact UFO may be resting on the seabed beyond the area painstakingly searched, remains a valid consideration.

Chapter 6 Endnote

1. UFO Sightings 1965–81, Telex from Maritime Command to CFHQ, October 9, 1967, RG 77.

SECTION 2

CONTACT

Chapter 7: Opportunity and Peril
Graham Simms

"We stand today on the edge of a new frontier—the frontier of unknown opportunity and peril. I am asking each of you to be pioneers toward that new frontier."
– President John Fitzgerald Kennedy, 1963

In trying to track down the root cause of the Shag Harbour Incident, it became obvious that we had to explore the possibility that advanced military saucer-type craft could be responsible. To do so, we needed to delve into the history of military research into constructing saucer-type craft and the effort to develop antigravity technology. While this history does not provide an ultimate explanation for the Shag Harbour Incident, it does inform us of what was brewing in the background at that time.

Shag Harbour witness Dickie Wickens and Halifax reporter Ray McLeod both suspected that the Shag Harbour UFO was a high-tech American craft. I decided to ask McLeod why he had this impression. In an hour-long phone conversation between myself and MacLeod in 2010, the seventy-year-old retired educator and journalist provided some insight into why the search was shut down despite no results and how the media is influenced and influences in regard to UFOs. MacLeod was not shy in expressing his opinions about the memorable incident. In fact, it vexed him. He was the thirty-three-year-old night shift reporter for the *Halifax Chronicle-Herald* when the Shag Harbour story landed in his lap, and he was surprised that his article was splashed on the front page, with a three-inch red headline. "I never expected them to go with this. I thought it would be on page three, maybe." said Ray. He was also surprised when the newspaper abruptly ended reporting on the incident a few days later. MacLeod told me that he strongly suspected that the mysterious craft sighted and searched for around Shag Harbour in 1967 was something that was known to and identified by the American military forces because it was their property. Why else would they call off a search when some sort of craft obviously crashed, he asked me. He believed it was a secret US military saucer-type craft that was being tested.

"Within two days the whole thing was shut down, discussion of the topic was eradicated," Ray said.[1] In his opinion, the decision to call an end to the search and the subsequent media blackout were part of an "organized effort to stop discussion" because "someone knew what it was" that crashed. "Why do you stop looking unless you know [what it was]? If something went down, then you keep looking. It was an interesting event. The story to me is that it was shut down. You don't do that unless you know what it was. And they still have not said anything; there has never been an explanation."

Ray felt the primary reason the story made the front page in the first place was because *Chronicle-Herald* managing editor Harold T. Shea pushed it forward due to his own up-close flying saucer sighting a few months earlier. Harold and his wife Elva were driving home to Halifax after attending a wedding in Chester, and as they passed Queensland Beach, they were terrified to see a low flying disc close to the shore. Shea stood by his decision to put the Shag Harbour story on the front page. "I have no regrets, I'd do the same thing today," he told Chris Styles in 1994.

So why did the *Chronicle-Herald* back off their initially positive inquiries into the UFO crash and start publishing stories debunking the possibility that the incident involved a real UFO? A meeting held in a smoky back room office at the *Chronicle-Herald* changed the direction the newspaper took in its reports about the UFO crash. According to Ray MacLeod, Harold Shea, and Truro office manager Wilkie Taylor (who heard the fight from just outside the office), after the first headlines about the likelihood of a UFO crash, the *Herald* was getting calls from concerned citizens. This upset Graham Dennis, the paper's owner and publisher, who called MacLeod and Shea into his office. Dennis was red in the face, smoking a cigar, and holding up a copy of the paper with the screaming headline "Could Be Something Concrete in Shag Harbour UFO—RCAF." He smacked the paper down on his desk. "You two should know better! We're not in the business of scaring people, and this is scaring people!" Dennis told MacLeod he was off the story and told Shea he was moving him to the day shift "where we can keep an eye on you." Mr. Dennis announced, "I'm going to give the story to David Bentley. He's British trained and knows how to follow orders."

Dennis then said something to MacLeod that Ray would believe for forty years. "There is no William Bain. You were conned," said Dennis. Ray had spoken to Squadron Leader Bain on the phone and had quoted him in the front page article. In fact, the three inch headlines at the top of the article referred directly to Bain's statement that "this could be one of those rare cases where something concrete is found." Was Dennis genuinely mistaken due to misinformation from someone else, or did he knowingly mislead Ray MacLeod about the existence of Bain? Regardless, MacLeod believed Dennis's misrepresentation regarding Bain's non-existence, right up until he ran into Chris Styles in the aisles of a grocery store in 2008. "Are you sure he was real?" Ray asked Chris. He didn't seem convinced. "Well, I spent three hours with him in Ottawa before his chiropractor appointment," Chris responded. "The man is real. He was in the military for thirty years. He worked at the Air Desk at HQ in Ottawa. There is no doubt."

Ray admitted to me that he was surprised and excited after his initial conversation with Bain, when he affirmed that there may have been something "concrete" that crashed at Shag Harbour. "Bain was taken aback when I contacted him." Ray was surprised again when Herald owner Graham Dennis convinced him that he had somehow been duped by someone and that in reality there was no Squadron Leader William Bain. Although it now seems almost unbelievable, in 1967 the publisher of the paper convinced his reporter of a falsehood, claiming that he had been pranked by someone impersonating a member of the DND Air Desk. Further, Dennis said the Air Desk did not exist, even though MacLeod's call had been transferred there by DND HQ.

Ray was of two minds. Part of him doubted Dennis's doublespeak, and the other part of him did not want to make waves or be a seen as a fool. Ray went against his journalistic instinct and decided to succumb to Dennis's insistence. So why would Dennis try to convince his employee that Bain and the Air Desk did not exist? We can speculate that Dennis had contacts with the Department of National Defence, who placed the weighty hand of government censorship on the newspaper's owner when it came to spilling the beans about a UFO crash. Tennyson and McNeil were going to be the new DND approved NRC point men for "non-meteoric" (UFO) reports, replacing William Bain and the Air Desk, who had done actual on-site investigations.

So Dennis gave the UFO crash story to David Bentley, the British-trained reporter. Dennis presumably directed Bentley to Father Burke-Gaffney and professors McNeil and Tennyson as the new, less exciting, government approved sources on the story. In his blog, Ray later added:

On the quiet, I was told David would have specific instructions and direct supervision. The next day, I ran into Bentley as the shifts changed. He drew me aside and apologized profusely, saying it wasn't his idea and he didn't like the smell of it. I asked him why he had not followed up some of my contacts, including RCAF Squadron Leader Bain in Ottawa whose comment had been used for my headline. Bentley stared at me and said Bain did not exist. I was never sure how to take that.

(raymacleod.blogspot.ca/2008/09/that-damn-ufo-and-me-part-2.html)

The next few weeks, the stories that appeared in the *Herald* following up on the Shag Harbour UFO search downplayed the original story. McNeil and Tennyson suggested the same explanation: there was nothing to UFOs, and a super-secret war-machine from the United States was responsible for the sighting and crash at Shag Harbour (Bentley 1967: 1). But this explanation was pure speculation, not based on the facts of the case. Burke-Gaffney shot down the "super-secret war machine" theory but also downplayed the likelihood that the Shag Harbour UFO was extraterrestrial in origin (Ibid.: 6). It is glaringly obvious that someone above Dennis pressured the *Herald* to alter its reporting on the UFO story. From that point on, the *Herald* went in a different direction in their reporting on the Shag Harbour story than that taken by the international press.

DND had been keeping an eye on UFO reports in the media at the time. Files reveal that DND clipped a newspaper article about Professor McNeil in which he admitted that he "could believe in UFOs." The hand-written note on the side, "this does not help the situation," indicates that the DND author did not appreciate the NRC investigator making this admission to the media.[2] The military wanted a single "scientific" UFO study so that it could be easily controlled—not a military office investigating UFOs and not an office which would give credence to the phenomenon as being extraterrestrial. The DND did not want the investigators fanning the flames of the public's belief in UFO reality. So government investigators Tennyson, McNeil, and Burke-Gaffney all disputed the UFO angle, and Tennyson and McNeil put forth the company line that the Shag Harbour UFO crash was merely a secret, American Cold War machine, which is what the *Herald* reported.

Was it possible that the UFO was an advanced military craft, or was that just a concoction of the cover-up? Some UFO researchers, like former DND employee Palmiro Campagna, have concluded that some to many UFO incidents and sightings, and specifically the Michalak case of 1967 (discussed below), were cases of secret military craft, presumably American, being tested in the barren north country (Campagna 2010: 59, 74). The possibility does exist that Soviet and American craft, likely derived from German technology (or crashed alien UFO technology), was developed and test flown in Canadian skies as early as 1967. That year, 1967, was the height of the Cold War, and the possibility of a secret high-tech Soviet craft has to be considered. Some researchers and many of the eyewitnesses of the Shag Harbour Incident still consider it as a real possibility. To my way of thinking it seems a greater possibility in explaining some of the other noteworthy Canadian UFO cases of the day, such as the Michalak case, than in explaining what happened at Shag Harbour and Shelburne.

The Michalak case occurred close to the time of the Shag Harbour and Putnam incidents. The Putnam encounter, explored in detail in the next chapter, occurred in Nova Scotia on October 25, 1967 (exactly three weeks after the Shag Harbour Incident) and Stephen Michalak's Falcon Lake, Manitoba, encounter took place May 20, 1967 (just less than five months before the Shag Harbour Incident). Both Putnam's and Michalak's case involved a type of radiation burn and poisoning from what some suspect to be a malfunctioning experimental military craft. The Michalak case was the biggest file in Records Group 77 and was well documented. The biggest weaknesses of the case are that it is a single witness and that the Canadian Department of National Defence has limited its cooperation. There have since been several similar cases in the US that have received widespread media coverage involving civilian lawsuits against the USAF over UFOs, or advanced military craft, causing radiation burns (Curtis 1985). The Putnam and Michalak cases also demonstrate that the Shag Harbour Incident was occurring within the context of a province-wide flap and a continent-wide uptick in UFO activity.

The Michalak Case
Early afternoon on May 20, 1967, fifty-year-old Stephen Michalak, a Polish-Canadian geologist who had trained as an engineer, was prospecting for quartz outcroppings in Manitoba's Falcon Lake Provincial Park. By the late afternoon he ended up suffering first degree burns to his chest from the exhaust of what he thought was an incapacitated American craft of advanced design. Mr. Michalak described what he saw: "Two cigar-shaped objects with humps on them…descending and glowing with an intense scarlet glare. As the objects

came closer to the earth they became more oval-shaped." One of the two landed 150 feet away and other "remained in the air fifteen feet above me for about three minutes, then lifted skyward again, amazingly quickly, silently, changing colour. Like hot stainless steel" (Michalak 1967).

There was a strong smell of sulphur in the warm air wafting from the exhaust. He identified the sounds of a fan motor and air intake. As he approached the object Michalak heard human voices. He attempted to communicate with the presumed occupants, "Okay Yankee boys, having trouble? Come out and we'll see what we can do about it." Although he heard voices he couldn't discern what they were saying or their language. He repeated the offer of aid in Russian, German, Italian, French, and Ukrainian. The exterior of the craft was seamless. He was close enough to touch it; it was hot. When the craft suddenly took off, the exhaust from the vent blew off Michalak's shirt, catching it on fire and burning a grid impression on his chest.

Although the Michalak case is the largest Canadian investigation file from 1967, the Department of National Defence was singularly silent about it. The case was brought up in the House of Commons during question period by Manitoba NDP Member of Parliament and future Governor-General, Ed Schreyer on June 29, 1967. He asked about the government's silence on the case. The Speaker cut off the subject without reply (Rutowski and Dittman 2006: Chapter 12). Cabinet members also made requests for information. On November 6, Minister of Defence Leo Cadieux simply stated: "It is not the intention of the DND to make public the report of the alleged sighting."[3] On November 11, Schreyer again presented his question in the House, this time formally on paper. The matter was commented on in editorials at the time. On October 14, 1968, a year and a half after the encounter, the President of the Privy Council Office, Donald MacDonald, refused MP Barry Mather's request for access to the Michalak case reports (Ibid.). Then on February 6, 1969, Mather was granted access by a member of the Privy Council to examine their file on UFOs but some pages had been removed. He was told that the release of the file "would not be in the public interest" and might "create a dangerous precedent that would not contribute to the good administration of the country's business."[4]

The USAF-funded Condon Committee of the University of Colorado's UFO Project did an investigation of the Michalak case. Their report says, "DND and RCMP investigation teams were unable to provide evidence which would dispute Mr. Michalak's story" (Condon 1969: 316). And they went to great lengths to try. The RCMP even tried getting Michilak drunk at a bar to

CHAPTER 7: OPPORTUNITY AND PERIL

see if he would slip up.[5] In his book, *The UFO Files: The Canadian Connection Exposed* (2010), Palmiro Campagna, a professional engineer with the Department of National Defence in Ottawa, says he feels it was a military craft being tested in Canada. Canadian UFO researcher Paul Kimball thinks it could have been an unmanned experimental military drone.[6] The Michalak case seems the most likely of those reviewed to have been a field test of a secret military fighter craft using conventional or more likely exotic technology. This conclusion is based on Michalak's description of the craft and its flight characteristics.

In addition to the RCMP, DND, and the Condon Committee, the Aerial Phenomena Research Organization (APRO), the Royal Canadian Air Force, the National Research Council, and the US Atomic Energy Commission all investigated the case.

"Never Approach a Flying Saucer"
If the Michalak UFO was a secret military test craft would it have been an American or Russian device? Military applications could be partially responsible for the increased amount of UFO sightings in the last half century but certainly not all of them. There doesn't seem to be much hard evidence as to whether or not the advanced prototypes were actually built and tested by either the German, Soviet, or American and Canadian forces. However, there are witnesses with relevant experiences as well as recently declassified documents that may shed some light upon this very question.

Both the Putnam and Michalak cases occurred around the time of the Shag Harbour and Shelburne incidents and both involved the main witness's painful medical conditions caused by a radiant energy that emanated from the UFOs. Radiation exposure from high-tech craft is well represented within UFO literature and has occasionally received media interest. There may indeed be cases of human exposure to radiation from both secret military and alien craft. There certainly have been civilian lawsuits against the military for this exposure. As Frank Edwards warned in his seminal 1966 book *Flying Saucers— Serious Business*,

> Near approaches of UFOs can be harmful to human beings. Do not stand under a UFO that is hovering at low altitude. Do not touch or attempt to touch a UFO that has landed. In either case the safe thing to do is to get away from there very quickly and let the military take over. There is a possibility of

radiation danger and there are known cases where persons have been burned by rays emanating from UFOs. Don't take chances with UFOs! (Edwards 1966: jacket copy)

It appears that there has been military aerospace research and production of UFO-like craft for over half a century. Apparently this military research, development, and application of saucer-like craft went underground, ostensibly due to security restrictions imposed by the escalating Cold War. Yet up to a time in the mid to late 1950s, the media, scientific literature, and patents and trademarks offices retained traces of some of the original research breakthroughs in this specialized field. Taking a look at these past examples may directly inform the present situation.

Early Electrogravitics and Antigravity Research
Government and industry were involved in postwar research of antigravity and electrogravitics fields with the aim of developing combat discs and antigravity technology.[7] Some of this work was initially relatively public, but by the period from 1954 to 1958, aerospace companies and defence departments were progressively more secretive about any details or discussion of the science involved and the fruits of their research. Today, after fifty years of silence, the media and scientific literature are once again buzzing with antigravity news. Recent publications like *Aviation Weekly* and *Jane's Defence Weekly* have provided significant insight into the hidden technological advances of this secretive black budget world, and so has the American Federation of Scientists and its publications. The information that appeared in print in the fifties was quite revealing. An October 15, 1955 news release from the United States Department of Defense quotes President Eisenhower's Secretary of the Air Force, Donald A. Quarles:

> [W]e are now entering a period of aviation technology in which aircraft of unusual configuration and flight characteristics will begin to appear.... The Air Force and other Armed Services have under development several vertical rising, high performance aircraft.... Vertical rising aircraft capable of transition to supersonic horizontal flight will be a new phenomenon in our skies, and under certain conditions could give the illusion of the so-called flying saucer.[8]

CHAPTER 7: OPPORTUNITY AND PERIL

The same news release also specifically mentions, as an example, the Canadian "Avro car," which was being developed at that time with USAF funding. But there was a lot more going on than the Avrocar.

According to the October 1955 Aviation Report produced by Aviation Studies, a privately owned, London based aviation intelligence consulting firm who marketed reports to aerospace companies and government defence departments, there was an international electrogravitics industry by 1955. Aviation Studies also sponsored gravitics research for use in "fighter saucers" (Perl 1956).

A month after the October 1955 Aviation Report was published, the *New York Herald-Tribune* featured a series by Ansel Talbert, the newspaper's military and aviation editor, on the aviation industry's interest in gravity control (Talbert 1955a, 1955b, and 1955c). The series admitted to a large-scale gravity-control research program among US aircraft and electronics industries. General Dynamic's Convair division (who built the B-36) and six other firms were specifically named as involved in the studies, including the Sikorsky division of United Aircraft, Lear, and the Sperry-Gyro division of Rand (Rand Gyroscopes). Talbert also mentions key scientists involved including Edward Teller, J. Robert Oppenheimer, Freeman Dyson, John A. Wheeler from Princeton, Václav Hlavatý, Stanley Deser, and Richard Arnowitt. Talbert quotes industrialist William P. Lear who explained the benefits of the artificial electro-gravitational fields, "fields whose polarity can be controlled to cancel out gravity," which he was confident were possible.

> All the mass materials and human beings within these fields will be part of them [antigravity fields]. They will be adjustable so as to increase or decrease the weight of any object in its surroundings. They won't be affected by the earth's gravity or that of any celestial body. This means that any person who was in an anti-gravitational airplane or space ship that carried along its own gravitational field—no matter how fast you accelerated or changed course—your body wouldn't any more feel it than it now feels the speed of the earth.... Aviation as we know it is on the threshold of amazing new concepts. The United States aircraft industry already is working with nuclear fuels and equipment to cancel out gravity instead of fighting it. (Talbert 1955a)

In the early 1950s numerous companies spoke reassuringly in the mainstream press about the possibilities created by past and present studies as well as existing prototypes that were being tested. The Talbert articles refer to antigravity research as being a growing international industry, stating that there were also French, German, British, Swedish, and Canadian companies who had also taken up the field of study (Ibid.: 6, 10).

In the February 1957 issue of the *Journal of the British Interplanetary Society*, A.V. Cleaver, assistant chief engineer at the Aero-Engine Division of Rolls-Royce, estimated that government and industry in the US were spending $5 million per year on fundamental research of electrogravitics (Cleaver 1957: 16). Around that time, industry's research of electrogravitics and antigravity went completely underground, where it kept on growing and expanding. The research didn't stop, but the publicity did. Antigravitics is just one of many possible exotic technologies that has been developed and used since that time (LaViolette 2008: 2).

Collectively and individually, these media reports and documents indicate that Canada and the US military and private contractors were involved in the research and development of saucer type craft using both current conventional technology and highly advanced types of unconventional antigravity technology that was swallowed underground into the US military aerospace industrial complex black budget programs after the mid 1950s.

1950s Avro-Canada and USAF Saucer Development Program: Project Y and Y2

In 1952 John Frost was the British aeronautical engineer who was chief design engineer for special projects at A.V. Roe Canada Ltd., later called Avro. Frost wanted to build a flying saucer using conventional technology based on information from Nazi Germany (Campagna 2010: 59). There were saucer and wing shaped aircraft being researched and developed from the 1940s in Nazi Germany. Conceivably, through the Defence Research Board, Frost could have acquired the German saucer designs from an American contact involved with Project Paperclip, the US program that imported Nazi German scientists.

Frost first proposed the Avro "Project Y." Mr. A.V. Roe and Dr. Omand Solandt, then head of the Canadian Defence Research Board, both contributed to the initial design and funding. Two years later Project Y evolved into Project Y2. The capability of the craft had also evolved and was highly advanced, more than Project Y itself. The Avro report from June 1954 called "Project Y2: Flat Vertical Take-Off Supersonic Gyroplane" from the Directorate of Scientific Information Services at DND demonstrates the development of the subsonic Avrocar into a supersonic version (Ibid.: 54). The

CHAPTER 7: OPPORTUNITY AND PERIL

USAF was looking for a craft that could take off vertically from a small space, as an improvement on the conventional helicopter. At that point the USAF became more interested than the Canadian military in developing the project's capabilities.

General O.P. Weyland, Commander at the USAF's Tactical Air Command at Langley Air Force Base got involved with AV Roe in 1955 when Avro's Project Y2 moved south and became a USAF contract called variously Project 11794 and Project PV. (The move happened in the same year as Air Force Secretary Quarles's USAF statement quoted in the last chapter.) In 1958 the USAF contributed a further $5 million to Avro and the project was renamed Weapons Research System 606A (Campagna 2010: 74). In August 1960 an early version of a dismissively unstable Avrocar prototype was displayed for the press. In actuality, according to Frost their later version would have been ready for test flights at the initially projected speeds of 2,000 mph and heights of 80,000 feet, but funding was allegedly pulled and the American government claimed the project was suddenly abandoned. Sudden cancellation of projects and use of multiple project names was often used as a diversionary tactic during the Cold War. Development of the SR 71, F-117A, and the B2 were all so-called "black projects," in other words, highly classified.

Silver Bug

In 1995 a technical report was declassified that clearly demonstrates the persistence of the Avrocar project at Wright-Patterson Air Force Base in Ohio in 1955. The February 15, 1955 document from the Air Technical Intelligence Centre at Wright-Patterson, was released to Canadian DND employee and UFO researcher Palmiro Campagna when it was declassified forty years later. Entitled "TR-AC-47, Joint ATIC-WADC Report on Project Silver Bug," the report shows that Silver Bug, Project No. 9961, was the supersonic version that Avro had secretly transplanted to the USAF.[9] More basic subsonic versions of the Avrocar saucers had been officially researched and developed in Canada. The successful research continued in the Silver Bug program, which involved highly classified supersonic saucer prototypes that were carefully hidden from public scrutiny. The Silver Bug report is technically similar to Frost's Y2 report but also discusses the USAF's desire to determine Soviet interest and state of development "in this specialized field."

Internationally from the 1980s into the first decade of the millennium there continued to be a growing number of UFO sightings of craft besides saucers with unusually advanced capability and design, especially giant triangle and boomerang craft including, and at times corresponding to, the triangle-shaped "Aurora" and "pumpkin seed" designs. Several advanced craft that have been shown to the public have had a combination of these unusual design and technological characteristics. Once again, as in the early fifties, the aerospace technology periodicals have begun to offer the public some tantalizing corroboration as to what is going on behind the scenes and in the sky. These magazines include *Aviation Week & Space Technology* and *Jane's Defence Weekly*.

So it is possible that advanced aerospace craft have been showing up in the UFO sightings. Secret prototypes are not terribly elusive if they are occasionally crashing and being witnessed by the public, and word is leaking out. The early and secret discoveries are already current if this technology is showing up on craft like the B-2 and the National Space Plane. Advanced aerospace designs could have been responsible for a small or indeed a significant percentage of sightings going back to the 1960s. They would not even need to be manned craft; some could be variations of advanced drones and unmanned aerial vehicles (UAVs). Secret exercises, operations, field tests, and accidents could account for a portion of witnesses' experiences. The USAF admitted as much as early as October 15, 1955 in Secretary Quarles's press release. But they could not account for all of the UFO sightings.

In Conclusion

Chris and I concluded that the craft involved in the Shag Harbour Incident was almost certainly not an advanced military saucer-craft, although such things did exist in 1967. There were secret, military, antigravity, electrogravitics "UFO" craft being tested and flown during the time of the Shag Harbour Incident, even in Canada. Yet the capabilities of the experimental military craft were not commensurate with the actions of the craft witnessed at Shag Harbour.

There exists the possibility that technology from genuine ET UFO crash recovery operations could have been merged with and advanced pre-existing terrestrial saucer/antigravity propulsion research and development programs by 1967. In certain more recent close encounters, eyewitnesses have reported inside-out American flags on the craft, military personnel, and military jet escorts. These craft are high-tech, but not as apparently high-tech as the reported alien vehicles. So, there are two possible classes of craft: exotic, secret, military aerospace machines and alien vessels. Both seem to demonstrate enormous acceleration velocity. They also exhibit rapid changes in direction and are generally almost noiseless. Some have buzzing, high pitched, or air pressure sounds. There is repeated reference to these extraordinary objects flying certain patterns, hovering, or moving suddenly at right angles, skipping, and even blinking in and out. Interestingly, both seem to break down occasionally. Triangle and boomerang craft have been seen more often since the later 1980s. Unusual aerial activity at Area 51 also increased from the mid eighties and continues into the millennium. Today, legitimate black projects seem to be subject to an informal level of government cover-up by perplexed bureaucrats. There are even suggestions of an illegitimate level of control and secrecy going so far as to suggest a parallel but separate quasi-military faction that is going "off world" and interacting with ETs. Historian, author, and researcher Richard Dolan calls this a "break-away civilization" (Dolan 2011).

From natural phenomena, simple explanations, exaggerations, misinterpretations, and hoaxes, to cover stories and cover-ups—for one reason or another, most UFO crash stories tend to evaporate upon close scrutiny. But the Shag Harbour Incident is one of the few cases that has remained strong. There are still fresh approaches to be taken and investigated in the Shag Harbour/Shelburne Incident as the UFO phenomenon in general is just beginning to reveal the full extent of its dark yet illuminating secrets.

Chapter 7 Endnotes

1. Unless otherwise indicated, quotes from Ray MacLeod are from a telephone interview with the author conducted in April 2010.
2. Handwritten note with DND press clipping in RG-77.
3. Canada, *House of Commons Debates* (November 6, 1967), p. 3919.
4. Canada, *House of Commons Debates* (February 6, 1969), pp. 5234–6.
5. From William Bain interview with Chris Styles, 1995.
6. Paul Kimball in conversation with the author, Spring 2007.
7. Wiktionary defines electrogravitics as "a proposed science involving the use of an electric field to charge (or polarize) an object so as to counteract the effects of gravity." The field was developed by Nicola Tesla and Townsend Brown.
8. US Department of Defense, "Air Force Releases Study of Unidentified Aerial Objects," news release, October 25, 1955.
9. TR-AC-47-(Unclassified), Joint ATIC-WADC Report on Project Silver Bug, Project No. 9961, February 15, 1955. Published by Air Technical Intelligence Center, Wright-Patterson Air Force Base, Ohio.

Chapter 8: The Twenty Year Picnic
Making the Case for an Extended ET Presence in Nova Scotia
Graham Simms

"Discovery consists of seeing what everyone has seen and thinking what nobody has thought."
– Albert Szent-Györgyi, Nobel Prize-winning physiologist

"One doesn't discover new lands without consenting to lose sight of the shore for a long time."
– André Gide

Ufology is a rich hunting ground. As philosopher of science and its revolutions Thomas Kuhn pointed out, "Discovery begins with the awareness of anomaly" (Kuhn 1962). That is why examination of anomalous phenomena, such as UFOs, may be one of the more profitable avenues for understanding the universe. The concept of any form of nonhuman intelligence stimulates something within that is both profound and primal. Humankind's quest to discover the existence of worlds and intelligent species other than our own may serve to challenge or even invalidate many traditional scientific and cultural dogmas. We should prepare ourselves with open minds and hearts to the full range of possibilities.

Chris Styles approached the Shag Harbour Incident as a ufologist. It would be my lot to "cast a wider net" and approach the case more as a theorist of the paranormal. I began by interviewing Chris, eventually dozen of times. We usually did this at his residence, and I recorded his stories and answers to my questions on digital recorder. Next I reviewed the available Canadian UFO data collections. The most extensive of these is known as Records Group 77 (RG 77) and is held at Library and Archives Canada in Ottawa. It was my hope that this insight into UFO sightings of the period would provide some kind of framework and context to further interpret the Shag Harbour Incident.

My introduction into the world of active UFO research was nothing like I imagined it would be. I was handling and sorting through hundreds of government documents, files, and microfilm. The eclectic demands of UFO research required a steep learning curve of intuitive and academic abilities, not the stuff of any high school or undergrad program. There was a lot of bureaucracy and procedure to just access the UFO files that contained huge servings of "alphabet soup," military and RCMP acronyms. There were the intricacies and frustrations of the interlibrary loan system. And then there were the "cheap tricks" that helped narrow the focus of a document search when the dates were "soft." You take your best guess and alternate microfilm reels one at a time both behind and ahead of your best estimate. And of course there are the endless poor copies, often illegible but always clearly marked with the label "poor copy." I gained an appreciation of the archival work done by those UFO researchers who have advanced the field in so many ways by doing their frequently mind-numbing homework and unearthing the necessary paper trails.

Chris provided me with further documentation such as RCMP files that were found amongst the Burke-Gaffney Collection held at Saint Mary's University in Halifax. There was also a plethora of press clippings and periodical articles. Many of these exhibit considerable repetition, including factual mistakes that get repeated time and again. However, some of the articles are significant and indispensable. Perhaps the best example is the Aerial Phenomenon Research Organization (APRO) Preliminary Report prepared for the late prolific investigator Jim Lorenzen. That eight-page overview contains a level of detail not seen within the press coverage. The APRO investigator spoke to the watch officer at Maritime Command who revealed details of the interest and extent of US military operations at the time of the incident in the nearby Gulf of Maine, not far from the area of the UFO crash. The report identifies all of its sources. Lorensen, director of APRO at the time, was one of the few researchers who followed up on the Shag Harbour Incident and is an unsung hero in the history of UFO research.

Sometimes in all the digging through documents you get "a live one." When you read between the lines and the writer allows a few "juicy" details, your hair can stand on end. Suddenly, a police report can become a very human story. I certainly got that tingle during my investigation into the claims of British UFO researcher Phil Hoyle in his letters to Chris, explored in detail in chapter 10.

It was fascinating for me to speak to and interview some of those who were in Shag Harbour at the time of the incident, such as Laurie Wickens and former *Halifax Chronicle-Herald* reporter Ray MacLeod, who wrote the October 7, 1967 headline story "Could Be Something Concrete in Shag Harbour UFO – RCAF" (MacLeod 1967). They both suspected the UFO was actually a secret

American craft. Although I do not agree, their views are understandable, given the specifics and that we now know there were secret craft being tested around that time, as discussed in chapter 7. In the interests of completeness and seeking a fresh perspective I decided to include an examination of local folklore. My mentor, Harvard's Dr. John Mack and veteran UFO researcher Jacques Vallee always spoke about the relationship between the UFO phenomenon and folklore, and it seemed a natural place to look. This approach yielded some surprising results, examined in chapter 9.

When Chris Styles and Don Ledger began investigating the Shag Harbour Incident in the early 1990s the National Archives RG 77 files were only available on microfilm, which had to be obtained through interlibrary loan. Now the collection is available online. There are even Archives web pages that exclusively feature the mystery of the Shag Harbour UFO crash.[1]

One of the first things to "jump off of the page" when examining the RG 77 files is the time frame. The collection falls between the early sixties and the early eighties. Perhaps the cut-off dates were arbitrary, but that span of two decades seems to coincide with the best estimate that Chris and many of the residents of Nova Scotia's southwestern shore have as the time frame when UFO incidents were most commonplace. That impression would solidify as I became more familiar with the document record and eyewitness accounts. Chris and I started to think of those two decades as "the twenty year picnic," a name inspired by Ray Bradbury's story, "The Million Year Picnic."

The quantity and in some cases the quality of the UFO cases found within RG 77 can be daunting. For the most part they are credible, believable accounts from all types of people. Details run the gamut from dry, slightly odd details to extremely bizarre encounters. Although each case is unique in some way, many exhibit certain consistencies across the nation throughout the twenty years covered by the collection. Extreme velocity, sudden acceleration, and disappearance are common features of the crafts' behaviour. The reports also seem to indicate patterns of behaviour in terms of geography, flight characteristics, and vehicle descriptions. Nocturnal lights outnumbered daytime sightings; structured craft and flying saucers were prevalent. The strongest overall impression I received from reviewing RG 77, was the persistence of UFO activity throughout the twenty year period along the Atlantic coast.

UFO cases in the Maritimes seem to vary slightly from "the norm." I paid special attention to the details, consistencies, and inconsistencies of coastal sightings over Nova Scotia's southwestern shore, which includes Shag Harbour and Shelburne County. Certain types of UFOs were sighted time and again.

Some of these types are commonplace in the field, such as orbs, often orange or yellow in colour. Recollections about the heyday of this type of UFO sighting are common when speaking with eyewitnesses along the southwestern shore. In fact Chris found that on Cape Sable Island many spoke of the parental concern of families that lived near the shore during the period. Moms and dads would sternly warn children, "If you see the orange balls, go the other way. Don't go near them or bother them." Other types of UFOs were much rarer but showed up repeatedly, such as a three sectioned type of craft that Chris calls "tea strainers" due to a translucent, mesh-like middle section that witnesses could typically see into. All of these manifestations of UFO phenomena were not just part of local folklore but an accepted part of everyday life.

There were several factors among the Canadian UFO reports from the 1950s through the 1980s that suggested a link among the activity around Nova Scotia. There were dense clusters of reports from the South Shore of Nova Scotia up to Newfoundland. Most of these sightings were associated with the ocean. In terms of the mainland of Nova Scotia, away from the coast, there was also a density of sightings reported around the centre of the province near the innermost area of the Bay of Fundy, around Stewiack, Debert—from Springhill to Truro. Both the coastal and land sightings were predominantly of the large illuminated orange balls, secondary only to disc sightings.

Nova Scotia UFO encounters have a different quality from much of the UFO literature of the time. There were many sightings that were almost but not quite close encounters. There was a marked absence of abductions yet plenty of interactions between witnesses and UFOs that suggest communication and an intelligence behind the craft. The UFO phenomenon in the Maritimes can be seen as modern folklore. The fact that a very high percentage of the population of the Maritimes has Celtic or Native ancestry—the two genealogies with the highest rate of UFO encounters—suggests a further link.

An Ongoing Operation?

After spending considerable time analyzing the data, it seemed to me that some of these UFO events had to be connected and not merely random in nature. Not only was there clearly intelligence behind the majority of the incidents, but I began to suspect that what unfolded during the Shag Harbour Incident and Shelburne flap may have been part of an ongoing operation and indicated a long-term extended presence by mysterious "visitors" attracted to the area.

CHAPTER 8: THE TWENTY YEAR PICNIC

UFO activity appears to have occurred not only throughout those recent decades but possibly for centuries when one allows for how UFOs might have been interpreted before the dawn of the so-called "modern UFO era."

In one memorable conversation, I chided Chris just a little. "Why didn't you and Don consider that Shag Harbour might have been part of an ongoing presence in the area?" It was a consideration that I did not recall reading in *Dark Object*. Chris explained that it had been discussed a number of times in the early nineties when the manuscript was coming together, but it was a time of information overload, endless interviews, and deadlines. Chris claimed that he felt that the possibility of an ongoing alien presence was a valid premise, but there was no time to pursue vetting it. He admitted that that sounded like a lame excuse, and it was a fair criticism. Chris went on to explain that the plethora of other cases did influence his understanding of the UFO phenomenon and in fact led to his "blended view," which allows room for both the extraterrestrial hypothesis (ETH) and a strong psychic component, that is, encounters that involve interaction with the consciousness of the experiencer.

One of my interviews with Chris yielded another reason to consider an ongoing presence throughout the '60s, '70s and '80s. Chris told me about his 1995 interview with William Bain, who was the Squadron Leader of the RCAF's "Air Desk" in Ottawa at the time of the Shag Harbour Incident in 1967. Bain provided some insight on the East Coast situation at that time and the authoritarian attitudes of some Canadians regarding UFOs. Bain and his colleagues at the Air Desk took the UFO phenomenon and their investigations quite seriously. Their on-site investigations sometimes employed considerable resources and civilian scientific consultants, as was the case with both Shag Harbour and the Michalak case discussed in chapter 7. Bain explained that he thought there had to be "something" behind the UFO phenomenon due to the well documented history of military pilots chasing and being chased by UFOs. In fact, William Bain admitted to seeing what he called "tricks of light" and other unknowns that he reluctantly attributed to the phenomenon when he was a young military pilot flying off of the coast of Nova Scotia. To my mind the very existence of the Air Desk back in the 1960s indicates Ottawa's acknowledgement of UFO reality and attests to the ongoing UFO presence off the North Atlantic coast throughout that decade.

Reports of UFOs kept the RCMP busy throughout the '60s, '70s, and '80s, especially in Nova Scotia. RG 77 and RG 18 abound with hundreds of these UFO reports. The Mounties had a standard form just for that purpose, known as the HQ-400-Q5 document. There are many archived reports of RCMP staff on active duty who filed UFO reports without any civilian complaint as a precursor. Officers on speed trap duty would witness a UFO event and simply write it up. And that is one of the great things about the RCMP. Everything they do generates a paper trail. In Canada, the Royal Canadian Mounted Police (RCMP) serves as a national police force and is often hired in some regions as a provincial or municipal force. It is a unique role, and the members are trained to a high standard. As investigators they are taught to "write what you see, nothing more." The result is that as far as UFO investigations go, they are a "disinterested" party that can be relied upon to report the unembellished facts. So the pool of archived RCMP UFO reports is a unique resource that can be an important starting point to launch a civilian investigation of any Canadian UFO cold case that involved the RCMP. I intended to fully exploit this resource.

In addition to the entire history of activity of UFOs in Nova Scotia, another straightforward reason to consider a connection between the Shag Harbour Incident and the ongoing presence of UFOs in the province is the sightings observed on the "Night of the UFOs," October 4, 1967. A number of both similar and dissimilar lights were seen in the skies that night across Nova Scotia, out at sea and over the Bay of Fundy, and even in the busy Halifax Harbour. UFO sightings persisted for days and even weeks in some Maritime locations. And new data continues to be discovered to strengthen the case for one of the busiest UFO flaps on record. Only in the fall of 2008 did Chris and I become aware, via our New Brunswick colleague, Stanton Friedman, of the UFO sighting of Pan Am Flight 160, forty-eight hours before the Shag Harbour crash (discussed in detail in chapter 16). The description of the UFO that the crew observed on October 2, 1967, at 39,000 feet, while Flight 160 was approaching the Nova Scotia coast about sixty miles from Shag Harbour, was extremely similar to that of the craft that struck the water two days later. At times over the six minute Pan Am event the UFO became a collision threat. The six flight crew aboard Pan Am Flight 160 witnessed the UFO depart with a manoeuvre that would be impossible for any conventional aircraft. The high number of such credible reports argues that UFO activity in the area was organized and persistent. It also suggests that the location of the Shag Harbour Incident was not random chance. Whether Shelburne County or the ocean off its shore was the location of some sort of UFO base remains unknown; however, it seems to have been at least a "traditional stopping place."

Another factor that led me to consider the premise of connection and inclusion is found within the hearts and minds of the people who live in the communities affected by periods of frequent UFO activity. We'll begin with the concerns of Mr. R. Grandy Irwin, who was an insurance salesman in the town of Shelburne in the 1960s. In August 1968 Mr. Irwin felt compelled to put pen to paper and send his concerns to the authorities.

The Irwin Encounter
On August 16, 1968, some ten months after the crash of Shag Harbour's mysterious "dark object," R. Grandy Irwin typed a report on his insurance company's stationary that he posted to the base Commanding Officer (CO) at CFS Barrington at Baccaro. His report describes repeated sightings of self-illuminated spheres by himself and others on the evenings of August 12 and August 15 in the Shelburne area. At one point he suggests that the authorities should search the uninhabited woods of Shelburne County near an isolated lake for the source of the UFOs. Nova Scotia has countless inaccessible lakes, and some may have never been visited by modern man except by air. Mr. Irwin states that "the area in the vicinity of Harper's Lake…would be a most likely place for an uninvited visitor to seek sanctuary during the daylight hours."[2]

Mr. Irwin observed the UFOs from the western veranda of his home on the corner of Water Street and St. Patrick's Lane in the town of Shelburne. The first UFO sighting, on August 12, 1968, occurred around 9:45 pm. Irwin was outside watching twilight disappear to the west. As true nightfall appeared so did a light between two stars underneath the planet Venus, which was in the northwest. Irwin describes the light as being as bright as Venus, and it was in motion when it appeared. It was thirty-five to forty degrees above the horizon and was headed southwest. It moved at enormous speeds, changing course in forty-five degree increments with no loss in velocity. The UFO was silent and left no trail. Irwin writes,

> The object was proceeding at an enormous speed and veered first to the left and then to the right at very sharp angles of approximately 45 degrees at each change in direction. These changes in direction were instantaneous and required no discernible lapse of time. It appeared to change direction about six times but always remained on its same general course toward the Southwest, where it disappeared from my sight. Whether its disappearance was by reason of the great distance it had traveled or whether the light had been extinguished by mechanical means, it is impossible for me to say. The elapsed time from the time of the sighting until the time of disappearance would have been about ten seconds.[3]

This type of motion is commonly reported and is reminiscent of the "skipping rock" motion described by Kenneth Arnold, whose historic UFO sighting, which occurred in June 1947 while he was flying his private plane near Mount Rainier in Washington state, is generally considered to be the first of the "modern UFO era." In fact the term flying saucer was applied by Arnold and the journalists of the day to describe the motion, not the shape, of the objects seen by Arnold. Arnold's UFOs were in fact shaped like flat crescents that resemble the Batman logo. The term "unidentified flying object," or UFO, is a USAF term and lay a few years into the future, circa 1952.

Grandy Irwin's second UFO sighting, on August 15, 1968 lasted for two hours. On that evening he had binoculars, and his wife was present and also witnessed the spectacle.

Mr. Irwin's report was forwarded from CFS Barrington to the Meteor Centre of the National Research Council (NRC) in Ottawa, where UFOs were automatically classified as meteors in name at least. It was later returned to CFS Barrington and forwarded to the Canadian Forces headquarters. Less than a week later it was sent to the NRC's repository where it would sit for decades, until Chris unearthed it.

History of UFO Activity in Nova Scotia

So how far back does the activity go in the area? Well, there is the classic Bay of Fundy case from the late 1700s. In his diary entry for October 12, 1796, Judge Simeon Perkins (1735–1812), a well-known politician and merchant from Liverpool, Nova Scotia, whose diaries are an essential primary source for historians studying Canada's colonial past, tells a strange story of a fleet of ships seen low in the sky slowly flying in formation over the Bay of Fundy (Innis et al. 1948). He recounts a man walking on the ground out front of the "fleet" with his arm and hand outstretched as if in greeting. There were several witnesses to the fleet of fifteen airships that flew slowly overhead at one o'clock that fall afternoon. It is one of the earliest recorded, non-indigenous sightings of an unidentified flying object on the North American continent. The local stories of illuminated spheres on Cape Sable Island and throughout Shelburne County seem to go back at least a century. Dates are not preserved in these local accounts recorded by witnesses, amateurs, and folklorists like the late Helen Creighton. But the legends of phantom ships go back at least as far as a century, if not two centuries.

One of the earliest UFO sightings found within the RG 77 microfilm involved a sighting from the summer of 1952 in Yarmouth, Nova Scotia, to the west of Shelburne County. In this case, a group of American tourists witnessed discs and half discs in formation flying just offshore over the ocean between Maine and Nova Scotia. The sighting was considered sound and serious enough to cause the FBI to alert the USAF, which contacted Canadian authorities. The RG 77 document, which was declassified in 1975, still had the witness identities blacked out. The witnesses, US tourists, had observed two formations of shiny silver crescent or bat-wing craft.[4]

Recently, another 1952 UFO encounter came to light that contains details that are staggeringly similar to the Shag Harbour and Shelburne incidents that occurred fifteen years later. These details demonstrate that the alien encounters at Shelburne were not an isolated incident, and lend credence to the likelihood that the US military, if not the Canadian military, was familiar with what they were dealing with when it came to the UFO crash at Shag Harbour and the UFO observation mission at Shelburne.

Richard French, a retired Lt. Colonel in the US Air Force, testified in May 2013 at the Citizens Hearing on Disclosure before former members of Congress in Washington DC about his work in the 1950s and a UFO incident he witnessed in Newfoundland. At that time he was a lead investigator of Project Blue Book, which came up with ways to explain away UFO reports for the USAF. French recounted that in 1952 a UFO incident occurred off the coast of St. John's, Newfoundland, that he was ordered to investigate for the Air Force. The case was eerily similar to the Shelburne Incident fifteen years later. "There were a lot of people assembled on the wharf, at least 100 people standing around just looking in amazement at the water, including several local policemen." French recalled that the water was clear and that he saw two circular craft floating below the surface of the water, twenty feet from shore. He also saw two beings in the water near the ships, which he presumed were being repaired. The two beings

> were about two or three feet tall, light grey in color, very thin, long arms with either two or three fingers. The top of their heads was much wider than their jaw line, their eyes were very slanted, and you couldn't see pupils in them. They looked the way [aliens] have been depicted in motion pictures. (*Huffington Post* 2013)

The craft eventually rose out of the water, and "It then accelerated to somewhere in the neighborhood of 2,500 to 3,000 miles an hour and disappeared" (French 2013).

Just like the Shag Harbour Incident, there were two UFOs underwater just offshore, in the Atlantic, being repaired by aliens. Both the Shag Harbour and St. John's aliens were viewed by highly trained military officials. Both UFOs then took off from the water into the sky. Given the steady stream of UFO and USO sightings in Newfoundland and Nova Scotia reported between 1952 and 1967, the time of these dramatic incidents, it does not seem to be a coincidence that these two incidents were so similar and occurred so close together.

The Putnam Encounter

There is a Nova Scotian close encounter (CE-4) case that is not as well known as the more famous Michalak case (see chapter 7); however, Raymond Putnam's UFO experience of October 25, 1967, is every bit as engaging. Like the craft from the Shag Harbour Incident, this craft seemed to be having technical problems.

Mr. Putnam was the rear brakeman, or flagman, on the CN Rail "Cabot" train, which ran between Truro, Nova Scotia, and Moncton, New Brunswick, along the Cobequid Hills. At 3:15 pm on October 25, Putnam and two others on the train—a sleeping car conductor and an inspector from Montreal—witnessed what he called the "thing" in a sighting that lasted forty minutes. Eventually military jets arrived on the scene and seemed to pursue the craft, which "took off" in an unusual manner. The appearance of the craft and the exhaust trail it left were also atypical. He described the object as being shaped like an acorn with two large wings pointing upward. The wings were estimated to be from 150 to 200 feet wide and steel grey in colour. A blue light was visible between the wings. The three jet planes approached from a "considerable distance."

Here is an excerpt from Mr. Putnam's RCMP report.

> It gave off a terrific radiation, as I tried to look at it I covered my face with my hands and peered through my hands with one eye and then the other. It seemed as I looked away from it that I could not believe my eyes and it was difficult to visualize what I had just seen. It followed along beside and at the rear of our train. From just ¼ mile past Wentworth nearly to Westchester and then followed the top of the mountain range toward the west. As it drifted

away from our train it tipped to a 45 degree angle, the rear top end to the left and later rolled on to ¼ turn so that the flat sides were up and down. Shortly, a jet from a high altitude came in sight, diving at the same angle the demon was positioned, and directly towards the exhaust end of the UFO. The UFO then levelled out and a thin short exhaust was seen from behind it until it took the shape of a cigar and it looked just like a cloud, with the jet plane pursuing it. The jet never caught up with it as far as I could see. They went out of sight toward the west and to the left of the sun, time 3:50 pm AST.

Two men on the train witnessed the "thing," a sleeping car conductor and an inspector from Montreal. I have their names.

One week after, the hair on the back of my hands disappeared and my hands seemed to wither up some, they felt funny. My eyes got sore and seemed swelled hard. Two weeks later I thought I was taking pneumonia. My chest or ribs in front got sore. My throat got sore and still is. My forehead got greasy and later seemed to dry up. Now my eyes are sore and I had to get my glasses changed but they are still sore. I reported this to the RCMP and thought the Air Force would contact me and I'd get some help but have heard nothing. It tried to talk to my Dr. and have asked him for penicillin but he refused. I guess he thinks I'm nuts. Can you tell me anything [about] the thing, what kind of radiation—Atomic, Electro-magnetic, solar or what? What medication? I would like to talk to the crew on the plane that chased it sometime. Any help you can give I will greatly appreciate.[5]

This case is somewhat unusual in that Putnam was not only reporting the experience out of concern and genuine curiosity but also due to his forty-minute exposure to some sort of radiation that had made him ill. He was looking to the military for advice on how to treat his resulting medical condition and to learn what it was that he had been exposed to. Ray Putnam never received any advice or special help. He was profoundly disappointed and was reluctant to speak of the case in his later years for fear of ridicule.

Putnam's "demon" UFO could have been either military or extraterrestrial. It may have been something less obvious than these concepts. According to the crypto-terrestrial theory put forth by Mac Tonnies, Putnam could have seen an advanced craft that was piloted by earth-based alien beings, long hidden away in underground or underwater bases (Tonnies 2010: 128). Another possibility is that the UFO may have originated from a postwar Nazi, German or Soviet effort or some unknown rogue group. Could the jet Putnam witnessed "chasing" the UFO have actually been escorting a military test flight? The way that Putnam's UFO was seen to change shape and morph into a cloud was unusual but is not unknown within UFO phenomena literature. To me it is indicative of an advanced technology but possibly less sophisticated than some other more dramatic modern sightings. Yet the contrail it left sounds fairly typical of current technology. Putnam's description of the flight characteristics would seem to imply that the craft was having some technical difficulties. Putnam thought that the jets were interceptors in hot pursuit of the UFO. Nearby at CFB Chatham there were a few Vampire trainers and tactical Voodoo jets that occasionally fulfilled this NORAD role.

Central Nova Scotia: Debert and Springhill

Near the innermost part of the Bay of Fundy is Springhill, Cumberland County. Springhill is 77 km from Debert and is on the line between Truro and New Brunswick where the Putnam encounter and several other noteworthy UFO incidents occurred during the Twenty Year Picnic. This spate of UFO sightings between Truro and Springhill included the nearby areas of Debert and Stewiack, which is at the centre of the province and exactly halfway between the equator and the North Pole.

Was there anything unusual about these areas that could have attracted the interest of possible aliens? During the Cold War, Debert housed the two-storey subterranean Regional Emergency Governmental Headquarters (REGH), nicknamed the "Diefenbunker" after John Diefenbaker, Canadian prime minister from 1957–1963. The Diefenbunker was one of five underground bunkers in Canada that functioned as government communication stations designed so that government could continue to function in the event of a nuclear attack. The only underground government bunker in the Maritime provinces, it opened in 1964.

Nearby Springhill is a historic mining area, with many unused subterranean mines. In fact the Springhill mines are still among the deepest underground works in the world, at over 15,000 feet below the surface. The Springhill mining disaster occurred on October 23, 1958, when a "bump" or underground earthquake collapsed some of the mines, killing and trapping miners. This was the most severe disaster in North American mining history and devastated the town. The Springhill mines, which were owned by a subsidiary of A.V. Roe, were never reopened. They were later flooded and today are used for drawing geothermal heat. Could groups of aliens have been interested in monitoring deep underground man-made recesses and structures, like the ones in Debert and nearby Springhill or in the natural abysses branching out from under the Bay of Fundy area?

The headline of the *Springhill Record* on Thursday, December 2, 1965 read "Strange Craft Seen On Springhill Boundary." Twelve-year-old Kevin Davis and ten-year-old Gary Jardine saw the object the previous Monday evening, November 29, 1965, hovering over the Surrette Battery Company in Springhill. They first saw the object "skimming along the skyline" over the former mining area. "It made a humming noise. There was a jet of fire going straight up from the tail, and a red dome on the roof blinked off and on." It looked like it was made of aluminum and had "porthole" type openings on the side. The air blowing out from under it as it hovered blew away snow and trampled bushes. The UFO released a smaller "probe" through a portal, twice. The newspaper stated:

> As the boys watched, a long bar of the aluminum-type material, with one end divided into two parts "like fingers," came out of the largest opening ... from the craft, seeming to be also supported by air pressure. It returned to the craft, which then ejected it for a second time.... The whole roof of the vehicle was encased in glass or some equally transparent material and "we could faintly see three arcs of aluminum, or whatever it was, inside the windows." (*The Record*, Springhill, Nova Scotia, December 2, 1965)

The boys returned with their fathers and a large number of their friends immediately after the initial sighting, but the craft was gone. The boys collected an assortment of "radio or electronic bits" they found on the ground near the area of the encounter and brought them to the office of *The Record* newspaper. The newspaper returned the "bits" to Jardine's father. The newspaper added that "a somewhat similar if less detailed report has been heard of something seen over Fenwick last week." Fenwick is seventeen kilometres away from Springhill, toward New Brunswick along the same stretch of sightings between Truro and New Brunswick.

A follow-up article appeared addressing "the storm of controversy" following the initial report. Other witnesses came forward. Two dozen teenage boys came to the office of the newspaper with questions and wanting to see the "electronic bits."

Several mothers called and said the story was frightening children, while another mother told us her son rushed in and said: "Gosh, Mum, get out the good dishes—maybe we'll have men from Mars for supper!" A local businessman came into the office with a composite drawing describing the same craft seen over various sections of the USA. (*The Record*, Springhill, Nova Scotia, December 10, 1965)

On August 8, 1967, at 1:15 AM residents of Bible Hill observed a "very large orange ball" five miles east of Truro, giving off white light that flashed approximately every two minutes.[6] By 1:30 AM residents of nearby Upper Stewiack also saw the "large orange ball flashing in the sky" "in the direction of Truro in the Camden Road area." The investigating RCMP officer, Constable Noseworthy, personally observed flashing on the horizon.

Two weeks later the RCMP were again notified by several residents of Upper Stewiack that on Friday, August 25, 1967, between 10:30 pm and midnight, unusual bright lights were observed low to the ground. The lights were on top of an object that could not be seen clearly. The lights "come from the top rather than the bottom of this object." Another witness said "there was a darkness below the lights." The lights ranged from blue-green to red and flashed or "pulsated" at times. Upon investigation, RCMP Constable G. J. R. Richard found other witnesses. Mrs. Cooper stopped her car when she saw the lights ahead of her, observed them for a few minutes in awe, then slowly drove in reverse back to her mother's house. Mrs. Cooper woke her mother, Mrs. Alvina Chisholm, and they both went outside to watch the celestial objects for more than an hour. The UFOs were silent, ascended occasionally in the air, and were between 100 and 1,000 feet above the ground.[7]

Roy Putnam's encounter was exactly two months later, on October 25, 1967, near the Wentworth Valley, which is between Truro and Springhill, his train having just passed Debert.

An RCMP synopsis of UFO reports from late 1967 entitled "Air Borne Phenonmeno[n]" makes a tentative link between Putnam's sighting and "a scene in the woods" on Debert Mountain from the year before, investigated on November 13 and 19, 1966, by the RCMP and Father M.W. Burke-Gaffney, S.J., the Jesuit who had been Dean of Engineering and Dean of Science at Saint Mary's University in Halifax and who had been secretly investigating UFOs. Debert Mountain is about 25 km from the Wentworth Valley. There were "irregularities" at the location, mainly a straight gash in the earth 1.5 feet deep with a "continuous ridge of soil ejected from the trench," which was eight to ten feet long and ended in an apparent explosion that tore the roots of trees as well as causing damage to the trees eighty feet above ground. The RCMP note that the ditch "appeared as if an object of unknown shape or size had come from the sky and exploded as it was in the process of burying itself in the ground." No shrapnel of metal or rock was noted in the area, and Burke-Gaffney's tests for magnetic effects close to the explosion were negative. Burke-Gaffney ruled out the possibility of the explosion having been due to a meteor. "Meteors land at a minimum of 10 miles per second and bury themselves deep in the ground.... A meteor would not skid along the ground digging a trench."[8] In his report to the RCMP, Burke-Gaffney speculated that the damage was caused by an explosion due to lightning. However, he noted that there were no indications of burning or scorching, which typically accompany lighting strikes.

What technology could have caused an energetic blast like the one on Debert Mountain described by the RCMP and by Burke-Gaffney? Under what circumstances would such a discharge take place? And what accounts for the density of activity in an area known for such recesses into the depths of the earth? We don't know what the astronomer priest really thought about these cases. In Chris's conversations with Burke-Gaffney's colleagues, friends, and family, they said he expressed skepticism. But in the October 18, 1967 issue of the *Halifax Chronicle-Herald* regarding the UFOs seen around Nova Scotia at that time, he said, "They did not come from outside the earth's atmosphere." Is he covering up, or is there some truth to his words? His statement does not necessarily mean the UFOs were not capable of space travel but may indicate that he thought they were based here on earth.

Connections

My impression from the case studies was that most of these objects were not just passing through, en-route somewhere, just flying over us. That they appear for thirty minutes, sometimes hours, up to days in an area and often return at intervals indicates to me that they are intelligently guided and involved in some kind of an organized activity. Regular routes suggest the same craft going and coming back rather than each sighting being of a new object. The high numbers of UFO sightings suggest a bottleneck, regular routes converging possibly from a common source.

Often the UFOs demonstrate a pattern of interaction—again a fundamental way of communicating—repeated patterns in movement, blinking, even playfully engaging witnesses. Many are very low to the ground.

Others look like stars and are seen from some distance. Some are low and then shoot up. Typical electromagnetic interference with television reception, tape players, radios, and car engines cutting out in the presence of UFOs is often reported. Craft sometimes commit massive accelerations and angles that defy gravity, even instantaneous jumps and blinking in and out. On the other hand some craft have a steady pace and seem to be travelling from one place to another. Besides the jumps or skips of massive velocity, generally one of the most regular features of witness descriptions is the craft demonstrating the ability to remain stationary and hover, often for significant periods.

It may not be obvious at first glance whether the RG 77 UFO cases from Nova Scotia are connected, yet I believe many demonstrate a connection. I was almost disappointed that there was no immediate answer to the puzzling questions I had about the "Night of the UFOs." While some of the cases were quite interesting, the reported observations were mostly fairly simple. No single explanation is going to account for all the reports. UFOs are a complex phenomenon and neither the craft nor the entities follow a simple or single pattern. But as I digested the cases there were distinct themes and similarities. RG 77's strongest threads are the similarities among cases and their common geography. The primary hotspots were the southwestern shore, the ocean off the south shore of Nova Scotia all the way up to Newfoundland, and the inner Bay of Fundy area. As I looked into the geography of these areas with the greatest degree of UFO sightings, I realized that they were also the places with the highest degree of magnetic and gravitic anomalies. These geological anomalies were mostly underwater but also on the mainland. The large, rambling, orange spheres did not receive much mention in the popular UFO literature of the day, but they show up frequently in these areas. Sightings of the spheres were just part of the local folklore and a relatively common occurrence along the south and southwest shores of Nova Scotia. Is there a connection between the illuminated orbs and the geological anomalies around Nova Scotia?

Indeed, the Canadian navy also devoted time to these enigmas. The navy would regularly chase high-speed unidentified submerged objects (USOs) off the coast of the province. During the 1960s some Canadian naval officers were even quietly saying that some UFOs were likely creatures descended from the upper atmosphere, perhaps from fifty miles up. Meanwhile, in 1966 the Canadian government started studying the magnetic and gravity anomalies off of the coast of Nova Scotia and Newfoundland.

The SOSUS and MAD technology used at CFS Shelburne indicated that there was underwater USO traffic in the North Atlantic off the shores of Nova Scotia. Canadian, like Scandinavian, American, and British naval officers and sailors reported ongoing UFO/USO activity on and below the ocean surface off Nova Scotia and in regular areas around the world since at least the 1960s. So these craft were not just dropping in from outer space but were equally at home underwater.

The Russian Navy has recently declassified some of its records of UFO encounters and commented on the matter. Former Russian Naval officials stated in 2009 that fifty percent of UFO encounters happen from oceans, with fifteen percent connected to lakes. They also said that the craft are most often seen in the deepest part of the Atlantic Ocean and wherever NATO fleets concentrate. (Russia Today 2009)

The Oz Factor
Since we are not really able to analyze the spheres or craft up close ourselves, we study the witnesses' claims concerning the craft and the effects of the UFOs on witnesses. What are the effects of these displays? In ufology there is a condition or reaction that is termed "the Oz factor." Often at the onset of an experience, the environment shifts, and the person feels strange and isolated. This isolation is experienced to varying degrees, from empty streets to alternate landscapes.

Jenny Randles, former lead investigator at the British UFO Research Association (BUFORA), described the Oz factor in 1983 as "the sensation of being isolated, or transported from the real world into a different environmental framework...where reality is but slightly different, as in the fairytale land of Oz.... The Oz factor certainly points to consciousness as the focal point of the UFO encounter" (Randles 1983). Time may seem to slow down, no one else is around, and subjects feel alone or isolated. Sensory isolation is a key indicator of the Oz factor. Carl Jung considered this state of mind to be "a very important precondition for the occurrence of spontaneous psychic phenomenon." Dr. John Mack noted the alteration of consciousness, experienced as a higher vibrational rate, to be a precursor of contact (see Mack 1994: 371; and 1996: 70–71).

Chris and I discussed personal and cultural versions of the Oz factor at work in the Nova Scotia cases. There are gaps of time within the close encounters that the witnesses couldn't fill in, which had a lingering effect on their peace of mind. Several Nova Scotian witnesses expressed high levels of confusion and disassociation during and after their encounters. They were excited that they knew they had experienced something but dismayed that they had so little context for it. There were strange experiences and persistent feelings after the encounter that they could not fully convey. Witnesses invariably found their UFO experience to be both emotionally devastating and surreal.

It is interesting to note how people typically react to close encounters, especially when there is no room in a belief system for such an experience. Our modern culture just does not provide the tools to deal with, understand, or even define anomalous phenomena that are denied by consensus reality. The experiencer's world tends to shrink and only accommodate thoughts of themselves and the UFO phenomenon. They are often unable to cope with family matters and work, and they are often filled with ambivalence toward the stuff of everyday life. Some witnesses cannot seem to get their heads around the notion of alien contact in spite of what their senses have told them.

How we see "them," the aliens or whatever intelligence is behind UFOs, is filtered by our Western cultural outlook. Culture precedes the experience, providing a powerful filter. Culture colours our world view, shapes what we think we see and how we define the terms and concepts of alien, UFO, and ET. Like the bewildered natives observing the first Spanish ships arriving on the shores of the new world, we can't really see the ships for what they are, the contact for what it is. There are varying degrees of resistance. There is cultural interference with the experience. We are steeped in the physical, material aspects of existence and lacking deeper context in which to understand anomalous phenomena, ET and UFO contact phenomena. How would the experience appear if we looked at it with no ideas, no preconceptions? And to confuse things further, the phenomena themselves are elusive and may mislead us. So we can't put it all together. We feel dissatisfied and adrift.

If we try to apply strict scientific reason, these phenomena laugh at our stuffy, limited methodologies and narrow pigeon holes. A formal education does not necessarily lend itself to understanding a phenomenon of this nature, especially if the education is limited to the traditional scientific method. Yet an open mind can be applied to any discipline, and science has basically not attempted to engage this topic yet. Atmospheric physicist James E. McDonald, an early investigator into the UFO phenomenon, said it best with his 1969 essay, "Science in Default: Twenty-two Years of Inadequate UFO Investigations" (McDonald 1969).

CHAPTER 8: THE TWENTY YEAR PICNIC

Serious consideration of UFOs and aliens has effectively been quarantined from mainstream culture, except as entertainment. This is part of the reason why any real debate or discussion is off the rails and how such a powerful concept is rendered impotent. The UFO phenomenon is somewhat complicit in keeping itself unknown as well. It shows itself at times, but that is usually the most it does. It teases and then disappears to leave the rest up to us. Certainly there are examples, like the Smith brothers encounter discussed in chapters 11 and 12, where the presence seems to actually set up the contact and allows itself to be observed and even attempts communication with us. On other occasions it seems to want to leave itself undefined, known only to exist, and then leave the interpretation up to us. It leaves the implications to stew in our collective minds.

Our collective consciousness could play a part in the Oz factor. Perhaps our consciousness is a subset of a larger consciousness. Contact may be an effect of bridging the waking conscious mind with the higher, psychic aspects of consciousness. It can be understood as a linking to and crossing over into or from the more subtle realms. Contact may serve to expand our perceptions and increase our ability to appreciate our full density of existence and our experience with finer levels of existence. Perhaps some people can't even see these types of reality. Some people may react with some sort of psychosomatic symptoms or illness. On the other hand the energetic emanations from the illuminated spheres or craft may also be causing such effects. The possibility exists that some psychological and even physical effects suffered by people who encounter UFOs may actually be the result of some energetic radiation. This is the premise of reality transformation and the Oz factor.

In several of the cases we examined, the Oz factor is part of a visceral reaction to the experience, and this is an indication of the reality of the phenomenon—how deeply it moves people. In this way the Oz factor supports the theory of ongoing presence in the area. This phenomenon certainly has a basis, or at least a foot, in our material world. And at the same time there is the greater psychic (not necessarily physically measurable), spiritual realm to consider as well. In a sense the UFO phenomenon forces us to broaden our understanding of reality beyond dualism, beyond what we think of as real or unreal. Real in what way? Not real in what way? There are camps of "believe" and "not believe," like some religious dogma. These narrow and arbitrary perspectives propagate this overly simplistic binary argument. The UFO phenomenon is not a matter of belief. As John Robert Colombo, Canada's "Master Gatherer" of stories says, "UFOs are a category of experience, not a category of belief" (Colombo 2004). And as Chris says, "Some don't have the luxury of belief." We know so little about what consciousness is, can we make determinations of belief and reality based on so little evidence? I certainly don't know for sure, and I don't pretend to know I'm completely right.

As Arthur C. Clarke says in *2010*, the sequel to *2001: A Space Oyssey*, the answers here are bigger than the questions. And there is a lack of answers all around. There can, however, be educated guesses as to valid theories.

CHAPTER 8: THE TWENTY YEAR PICNIC

Chapter 8 Endnotes

1. National Archives Shag Harbour UFO Incident webpage: collectionscanada.gc.ca/ufo/002029-1500.01-e.html.
2. R. Grandy Irwin report, August 16, 1968, RG 77.
3. Ibid.
4. Account of tourist sighting in Yarmouth, NS, 1952, in RG 77.
5. Putnam RCMP UFO report, 1967, RG 77.
6. RCMP Air Borne Phenomenon file. Debert Mountain and Springhill cases, 1967–68.
7. RCMP file 67-400-43, 67T-400-83 Bible Hill, 1967.
8. RCMP report, Debert Mountain, 1967–68, Burke-Gaffney Collection, Saint Mary's University archives

Chapter 9: UFOs and Shelburne County Folklore
Graham Simms

"If the facts don't fit the theory, change the facts."
– Albert Einstein

"Where facts are few, experts are many."
– Old Chinese Proverb

Human experiences with visitors from the stars are woven into the fabric of our world's diverse cultures. Today such stories persist in both rural and urban areas, among both advanced and primitive cultures. The terminology and chronicling methods of such claims and occurrences have changed, but there is little difference between purported tales of alien contact and abduction and similar stories of interaction with the various beings of ancient folklore and mythology.

Ufologists recognize several waves of peak UFO activity during the 1960s, most notably in 1965, 1967, and 1969. Southwestern Nova Scotia, Shelburne County, and the Shag Harbour area was no exception. In retrospect, the notoriety and subsequent media attention given to the Shag Harbour UFO crash often served to eclipse the myriad of other concurrent UFO cases of the day. While in Nova Scotia generally there was a noticeable lack of contact by typical "greys" and very few claims of abduction, there were many other forms of close encounter cases (CE-3 and CE-4; see the Appendix for definitions of these terms). There were widespread encounters with both small and large orbs that seemed to exhibit intelligent manoeuvres. In some cases, the "Oz factor" and physical side effects were both long-term and severe.

Native Folklore of North America and Civilizing Visitors Throughout History

Unexpected contact is by no means just a modern phenomenon. It is embedded in written history, oral history, and folklore. Native cosmology is a rich source of creation stories often filled with interactions with spirits and peoples from the skies. Most of these Native cosmologies predate European and American folklore and science.

Cross-cultural tribal history and mythology overwhelmingly recount stories of celestial beings imparting the ways of the planet to humans. Throughout Canada's maritime region and areas of the Wabanaki Confederacy, the primary civilizer god of Native legend is known as Glooscap. Other similar examples from the American continent would include Kukulhan of the Maya, and Viracocha of the Andes and Quetzalcoatl. In the old world these archetypes appear as Egypt's Nadir and Osiris and throughout Sumerian, Hindu, and Japanese mythologies. As with the South American Indians, the North American Native cultures are riddled with references to the ancestors who came from the sky and taught them their ways and provided knowledge. These legends recount a rippling memory of other types of beings who travel between our planet and other worlds, rolling out to be repeated orally for generations. The result is an almost universal core of legends with a spiritual and unexpectedly physical dimension beyond Native ancestors, protector spirits, and nature spirits.

In the 1790s in British Colombia, along Canada's Pacific coast, the Nootka tribe held an interesting oral history of an unnamed civilizer god who came from the sky in a copper canoe. The god taught the Nootka how to smelt and work copper. This early legend was collected in the diaries of John Meares, a Royal Navy lieutenant who chronicled his voyages between China and North America in the late eighteenth century. Meares's *Voyages Made in the Years 1788 and 1789, from China to the North West Coast of America*, published in 1790, received widespread attention.

The "sky visitors," "phantom ships," and large illuminated orange orbs are the lore of the Nova Scotians of the southwestern shore. Their details are still echoed in modern UFO reports. All too often the gods of mythology arrive "from the ocean" or "from the sky." But where were they really coming from, and who were they?

Shelburne County Folklore

Much of the folklore of Nova Scotia is of the Celtic strain. Rich in imagination and romantic elements, it was brought largely by immigrants from Ireland and the highlands of Scotland. Parts of the Norse sagas were set in the Maritimes as this land of forests was the first part of America visited by Europeans. The French Acadians and indigenous community also contributed to the folk beliefs.

CHAPTER 9: UFOS AND SHELBURNE COUNTY FOLKLORE

Famed Nova Scotia folklorist, Dr. Helen Creighton (1899–1989), collected true lore from the province from 1928 to 1946. She found the province to be rich with stories of other-worldly occurrences, perhaps due to its strong Celtic roots.[1] She observed, "People of Celtic descent…seem to have an understanding of the occult that is denied to the rest of us" (Creighton 1976: 16). Besides the hovering and flying objects and lights found in the folklore of the southwestern area there are also typical ghost type encounters including apparitions and forerunners. Ghost experiences often involve hauntings, while other apparition phenomena may be perceived as spiritual events. Forerunners—from a picture that falls for no apparent reason, to an invisible knocking, to a sighting of someone who is not actually present—are taken as signs, usually of impending disaster and death. Creighton wrote,

> It is not everybody who is gifted with seeing or hearing forerunners, just as ghostly visitants are only seen by certain people. Nor do they appear only to the unlettered and uneducated folk…. Certain individuals, families, or dwellings seem to be particularly sensitive to these manifestations. (Ibid.: 24)

Creighton defines forerunners as supernatural occurrences that announce or warn of a coming disastrous event. A common example would be when someone sees a friend who is not actually there, and later they find out that the friend died at that time or shortly after. It is a sign of something occurring elsewhere or in the future. The sighting of an unusual light in the sky or on the water would often be taken as a forerunner or a sign of something buried. "They are known in other places as tokens or visions, but all over Nova Scotia among people of all descent, the popular name is forerunner. Occasionally, they foretell happy events; more often they predict death" (Ibid.).

A forerunner may be similar to a doppelganger, and may also have German roots, so there may be some overlap; the South Shore of Nova Scotia has a significant number of German settlers. Doppelgangers are the apparition of a person manifest in a location other than the actual location of that person, similar to bi-location. A person undergoing death or intense emotional distress may project a crisis apparition, just as they may have a near death or out-of-body experience. Many ghosts appear elsewhere at the very moment of their death. This is known in paranormal and near death experience research as the point-of-death phenomenon.

In some cases, people report "typical" encounters with deceased relatives who convey gentle messages coming from a place of great compassion. In other cases, deceased relatives convey warnings of danger. Along the southwestern shore, where almost every family would have experienced the loss of a loved one at sea, the foretold danger often concerns the ocean.

Along the southern and western shores of Nova Scotia, unusual lights or orbs have long been associated with the ocean, nautical disasters, and lost mariners. Creighton calls them "ghost-like lights" (Creighton 1976: 34). Before the Second World War there was limited air traffic over rural areas, and any technical concept of the UFO was unknown. Likewise, before the automotive age, people in the rural coastal areas of Nova Scotia would have had little other framework for the experience of an otherworldly craft than to describe it as a ship. Up to one hundred years ago, many families of the area knew of ghosts and knew of boats, the connecting nexus that allowed them to relate to the UFO phenomenon as phantom ships. And while it could be that some of the early twentieth-century reports of ships and lights in the air are attributable to early airplanes, balloons, Zeppelins, and submarines never before witnessed by the local populace, it does not explain earlier incidents.

The ghost ship is a common apparition reported along the southwestern shore of Nova Scotia. Although the ships are sometimes reported to be stationary, they are also seen moving above the water. Helen Creighton notes that phantom ship lights occasionally pass close to the witnesses, buzzing them or dancing wildly around them. Such displays remain teasingly just beyond the observer. Likewise, in the cases where voices are heard, they are not understood. Ocean lights were often observed just before storms. Creighton wondered if the cause of the lights was related to atmospheric conditions and concluded that while this may be true for some cases, it could not account for all of the reported incidents.

Over the last two hundred years in Nova Scotia and elsewhere in the Maritimes, there have been numerous cases of multiple witness sightings of what the people refer to as ships of fire or phantom ships. In more modern times we hear reports of phantom cars and even phantom trains. Usually the vehicle itself is not seen, only the lights associated with it. Perhaps the best known story, a famous legend that continues into the present day, is that of The Teazer or The Young Teazer. The *Young Teazer*, an American privateer schooner, was trapped by a British warship in Mahone Bay on the South Shore of Nova Scotia, on June 27, 1813, during the War of 1812. Rather than be taken captive, its captain blew up the ship. Shortly afterwards strange lights began to appear on the ocean that were attributed to that disaster. While some sightings of ships on fire or ghost ships may be attributable to a full moon low in the sky, illuminating a fog bank, most of the sightings contain specific detail and dramatic visual and emotional components that can not be explained by such a simple, natural occurrence.

Dr. Creighton makes a distinction between the lights of ghostly encounters and the lights of phantom ships. Within the category of phantom ships there seem to be at least two or three main groupings. Some are craft witnessed during the day. Most ghost ships are simply described as fire balls or spheres of intense light with unusual qualities, but occasionally there's mention of sails, ropes, and rigging on the burning ship. To me these types of sightings constitute a true paranormal ghost ship, as if a nineteenth-century incident was replaying itself through a window or tear in the fabric of space-time. Witnesses have never, to my knowledge, described seeing a ghostly crew, although in some close up encounters, a presumed crew is heard speaking; their language is always strange and indecipherable.

Creighton documented a case told to her by aging fisherman where the South Shore crew approached what they took to be an oncoming fellow fishing boat under sail. They saw mast mounted lights and other required lights on the vessel. The ship passed by them at a distance close enough to dip flags, the vessel visible as a single sphere radiating an unusual light, which the witnesses could only describe as "fire-like." To these men, balls of fire and ghost ships were one and the same.

> On a long cruise a vessel might go well out of its way to dip its flag to another ship, just for the pleasure of its company on the mighty deep. Some Tancook men were on the Banks off Newfoundland one night when they saw a ship bearing down on them with masthead lights showing. She was full-rigged and had all the lights she was required to carry, no more and no less. The captain and watchmen stood uncertainly as she approached, waiting to see what she would do. They were tacking at the time, and the ship passed them like a ball of fire. They knew then that this was no friendly gesture, but that they had seen a ghost ship. They feared it was a forerunner of disaster and they were nervous until they got back to their home port. (Creighton 1957: 122)

The lights were not seen to be sailing ships, just assumed to be a type of vessel by some, although the likelihood of the objects being paranormal in nature was also accepted by many in the area. "You couldn't see the vessel, only the light, but you'd know it was the vessel by the feel of it" (Creighton 1957: 122).

Dr. Creighton also collected this story, which happened to a fisherman from Port Medway near the turn of the century. The fisherman and his son were sailing from Port Medway to Lunenburg and the incident occurred near Hell Point, sixty-seven kilometres from Port Medway, not far from Lunenburg, on Nova Scotia's South Shore. He saw what looked like the hull of a boat that was shining and sparkling, floating just above the surface of the water and bearing down on him at high speed.

> One time I took a load of fish to Lunenburg in September. We left in the middle of the night. When we got down to Hell Point my boy was asleep in the cuddy. It was as pretty a morning as you could see. Here come a boat, spurs, just a hull. It looked to be all sparkin' like there were little sparks all over it. I put my head in the cuddy to wake my son to tell him it was going to run us down and when I looked back it was gone. Next day in Lunenburg I mentioned it and the Dutchmen laughed at me. They said they'd seen it lots of times, but they didn't say what it was, and that's all I ever knew about it. (Ibid.)

In the literature of folklore and the paranormal there are bizarre experiences that don't fit neatly into any known category. A favourite example, collected by Marion Robertson, comes from Shelburne County and was recounted by an elderly woman from Barrington Passage, just outside Shag Harbour, who taught English literature at an American university. Her story seems to involve some type of gravity anomaly.

> As a little girl in Barrington Passage, she discovered one morning, on her way to school, that by lifting her feet as she stepped onto a ledge of a rock that extended diagonally across the road, she glided from one side of the ledge to the other as if drawn by a magnet. She was astonished, but she dared not tell the other children. Every day, when she reached the ledge, she would lift her feet and glide to the other side of the road. (Robertson 1991: 21)

Marion Robertson's Shelburne County Folklore

Marion Robertson (1910–1998), another folklorist who studied Shelburne County's local mythology, noted the large number of paranormal experiences before 1950 that involved unusual types of airborne craft and orbs. Ms. Robertson hints that there these strange sightings may have involved some sort of "presence": "Of the privileged few, who have rubbed shoulders with a strange 'something,' some have heard sounds or seen moving lights; others have been aware of a presence, 'an even darker darkness in the dark'" (Ibid.: 1).

Tales of countless sightings of strange lights, hovering over the waters off Shelburne County, are found wherever records were kept; some go back from before the turn of the century, to perhaps over two hundred years ago. Many of these stories involve the sudden appearance and disappearance of mysterious lights. Just such a light has been seen repeatedly from the shores of Ingomar, located about fourteen miles south of Shelburne. In one experience recounted by Robertson, when locals went out in a boat to investigate, the light suddenly disappeared. They searched the location, but there was, "no boat or buoy from whence the light could have been shining" (Ibid.: 9).

Another example of unusual aerial light phenomena in the area is "the Dunns," which used to be seen over Shelburne Harbour. A rather dark folktale explains why these beautiful lights were called the Dunns. As the story goes, a man by the name of Dunn pushed his wife into the water from his boat, and she drowned.

> The next morning he threw himself into the harbour from a rock near the Sandy Point lighthouse that still bears his name. In the years since, some have seen lights on the harbour dancing toward each other, twisting and twining, then disappearing into the water. (Ibid.)

Two more recent (though undated) cases involve "phantom autos" and occurred on roads leading away from Shelburne County's Sable River. One of the cases occurred on the old Route 3 from Sable to Allendale.

> A car with four passengers and a driver was headed along the road toward Allendale. As they drove along, they saw ahead a very old car. They remarked that it must be an old Ford, one of the first, with its tail light centred on the

back, jerking with the motion of the car. The driver followed behind the old Ford until the road curved just before a long stretch of straight road. Then, suddenly, the car was not there. (Ibid.: 19)

The other case (also undated) happened on the older Sable to Jordan road. Originally a dirt road connecting Sable and Jordan; it eventually became part of Route 103.

One night a couple, driving toward Jordan, saw an old car coming toward them. It was being driven on the left-hand side of the road as was the custom in the early years of automobiles. It continued on the left, the couple in their car holding as far as they could to the right. The car came on, until within a few inches of contact, it disappeared. (Ibid.: 20)

In the first case, a jerking light is seen on the road ahead of the witnesses, but it is in the centre of an unseen dark mass that is assumed to be an unusual car. In the second case the writer says that they saw an old car, although this may also be an assumption based on the behaviour of the object itself. The report does not specify whether the event occurred in the evening; if it did, it sounds like another case of a light that approached the witness and suddenly disappeared just before contact. It also sounds like an ill-defined mass that was perceived as an unusual type of car.

Connections Between Folklore and Modern UFO Cases

The reports of Helen Creighton and Marion Robertson are also reminiscent of several modern cases of UFOs on roads and on the water among the RG 77 reports. In UFO cases involving reality transformation, craft and beings are perceived as something else— a bus, a car, or a boat—but were actually an illuminated mass or sphere "screened" by something more familiar to the experiencer. In some cases there was an interaction between the orb and the witness; it has been suggested that the light forms took on or projected the expectations of the witness. Do such incidents constitute a form of close encounter?

Illuminated spheres or orbs are commonly reported facets of the supernatural. They appear throughout the modern record of human experience. Supernatural phenomena have demonstrated a consistent tendency to manifest as orbs of various sizes ranging from that of a baseball to the size of a house. Smaller lights may be consistent with the earthlights phenomenon, which is limited to certain areas under certain circumstances. Some researchers feel that the orbs that are photographed may be attributed to characteristics of and glitches with modern digital equipment. Often orbs are described as balls of light or fire. Some are not very bright, barely visible. Close up they appear to have some substance to them. In fact many classes of supernatural events are characterized by their light. The large spheres, ten to sixty feet across or greater, may not be attributable to earthlights, described below.

Illuminated orbs come in different varieties. There have been reports of ghost orbs, fairy orbs, photo orbs, orbs that are associated with UFOs, and even balls of plasma that can impact physical matter. Sometimes the orbs can grow in size and flare up, spit sparks, and fly around. Curious events have been reported by those who have approached the orbs. Some experiencers and researchers have found that despite their physical appearance, the orbs act as manifestations of or vehicles for intelligences to cross over, to connect, to communicate with our world from other realms. The descriptions of many modern UFOs have deep similarities to the large phantom ships and fire balls of southwestern Nova Scotia and other locations where such activity has long been in evidence.

Veteran UFO researcher Jacques Vallee writes,

> The visitors seem willing to conform to whatever mythology or beliefs they find; they become what we want them to be and tell us what we want to hear. Modern mythology having shifted from the magical to the scientific, it's only logical that the visitors would pose as scientifically advanced beings from space. (Vallee 1979: 243)

The Shag Harbour Incident can be seen as a forerunner, an early forerunner to some future event. The words of Helen Creighton also have a particular resonance for those who study UFO encounters.

> You may wonder how people recognize a phenomenon. It is difficult to explain and I suppose it needs to be experienced to be fully comprehended. I expect

that in most cases it comes as it does to me, not as a telling by a voice that is heard, nor as a sign by anything that is seen. I can only describe it as a knowing. It is conveyed by some strange means of communication or transference of thought, and is so strong that the recipient has no doubt of its veracity. (Creighton 1957: 19)

Earthlights

Natural light phenomena have been called mystery lights, spook lights, ghost lights, will-o'-the-wisp, ignis fatuus, and jack-o'-lantern. Some of the light phenomena can be attributed to St. Elmo's fire, ball lightning, and even northern lights. The explanation for true earthlights is far more involved and has some bearing on the lights sighted off the coast of Nova Scotia over the centuries.

The earthlight phenomenon has been regularly observed in places as far flung as Silver Cliff, Colorado, Henjelven in Norway, and Marfa, Texas. The phenomenon in Brown Mountain, North Carolina, was investigated by the US Geological Survey in 1913. Earthlights have been observed throughout history, but only recently have they been studied scientifically. They seem to arise from exotic geological disturbances somewhat like earthquake lights (EQLs). This phenomenon can produce glowing orbs and plasmas in sphere or disc shapes. Earthlights have also been associated with rock friction, faults slippage, and tremors. They are believed to be caused by tectonic strain on geological rock formations and by the piezoelectric effect, the production of electricity from the application of mechanical stress to certain crystals. Tectonic Strain Theory (TST), put forth by Canadian scientist Michael Persinger, concerns the tectonic strain fields that trigger quakes in weaker regions but result in lights on the surface when they pass through stronger, more resistant geology. According to Persinger, this also produces powerful electromagnetic (EM) fields that can cause paranormal hallucinations via the temporal lobe. While earthlight is a term used to describe a broad class of primarily geomagnetic phenomena, in its most true form, earthlight and the conditions that give rise to it may also facilitate some forms of paranormal contact. The surrounding geological, magnetic, and atmospheric conditions seem to allow for geomagnetic and geogravitic increases and decreases that may facilitate the crossing over of a variety of anomalous phenomena including UFOs, poltergeist activity, and extrasensory perception (ESP) type experiences.

CHAPTER 9: UFOS AND SHELBURNE COUNTY FOLKLORE

A 1968 article by French writer Ferdinand Legarde in the journal *Flying Saucer Review* linked UFOs and geological factors (Lagarde 1968). Legarde based his argument on measurements made during the great 1954 UFO flap. In 1969, John Mitchell postulated the relationship between magnetic disturbances, faults, and UFOs in his book, *View Over Atlantis*, which helped launch the concept of earthlights as a subcategory of the larger study of earth mysteries. UFO researcher John Keel and others have noted that UFOs tend to be observed between the highest hills and close to natural faults. Michael Persinger—a neuropsychologist from Laurentian University in Sudbury, Ontario, who has devoted his career to studying environmental effects on human consciousness, focusing especially on altered states of consciousness, UFOS, and nonhuman intelligences—and Gyslaine Lafreniere, also from Laurentian, feel earthlights are caused by a combination of terrestrial and extraterrestrial forces that accumulate in a seismic area (Persinger and Lafreniere 1977).

Author and researcher Paul Devereux has studied the earthlights phenomenon since the late 1960s; in his 1982 book *Earth Lights*, he argues the UFO phenomenon is largely attributable to the earthlight phenomenon. Meanwhile other researchers were also beginning to consider the relationship between geophysics and consciousness. Unusual effects of geoactivity have been seen to magnetize door latches, make objects levitate, release mists and gaseous vapours, and produce balls of light and fire balls. In some cases the earthlight phenomena have been seen as moving with some degree of playful intelligence.

Researchers Michael Persinger and John Derr did a study of UFO reports of sightings based around Uintah Basin, Utah, from 1965 to 1971. They found that the timing of sightings was related to geological seismic fault activity. Interestingly, they discovered "that total numbers of reported sightings peaked in February and April and, to their greatest extent, in October 1967" (Persinger and Derr 1989), the time of the Shag Harbour Incident.

Persinger, Devereux, Russel Targ, and Hal Puthoff all put forth the theory that the electromagnetic fields surrounding the light phenomena will affect the brain and its perception, specifically the part of the brain associated with altered states of consciousness, ESP, and mystical experiences. This informs Devereux's experience and is why he believes interaction with earthlights can be mistaken for contact with UFOs, ETs, and "alien abduction."

The studies of Persinger and others suggest that poltergeist effects tend to occur during times and areas of high geomagnetic activity, while more spontaneous telepathic and clairvoyant experiences happen on days of low geomagnetic activity. Earthlights activity and, according to Devereux, UFO activity, occur during high magnetic field activity. Persinger speculates that "Tectonically generated fields would probably be accompanied by alterations in gravity." This may explain the purported levitation at Barrington Passage recorded by Helen Creighton.

In *Earth Lights*, Devereux mentions his primary experience with the phenomenon while in art school and his subsequent sightings on expeditions to regions exhibiting earthlights. In his first sighting, the light phenomenon seemed to take on a "proto-human" form. The light apparition appeared differently to him than it did to other witnesses. This helped Devereux develop his theories suggesting that the light forms interact with human biofields. These demonstrations indicated to him that the forms are sensitive to the experiencer and even react to an individual's thoughts. This could be one explanation for the vivid, detailed visions of phantom light forms appearing as legendary ghost ships or soldiers in the sky.

According to Devereaux, consciousness may be capable of interacting with plasma clouds. These shape-shifting entities are born from the interactions between magnetic and piezoelectric, shifting stones and the massive energy fields emanating from the earth and sun. Consciousness can be seen as an interpenetrating natural energetic field that permeates space throughout the universe and interacts with space-time in ways that we do not yet understand.

A similar phenomenon to earthlights has been demonstrated in upper atmosphere light forms, which are similar in description to former astronaut John Glenn's "creatures," which have been repeatedly reported in space. Astronaut Scott Carpenter thought these were living "critters" as did shuttle pilot Story Musgrave. Some characteristics of both earthlights and UFOs were found in light phenomena seen in space and caught on NASA cameras during the STS-80 space shuttle missions. Sometimes the "critters" seem to move in a choreographed style.

In the 2001 documentary, *The Secret NASA Transmissions: "Smoking Gun,"* Martyn Stubbs of Vancouver explains how he accessed the down-link transmissions from every NASA mission, recording over 2,500 hours of footage (Birdsall 2001). The footage demonstrated three different forms of phenomenon. Two types were large, luminous, and circular and seemed to move through space intelligently, in a coordinated way. A third form was almost invisible except for an image captured on a charge-coupled device (CCD) camera and visible in only one of several frames, moving very fast within the scan field. In some of these missions, NASA used a type of multi-spectrum camera, which included infrared that successfully enhanced light forms.

Magnetometers, ultraviolet, and infrared NASA cameras have picked up unusual spheres both on the ground and in space. So has select NASA space shuttle footage. The NASA Origins Project considered plasma-based life as a valid possibility. Then there are the mysterious blobs and "rods" (also known as "skyfish" or "solar entities") that have been captured on both film and video around the world. The late sci-fi author Philip K. Dick wrote over 500,000 words of non-fiction about his encounters with what could be considered electromagnetic beings and plasma life forms.

Geological phenomena like earthlights may or may not be related to some UFO sightings around Nova Scotia, like the orange orbs seen coming out of the ocean or small flying plasma orbs, but they do not seem to explain the concrete nature of the Shag Harbour Incident. Yet the well-known story of the Barney and Betty Hill abduction began with a light in the sky and ended with an orange ball of light. And in between those balls of light was the dreamy encounter with the alien and the UFO. There is obviously a variety of overlapping facts and theories that may apply to the UFO phenomenon, which will eventually illuminate and impact a wide swath of cultural and historical, scientific, and academic disciplines.

Ghostly and ethereal apparitions are occasionally detected by our advanced technologies. They may not prove either solid or of this earth, but their scientific impact could be huge. What is needed is basic honesty from NASA and other agencies to admit the existence of that large body of anomalous data that is held yet withheld from the public. Occasionally, something slips through the grip of official censorship such as the Mars Rover photo of "something" streaking across the Martian sky that is neither a meteor nor one of the ten objects that man has put into orbit around the red planet. When the story first broke in the media, NASA officials embarrassingly referred to the image as, "the first photo of a UFO from another world." It's nice to see that NASA still has a sense of humour, if not a sense of scientific duty and integrity. You can only keep the cork in the bottle for so long, especially when the contents are so full of ufological "fizz and sizzle."

What is it about Nova Scotia?

There are unusual oceanographic, geological, and geographic factors in Nova Scotia that make it distinct and that may be related to the anomalous activity there over the years.

Stewiacke, Nova Scotia, is located midway from the equator to the north pole, along the forty-fifth parallel north, and is at the centre of the province. The areas of Stewiack, Springhill, Truro, and Debert line the innermost part of the Bay of Fundy. The Bay of Fundy, extending along Nova Scotia's southwestern coast, is in a sense the original navel of the planet. Home to the legendary Native figure Glooscap, the bay also boasts the highest tides in the world. In addition to its Aboriginal heritage, the Fundy Shore is known for unique geology, semi-precious stones (including quartz-amethyst and rare zeolite crystals), and dinosaur bones. In 1852 geologists made one of the most famous fossil discoveries in paleontology, the remains of the earliest reptile then found, *Hylonomus lyelli*, in the layered, fossil-bearing cliffs of the upper bay. Charles Darwin mentioned the area in *The Origin of Species*, first published in 1859. The Bay of Fundy was roughly the centre of Pangea, the supercontinent, where the original breaking up of the continental crust occurred around 190 million years ago. On this original huge single continent, when the European, African, and American continents were joined, the mainland portion of Nova Scotia was connected to what is now Africa, while the Cape Breton Island portion of Nova Scotia was originally located near Scotland. But what are the implications of the Nova Scotia being a centre of Pangea? Is it significant that the province opened up to reveal the deep recesses of inner Earth and form the Atlantic Ocean millions of years ago?

The province is home to the Cobequid Mountains, which are the top of the Appalachian Mountain chain, a fault line that runs up the entire east coast of the North American continent. Offshore of Nova Scotia is the Scotian Basin, which extends 1,200 kilometres north into the waters off Newfoundland. On average, the Scotia Basin is 250 kilometres wide, and half the basin lies on the continental slope under water up to 4,000 metres deep. The Scotian Basin consists of highs and lows, with an especially deep valley called the Orpheus Graben bordered by faults that run even deeper into the earth. The Orpheus Graben (also know as the Orpheus basin or Orpheus rift) extends in a remarkably straight line from Chedabucto Bay (between mainland Nova Scotia and Cape Breton Island) up to Newfoundland. Like the entire Scotian Basin, the Orpheus Graben was formed when North America split from the African continent, so it is older than the formation of the Atlantic Ocean.

CHAPTER 9: UFOS AND SHELBURNE COUNTY FOLKLORE

During the 1960s, oceanographers discovered that the Orpheus Graben contains a massive gravity anomaly. The Orpheus rift valley of Pangea is one of the deepest in the world, and its gravity anomaly is one of the most significant of its types. The main gravity anomaly on the mainland of Nova Scotia is in the southwest, near the conjunctions of Shelburne, Annapolis, Lunenburg, and Queens counties. Could these anomalies hold significance in relation to the extended presence of UFOs and USOs around the province and the possibility of an underwater base of operation?

During the summer of 2008, I attended a conference on the legendary Oak Island, one of hundreds of islands in Mahone Bay, on the south shore of Nova Scotia. The purpose and origin of the labyrinth of booby-trapped manmade caves under Oak Island and what they conceal is one of the world's greatest unsolved mysteries and treasure hunts. I camped out there with Paul Kimball and radio host Tim Binnall of the paranormal show, *Binnall of America*. The island's history is full of ghostly apparitions, time bleed-throughs, and a myriad of hauntings. I noted one fascinating UFO report from the water next to the island in the RG 77 file from the early 1970s where a craft shot up from the surface of the water into the sky when approached by witnesses. Paul filmed my interviews and the presentations of engineers, a historian, author and journalist Darcy O'Connor, and psychic Eugenia Macer-Story, who were all speaking about the mysterious inner earth workings, surface clues, and history of the island.

Eugenia's overarching explanation for the strange history of paranormal occurrences around Oak Island specifically and around the province generally caught my attention and stuck with me. She told me that the cause of the anomalous activity, from UFOs to ghostly apparitions and psychic experiences, is mainly due to an oceanographic and geological area just southeast of the Nova Scotian shelf where the ocean floor suddenly gets unusually deep. It is one of the deepest rifts on the planet. This is the location of the gravitic anomaly called the Orpheus graben or basin. There are also wide swaths of magnetic anomalies in this area. The Bedford Institute of Oceanography (BIO) has studied this anomalous feature going back at least to the 1960s. Their published scientific studies confirm gravitic and magnetic anomalies in the area and postulate a likely geological origin. The scientific studies indicate that the gravitic and magnetic anomalies from the Orpheus basin affect the area, including the mainland of the province, due to magnetic lines of force that generate from the layering of metallic and non-metallic sediment that formed as the earth's crust settled and cooled in the area millions of years ago.

Is there a link between the magnetic and gravitic anomalies in that area, the secrecy at Shelburne Station, and the UFO activity around Nova Scotia during the period of the twenty-year picnic? Could the area of the Orpheus basin be home to an underwater USO base or at least an area of USO activity and traffic? We can't say for sure, but hypothetically it would be a good location for such activity. The nearest other significant rift is the Puerto Rico Rift. This island is famed in UFO lore as the location of underground alien and government bases. It is difficult to verify this claim, although there exists unusual undersea scans of the base of the island of Puerto Rico as well as otherwise unexplainable paranormal, cryptozoological, and UFO activity on the island. Other deep underwater trenches or rifts around the world, including off India and the Marianas Trench off the coast of the Philippines, have also been the sources of significant USO sightings and activity. According to Eugenia Macer-Story, the rift off the Nova Scotia coast provides a "window" for all sorts of paranormal activity in the province. What type of geological seismic activity was going on around Nova Scotia during the UFO flap of the mid 1960s to the early 1980s? This is an area of research that has yet to be explored.

A final factor when examining anomalies particular to Nova Scotia is that the province is at the top of the east coast "ley line" or axis. This line, which perfectly bisects the province, continues down the American east coast and aligns with many interesting sites, including most major cities going down the eastern seaboard. In addition to the cities along this line, a sacred geometric grid of temples, churches, American and Native American cemeteries, and burial sites are based on this central axis. The origin of this sacred geomantic line and related sacred geometry seems to be the early Freemasons and before them the Knights Templar. This geomancy seems to have its pre-Templar origin in Celtic, European, and perhaps even Egyptian tradition.

Eugenia has written about how geological anomalies and inter-dimensional realities may explain various types of paranormal activity. Other dimensions are in our physical universe, but typically we can't perceive them, and these dimensions may be inhabited by beings of varying intelligences. Eugenia has theorized about the denizens of dark matter, that some "ETs" may originate from realms or dimensions within dark matter.

A myriad of factors surrounding the geological stress and the magnetic fields of an area bear relation to paranormal portals and UFO flaps. Magnetic fields may be deviated by certain crystal and metallic elements. Like interference with car engines, radios, and compass readings, negative magnetometer readings are caused by negative drops in normal magnetic fields, which in turn can be due to striations in geology. Space-time distortions may occur along magnetic lines of force, and within these distorted conditions inter-dimensional, UFO, and paranormal phenomena may manifest themselves.

Aviation scientists around the world have been studying magnetism and gravity in relation to advanced propulsion systems. Back in the 1950s Canadian scientist Wilbert Smith was studying geomagnetic release in relation to UFO activity. Michael Persinger found geological factors were causing gravity disturbances that could give rise to plasmas that interact with the human central nervous system and brain electrical activity resulting in perceived contact. He also linked seismic activity and UFO sightings, both of which peaked in October 1967, the exact time of the Shag Harbour Incident (Persinger and Derr 1985: 143). Marine scientists have studied geomagnetic and geogravitic anomalies off the coast of Nova Scotia. UFO, psychic, and paranormal activity is linked to the phenomenon of these anomalies in the same area. Scientists have even hypothesized that solar flares can cause electromagnetic "wormholes" to earth.

So where does this lead us? Can magnetism and gravity anomalies on earth, when sufficiently charged with energy from the sun or geological stress, result in "windows" where the known laws of physics can diminish enough to allow breakthroughs from mysterious, higher realms? Something is causing these bizarre encounters and related phenomena, and someday science may catch up with the causes. Perhaps science will eventually open up to include consciousness studies and some areas that are deemed pseudo-science, like near-death studies and earth mysteries. Until then we can only prepare ourselves by evolving spiritually so we can properly handle the coming technological and information breakthroughs. According to esoteric aspects of eastern religions as well as the new quantum physics, consciousness is not limited to humans; it permeates earth and space and allows energies to take forms that can interact with human consciousness. What we are learning is that life is not limited to human beings or traditional concepts of conscious life, and we can interact with a myriad of life forms in ways we are just beginning to understand.

Chapter 9 Endnote

1. Indeed, modern researchers including Dr. Richard Boylan and Thomas Bullard have noted that UFO contact occurs in higher percentages among peoples of Celtic and Native descent. See Pritchard et al. (1994).

Chapter 10: Contact
Graham Simms

"Men really do need sea monsters in their personal oceans. An ocean without its unnamed monsters would be like a completely dreamless sleep."
– John Steinbeck, The Log from the Sea of Cortez

"It's an important and popular fact that things are not always what they seem. For instance on the planet Earth, man had always assumed that he was the most intelligent species occupying the planet, instead of the third most intelligent. The second most intelligent creatures were of course, dolphins."
– Douglas Adams, The Hitchhiker's Guide to the Galaxy

In casual discussions with friends, I've noted that most have had some unusual experiences that could be classified as paranormal. In more intimate relationships, I've discovered that some have had highly unusual experiences. Certainly most people have had some sort of psychic and intuitive experiences in their lives. A few friends remembered they thought they had seen a ghost. Anna had seen something she didn't think seemed human in the woods of Maine. Several had seen inexplicable lights, craft, or discs in the sky. Kathryn had seen a basketball-size orb of plasma-like substance fly low and hit a house in Nova Scotia. Several friends had seen 2 foot wide sparking and spinning energetic balls of light that moved with intelligence on the ground and in the sky around Halifax. Three friends eventually admitted, separately, that they had each had a close encounter with what they clearly thought was a UFO and experienced some sort of communication from it. Two of these encounters were in the Maritime provinces. The experience was powerful for each of my friends, yet they were all reticent to talk further about it. Although I had met several well-adjusted, honest men and women whom we at PEER (the Program for Extraordinary Experience Research at Harvard's Cambridge Hospital in Cambridge, MA) believed to be multiple experiencers, I was humbly grateful for the further understanding I gained when one of my close friends confessed that he, too, was a full on experiencer of contact with "star beings." My friend Albert is a West Coast Nez Perce Native American I met through common friends when we both lived in Boston. One day he took my hand and put it on his neck, where I felt a small lump that he said was an implant. His grandparents had told him that encounters with star beings were a hereditary trait of their lineage that they had experienced as well. By that point I was not particularly shocked, but his fascinating story brought the phenomenon home for me in a profound way.[1]

On July 17, 2005, two years before before the Halloween party where Chris Styles and I first met (described in the Preface), something significant happened to me. Dr. Mack had been hit and killed by a drunk driver a few months earlier, and I had been more involved in Buddhist training. Despite the immense inspiration I felt from Dr. Mack, I wondered where my interest in studying the UFO phenomenon was going. Was it a pointless indulgence? How could I channel the importance I knew it held? Similarly, I wondered about my commitment to my spiritual path. So I put out a question, a plea, to the universe, not in a heavy-handed way, but very subtly, forming a question even without words but with intent and radiating it out: Is this the right path? Please give me a sign.

Two days later I was on the balcony at my residence in Halifax with my friend Tony when I received an answer. (Later I would find out that Chris Styles had lived in the same residence years earlier, and we had the same room. The house used to be a nurses' training residence for the old Halifax Infirmary, and the room Chris and I had lived in at different times used to be the child-birthing room.) Tony and I were on the back deck on the top of the building with an unobstructed view over the city. It was dusk, and the stars were just coming out and the moon was low in the sky. I noticed a strange light, quite low and moving in an irregular way. It seemed roughly over the Northwest Arm, the stretch of water that borders peninsular Halifax to the west. Tony witnessed the first half of the action as well. As soon as I saw the strange, low flying, solid yellow-white glowing object, without blinking lights like any aircraft or helicopter, I felt a link in my consciousness with it, a feedback and a "locked on" sensation. The light immediately flew lower and began moving in jittery, random movements toward us, perhaps two thousand feet up and out. I communicated silently with the object, thanking it for showing up and asking it to show itself to me.

I asked Tony what he thought about the object and he was mystified. It was not a plane, not a helicopter. Then it ascended higher into the sky, slowly and

CHAPTER 10: CONTACT

steadily, until it crossed Orion. At that point, suddenly, with breathtaking speed it shot across the sky at an upward angle, past the moon and up until it was no longer visible. Tony turned to me with raised eyebrows. We were both awestruck. Suddenly, behind Tony, the presumably same celestial craft reappeared, in a sort of spiral shock wave and blast of light that radiated through the spectrum of rainbow laser light, one colour after the other, leaving a blazing tracer like a white sword across the sky, unfurling toward the southern horizon. The tracer lingered for a few seconds before the light rolled up behind the craft, and it disappeared in a flash. Whatever the source of the display, the airborne craft was of a very high technology.

Although I was experiencing some degree of excitement, even more I felt deeply grateful and humbled. There was no desire to run around and tell everyone what had happened. But it seemed like a response to my question of two days earlier. It was not particularly about me, it was so much bigger. In fact, there was a predominant sense of heavy, profound responsibility. There was a lot of work to do. And although I did not know how that work would manifest itself, I trusted the universe would open its doors if I had faith, did my part, and remained open to it.

Phil Hoyle and Paul H.
The universe opened another door for me when, a couple of years after my balcony sighting, Chris handed me the package sent to him by British UFO researcher Phil Hoyle. I became familiar with Phil's material and quickly got in touch with him in England. The experiences of the abductee he has been working with, named Paul H. (his last name is unknown to us at this time), seem consistent with the demonstrated and documented patterns of other abduction and alien encounter experiences, patterns that were recognized and documented by researchers like Dr. John Mack who seriously studied the experiences of a relatively large numbers of witnesses over significant periods of time. Phil filled me in on the situation regarding the encounters Paul H. has been having with the aliens that claim to be involved in the Shag Harbour and Shelburne incidents.

In his early fifties when I first made contact with him, Phil Hoyle is an Englishman who has had a lifelong interest in contact phenomenon and has been researching the UFO phenomenon for the majority of his adult life. He operated the UFO Investigations and Research Unit (UFOIRU), which investigates sightings, contacts, abductions, crop circles, animal mutilations, and holds sky watches. The main emphasis of Phil's work is UFO abduction-contact and sightings cases. In the last five years Phil's unit has devoted more time to the crop circle phenomenon and its apparent links with unknown lights, spheres, and discs in the Midlands area and in the famous Wilkshire area. UFOIRU records their night sky watches, sometimes using a five million candlepower light to signal skyward. Phil also sent a video of footage he and his unit had taken in his local area, the Shropshire area, as part of their close encounter of the fifth kind (CE5) sky watch project ongoing since 2001. Many of these UFO sightings and encounters and animal mutilations have been documented along what Phil calls "our animal mutilation corridor."

In the Hartlebury Common sighting video taken in front of the 407 metre (1,335 foot) hill called The Wrekin, lights appear that blink on and off. Alignments or strings of low stationary lights blink in for several minutes and then out, several times. Phil wrote that there are reports of animal mutilations in the Shropshire valley where Paul lives and that the sky watches there have been strange; the area seems heavily monitored by unusual high technologies.

Phil received new information from Paul in May 2004 that prompted him to write his letter to Chris. Paul had recently had a contact experience where the intelligences mentioned Shag Harbour, first as an example of how their craft could operate underwater. Paul claimed the beings involved in his contacts said that they are the same ones involved in the 1967 Shag Harbour Incident and that they could prove this. Paul gave Phil information regarding something that happened from the beings' perspective in October 1967 while the naval flotilla held station over the submerged craft near Shelburne's Government Point. Phil sent this information on to Chris, wondering if he would confirm two points.

> During the incident when the craft was on the seabed and military divers were sent down to investigate the object, the beings claimed that their own people wearing diving suites [sic] were working outside the craft and actually met face to face the military divers coming down to investigate. There was an apparent communication where the beings told the divers or one in particular that their craft was damaged and they wanted no confrontation and only wanted to repair the craft and they should be out of the area as quickly as possible. They also told my witness that one of the divers' names was Karol; I have asked my witness to clarify if this is the diver's surname, and he was sure it was his Christian name. Do you have any unpublished information that might confirm this statement? Also regarding the Shag Harbour Incident the intelligences in con-

CHAPTER 10: CONTACT

tact with my witness stated that a ship called HMCS *Skeena* was at the location at the time of the crash incident; is it possible to confirm this?[2]

Later Paul thought the diver's name could be Carol, and he thought it must be a last name. When Phil emailed Don Ledger, he reportedly confirmed some sort of link to the name Carol. The name the aliens supposedly gave Paul was not exact but relatively close to the diver's name.

Chris had of course spoken with two of the main navy divers who dove at Shag Harbour and then secretly at the nearby Shelburne mission. At least one of the divers observed the two craft next to each other under the navy flotilla, one presumably aiding the other. He also reported that beings were manoeuvring between the crafts. The diver even shot film footage and took still photos of those underwater events. The military command wisely took no action against the crafts, just observed them. On October 11, the fleet moved to intercept a Soviet sub breaching the twelve-mile limit. Soon after that point, at 8:30 pm, the objects were seen by many witnesses—including some, like the Cameron family, who made police reports—to break the surface of the water and streak through the sky above the Gulf of Maine.

The HMCS *Skeena* is a well-known Canadian navy ship that has been based in Nova Scotia since the 1960s. Chris has not been able to determine whether it was the ship present during the Shelburne operation. Karol or Carol as a surname of one of the divers was not an exact hit, but one of the primary divers in the operation, with whom Chris had spoken repeatedly, had a first name that was very close, a few letters more than Carol. He had told Chris that he delivered the film he had shot to the Defence Research Board (DRB) in Dartmouth.[3]

Although Chris admitted that Paul's account was interesting, we were still curious to know at what exact point Paul was first exposed to Chris's book, *Dark Object* or to other sources of information about the Shag Harbour Incident. Chris was worried that information may have reached him through other sources and influenced the information he passed on to Phil. In other words, Chris was worried about contamination. For me, the main concern, besides the truth, was the possibility of a "disinformation operation" or a military abduction (MILAB) psychological operation (PSY OP) with memory implants, apparently also used for disinformation purposes; however, I have no indication of this, and the situation presented by Paul seems more likely to me.

Paul H. and Shag Harbour

According to his letter to Chris, dated May 24, 2004, Phil Hoyle was first in touch with Paul H. in December 2003. Paul is a father in his mid fifties; he was in the Royal Navy for nineteen years and served as a marine engineering mechanic between 1964 and 1974. Paul was referred to Phil by Yvonne South from UFORM (Midlands). She knew that Phil had been investigating an older case that Paul believed was related to one of his contact experiences in terms of location and time frame. Phil conducted an initial interview with Paul over the phone. Paul had only recently acknowledged what was happening to him and was beginning to recall lightly blocked memories. He was developing a shaky understanding from being aware of the patterns of anomalous phenomena throughout his life that had now become obvious. He was experiencing the positive and negative side effects of the ordeal; the trauma and the transformation.

The following is a synopsis of Phil Hoyle's reports culled from his initial correspondence as well as my subsequent conversations with him.

In July 1981, Paul was working with his father as a commercial vehicle mechanic. One night, they were travelling through County Wellington, Telford, Shropshire, on their way to remove a faulty gear box from a truck before morning. At 9:00 pm they stopped for coffee at the Shamrock Cafe in Overley Hill. They noticed a very large light hovering in the sky above the trees of the wood lot opposite them, only a few hundred feet away. It looked like an illuminated double-decker bus. They saw a narrow beam of blue-green light coming from the object and sweeping around on the ground of the dark woods. The object then moved perhaps a half mile away, rose about five hundred feet higher, and disappeared from sight very rapidly. This is all Paul and his father remember seeing. The next thing they knew, it was about midnight and they had lost "a good three hours" of time. They noticed that suddenly there was another car parked nearby, and the coffee they had been drinking from a flask earlier in the day was much warmer than it had been earlier. They were puzzled as to where the three hours had gone. They decided to drive on to their gearbox removal job in Wellington. Over the next few days Paul and his father did not discuss the incident. They knew something had happened but had no clue as to what.

A week or so later Paul's father brought his attention to something in the paper. There in the *Shrewsbury Star* was an article by Val Walters and Rosemary Hawkins relating their own encounter with a UFO almost exactly when and where Paul and his father had their sighting, Overley Hill. The newspaper

CHAPTER 10: CONTACT

article came as a shock as it confirmed their worst fears, that something had taken place, something mysterious involving a UFO. Perhaps that is why they decided not to discuss it again and to try to put the incident to the back of their minds. Twenty-two years later, Paul was still troubled by the incident. His father passed away in 2000 and in 2002 Paul finally confided in a friend about the encounter. That is when they searched out local UFO groups and found UFORM in the Midlands, where they sent a request for assistance in researching experiences documented in that location and time frame. Yvonne from UFORM then redirected the request to Phil Hoyle's UFOIRU as she knew they had investigated the case involving Val Waters and Rosemary Hawkins in a nearby area in the same time frame.

In the days following Paul and Phil's initial interview over the phone, Paul recalled a sighting when he was a small boy. He was about eight or nine years old at a junior school in Minsterley, near Shrewsbury, where he and several other students and teachers witnessed a silver cigar-shaped UFO, forty to fifty feet long, that hovered at about five hundred feet for about five minutes above the Long Field Terrace.

Days after this recall Paul started remembering other incidents he thought were related, including one that occurred in February 2003. Paul was alone, travelling to Redditch for work, when he saw something odd and then suddenly found himself by a garage to the south of Ledbury, in Herefordshire. He didn't remember anything since he passed the town of Kidderminster, over two hundred kilometres and two hours earlier. He couldn't understand why he was there instead of Redditch and felt queasy, as if he had motion sickness. Paul stumbled toward a man at the front of the garage and asked him, "Where the fucking hell are we?" The man asked him, "Have you been brought here by aliens?" Paul responded, "I don't know how I got here. I feel unwell. I think I'm going to be sick." The man from the garage replied, "Well, you are in Ledbury." Paul never made it to Redditch. He got sick in front of the garage then got back in his car and headed home, stopping several times to vomit along the way. He also found he had a rash on the front and back of his body, which was itchy for a few days.

Since recalling the series of strange lifelong incidents that now seemed to be related, Paul had also been recalling recurring vivid dreams that always focused on the same themes. These dreams included specific places near his home, like Devil's Chair and Squilver in Shropshire, and multiple UFOs coming out of storm clouds. His recall of past experiences increased as additional alien contacts revealed themselves more completely (see below). As the information content of the contacts increased, Paul began to feel more comfortable with them. He was having more questions answered.

Phil Hoyle conducted a second interview with Paul on February 2, 2004. Paul and his son Ross had recently recalled a multiple-witness sighting they had experienced together during the summer of 1997. They were driving up to the Welsh Border Golf Club and Driving Range in Middletown when Ross asked, "What is that over the top of the driving range, Dad?" As they approached a gap in the hedge where they'd be able to get an unobstructed view of the sky, they clearly saw a cylindrical cigar-shaped object with holes in one end suspended in the sky. Paul pulled over and jumped up on the gate to get a better look. Two people at the club also observed the unusual aerial object.

"What the hell is it?" one asked the other.

"What do you think it is?"

"A space ship," answered the first. The other agreed. The object started to move very quietly in the direction of a nearby hill and then took off very quickly. When Paul and Ross arrived at the golf club they saw that people coming off the course had also been watching the strange craft.

Paul was now recalling details of the inside of the craft and of his interactions with some of the beings, who showed him the flight consoles and navigation screens and gave him a general explanation of how they used them. Paul recalled his father being on board the craft with him in at least one early memory. He recalled grey beings with three or four long pointed digits. "The entities that Paul claims to be in contact with are the typical grey type, and he claims they are not hostile."[4] Paul has said that some of the beings have the capacity to be nasty. He also recalled seeing a dark cloak or hooded being. During many of his contacts he remembers seeing what he can only describe as an eye, similar to an Egyptian eye. He stressed how important the beings' eyes were to the contacts.

> Their eyes are an eye, as we know it. I get a flash now and again because I can remember being absolutely riveted by looking at them. And I get a flash even now as I am talking to you, a flash of their features of which the eye is very, very prevalent. They don't ever appear to blink, and yet something happened in those eyes, I don't know what it is. It's like a movement within the eye. I don't know, that is, I shut up shop before I get to see it, to come to that degree. The eye is very important to them.[5]

CHAPTER 10: CONTACT

On Sunday, March 7, 2004, Paul had an unusual experience that frightened his son Ross. For the previous two years Paul had been suffering from a urinary problem; he regularly passed blood. The problem was being investigated by his doctor and was symptomatic of a kidney problem. On the night of March 7, Paul was sleeping downstairs on the sofa. In the early hours, Ross awoke to the sound of Paul screaming. Ross rushed downstairs. When Paul regained his composure he told his son that he had been having a dream where the small grey humanoids were operating on the lower right-hand side of his back. When Paul pulled up his shirt to show Ross the area in question, Ross was shocked to see a scar line and an elliptical area with a teardrop shaped hole in the middle. Within a few hours the scar over his kidney had faded. Since that night Paul has not suffered from the passing of any more blood when urinating. This type of quickly healing wounds is common in abduction encounters.

Around the time of this experience, Paul noticed intense energy in his hands and came to believe that he was developing healing power. He reported success in using the energy for healing on his friend Kevin who confirms a reduction in a ganglion tumour and feeling heat from Paul's hand.

On April 19, 2004, Phil Hoyle conducted another interview with Paul who recalled that around the ages of eight to ten years he had experiences with spheres of light that came through the walls of his bedroom. The spheres of light ranged from very small to soccer-ball size and changed colour from orange to blue. Sometimes a sphere would settle into his hand and he would have a "really great feeling."

On April 29, 2004, the general executive committee of UFOIRU had a meeting. The main topic of discussion was Paul's most recent ship-board contacts; now he remembered full past experiences, or he was having new experiences with a higher authority on board the craft. Behind the greys was an archetypal figure, a bearded being with long white hair that carried a crook or staff; after decades of contact with the greys Paul finally recalled meeting someone else from the craft who seemed more human and in charge. This archetypal figure was like Gandalf Greyhame from *Lord of the Rings*, the film adaptation of which was circulating at this time. Was Paul's recall only a screen memory?

Paul said that on March 23, 2004, he was parked in a car with his coworker and friend Kevin, apprehensively watching gathering dark clouds. He sensed "their" presence but could not see any craft and wondered if they were hidden in the storm clouds. Suddenly he felt an intense pressure on his chest and a funny sensation inside the top of his skull like it was itching or being tickled. He felt that a large amount of information was downloaded in to his subconscious and that his mind was overloaded. Paul started to talk about subjects that he had no experience with, and Kevin started taking notes so they could study the experience later. Paul felt like another intelligence had entered his body and was communicating from within him. He started to speak in a distorted way and his tongue was rolling. He saw an image of a tribal mask burning, which he understood as representing the suffering and problems Africa has been left to deal with, and further information was related through him that concerned the state of Africa.

The intelligence talking through Paul spoke about a world at war and warned about the Middle East burning and that things needed to be done quickly to stop the fighting around the world. They spoke from concern for man's plight and the suffering he has caused. Concern was conveyed about genetically modified (GM) crops and their detrimental effect on bees and cross-pollination of GM with non-GM food crops. Paul got the impression that "they" could choose to be nasty if Earth's elite continued their persistent destruction of life on Earth and ignored their pleas for peace and harmony with the planet.

Paul would later note that some greys acted almost like automatons, and theorized that perhaps they were designed for travel in time/space and to perform specific tasks. Once when Paul lost his temper at one of the small greys and threw it against a wall, he noticed that it had what seemed to be an artificially constructed torso. "You broke him," he was told. He noted that other greys are not automatons and seem to possess great wisdom and even compassion, despite their intellectual bent.

Paul would come to provide more details to Phil about the emerging lead character from this contact scenario. This entity was apparently the one behind the scenes directing the activity in the area, a person of authority behind the greys. Phil noted that the humanoid male as described by Paul resembles an elderly biblical character with a long white Middle Eastern style robe, long white or grey beard and hair, and shepherd's staff. He communicated to Paul, providing details about the situation of Earth today in relation to the cosmos. His name is Malak or Malik. Watching over Earth was his responsibility as part of an organized, governed universe society. Malak means angel in the Semitic languages and more specifically "directed messenger" (from God) in Hebrew. It is a name that appears several times in the Bible. Phil Hoyle says that this group has been described in the existing UFO literature over the last fifty years.

CHAPTER 10: CONTACT

It wasn't a stretch for me to accept Paul's story as so many other experiencers of contact have conveyed similar information. Paul's encounters strongly suggest that the environmental crisis has played a roll in the intervention, a point that has been consistently demonstrated throughout this phenomenon. I believe that it cannot be overstated that UFO activity is clearly occurring in the context of a planet in environmental crisis, on a trajectory of collapse. Contact revelations like Paul's and Phil's also seem to fit the universal society "quarantine" scenario, which is a key feature of the exopolitical theory.[6]

Contact has been occurring regardless of the veracity of some contactees and their myriad claims. On the whole these contacts overlap and mirror the affiliated UFO sightings. People have made contact and have been contacted in an apparently organized program that has been underway for decades, if not much longer. The research of famed English ufologist Tim Good has traced the history of the modern contactee phenomenon to the 1920s—even in Canada (Good 1998: 30). He has also concluded that there are several alien bases on earth—many underwater, including in the Atlantic. The UFO contact and contactee phenomenon can be seen as a grassroots introduction that has effectively bypassed the typical control mechanisms of our modern Western culture. One can conclude from the hundreds or even thousands of first person encounters and the waves of UFO sightings that we are being acclimatized to the alien presence. While the news media has been complicit in minimizing and covering up evidence of UFO reality, science fiction books, films, and television shows and even advertising have mirrored the rise of the UFO and ET archetypes in collective culture. The reality of contact between humans and ETs has gradually permeated our culture and society.

Chapter 10 Endnotes

1. Albert ended up training with a highly elite military unit outside of the country.
2. Philip Hoyle, UFO Investigations and Research Unit, in a letter to Chris Styles, May 24, 2004.
3. Although we were told that the film would be archived at Library and Archives Canada, it has not shown up there.
4. Hoyle letter, May 24, 2004.
5. Ibid.
6. Exopolitics concerns political relations within the scope of the universe. See works by Canadian futurist Alfred Webre: the online e-book, *Towards a Decade of Contact* (2000) and *Exopolitics: Politics, Government, and Law in the Universe* (2005). Wikipedia: "The exopolitics model functionally maps the operation of politics, government and law in an intelligent universe, and provides an operational bridge between models of terrestrial politics, government and law, and the larger models of politics, government and law in the proposed society of the greater universe."

Chapter 11: Shag Harbour's Subtle Realm
Graham Simms

"In all affairs it's a healthy thing now and then to hang a question mark on all of the things that you have taken for granted."
- Bertrand Russell

"Reality is that which, when you stop believing in it, doesn't go away."
– Phillip K. Dick

During a June 2009 visit to Chris's Dartmouth residence, I was relieved to find that Chris felt my research into the RG 77 UFO files had been worthwhile. He explained that although he and Don Ledger had viewed the files several times in their research for *Dark Object*, they had not actually made a concerted effort to probe the sighting details and timelines for tentative or even definite connections. As he had in the past, Chris explained that things had unfolded so fast in their investigation of the Shag Harbour Incident that he and Don struggled with massive information overload. But I still couldn't see how a "dry" effort advanced or helped the case for new evidence. Chris went on to explain that all worthwhile premises must be explored in the interest of completeness, even the ones that don't pan out.

I did feel upbeat about one observation Chris made during that summer meeting. He felt, as did I, that there was a connection linking the evidence. We just didn't have the complete thread or definite common feature that connected and made sense of it all. I felt that if this had been a legal case and I was at the point of delivering my summation in a court of law, I would have failed to make my case. However, if I was running out the clock in a formal debate, the composite evidence inferred by the RG 77 files was strong. Chris and I were both struck by the consistent detailed witness accounts that described sightings and events that were somewhat uncommon within the bulk of UFO literature. For example, there seemed to be an usually high incidence of large orb sightings near the water and multiple witness cases that involved three-sectioned, lozenge-shaped craft. Many of these incidents involved lengthy time frames and police or military involvement. A large portion of the cases were associated with the ocean. All of this was interesting and possibly significant, but where did it leave us?

I asked Chris what we could do with what we had found. And, what should we do next? He said he didn't know, but he thought that I might have an insight for our next step. Though relieved to hear of his approval of my archival efforts, I wasn't in the mood for a riddle. But then he posed a question that got his point across and put the ball in my court. "What would Dr. John Mack have made of it all?"

Chris's question would have significant meaning for most UFO researchers or enthusiasts who were aware of the work of the late psychiatrist Dr. John Mack. Dr. Mack was a famed professor of psychiatry at Harvard Medical School at the Cambridge Hospital and a founding director of the Center for Psychology and Social Change. In 1993, Dr. Mack founded the Program for Extraordinary Experience Research (PEER) within the Center to continue his work with experiencers and to explore the larger context in which to place the UFO abduction phenomenon. Chris's question held additional context and meaning for me as I had served in a paid work study position in Dr. Mack's PEER program while taking night courses at Harvard. Chris went on to remind me that he had presented a paper at the 1996 MUFON International UFO Symposium that was held in Greensboro, North Carolina, where Dr. Mack was also a speaker. Mack had presented his seminal paper, "Studying Intrusions from the Subtle Realm." Among several presentations at the symposium that dealt with the topic of UFO abduction, Dr. Mack's was the only one that had truly impressed Chris.

I started to answer Chris's dangling question when he abruptly cut me off. "That's why you're here. Just like Phil Hoyle and those tentative file connections, this is your baby. You understand the subtle realm. I just acknowledge it and then grapple with my prejudices to make sense of it." I knew that I had my next assignment.

There is one slippery problem with the concept of "the subtle realm," and that is defining it. Even Dr. Mack struggled to convey the idea's full meaning in terms and language that at least provided a commonality of understanding for the use of believer, doubter, and skeptic alike. The problem stems from the fact that we are aware of the subtle realm only by means of suggestion and implication. Sources of suggestion would include such phenomena as clairvoyance, out-of-body experiences, near death revelations, telekinesis, and alien abduction. These various intrusive experiences would seem to originate from another dimension of existence. The subtle realm is all that is obviously not part of the gross, manifest, self-evident material world. It includes all that is separate and uncertain and yet "felt" by many through what may be described as an "opening of consciousness." One could simply view the subtle realm as the spirit world.

I pointed out to Chris that while Dr. Mack's methods were applied to individuals, his work encompassed a cross-cultural perspective, and that he came to a transpersonal, spiritual point of view. Chris said that we could try and apply that outlook to the Shag Harbour Incident and the "twenty year picnic." He wondered aloud if the "pattern" of UFO sightings and encounters within southwestern Nova Scotia throughout the "twenty year picnic" from the 1960s to the 1980s was one of an intrusion of themes from a collective unconsciousness or a set of reality transformations run wild. Suddenly a few speculative concepts began to take root. Looking back at that afternoon get-together, I believe that we were both more than ready for a new approach after the long dry spell of development that had evaded us in our examination of the archival record of the twenty year picnic.

In his teachings, John Mack pointed out that consciousness itself is not the sole dominion and by-product of the human brain. Certainly consciousness would be a part of any superior technological species, but mightn't it arise from other wholly different and non material life systems of sufficient complexity? Even NASA's Origins Program allows for the possibility of life from crystalline and plasma structures. In fact, biologists still struggle with a truly inclusive working definition of life itself that properly encompasses it within multiple ecosystems.

The works of John Mack and veteran UFO researcher Jacques Vallee suggest that sometimes entities or intelligences may "cross over" between the subtle realm and the physical world. Perhaps that is the essence of events like the Shag Harbour Incident. Could they be actions or effects related to temporary overlapping of different realms or dimensions? If so, it might help explain the other spiritual and paranormal activity in the area at multiple times. It would certainly help explain the transience of physical evidence, from the dissipating yellow foam to the sudden disappearance of the UFOs on the night of October 4, 1967. For a time what was observed by witnesses seemed all too real or physical in nature and then, they just disappeared.

However Jacques Vallee's body of work, with his concept of "reality transformations," whereby UFO witnesses experience a transformation of their sense of reality, muddies the waters even further. Vallee believes that some UFO incidents exhibit witness perception control by unknown means. In fact, he suggests some UFO sightings and events may not have any objective physical reality, and yet they are not wholly internalized. They may be precipitated by whatever consciousness ultimately lies behind the UFO phenomenon itself. Vallee has provided evidence suggesting that witnesses of UFO phenomena undergo a manipulative and staged spectacle, meant to alter their belief system (Vallee 1969: 149).

Vallee is known for popularizing the possible UFO connection behind the reputed appearances of Jesus' mother, Mary, to three shepherd children at Fatima, Portugal, in 1917 and some other religious apparitions or miracles, as well as the potential link between UFOs and folklore, mythology, and the occult. He helped popularize the notion the UFOs and aliens are likely multidimensional rather than extraterrestrial. He later came to focus somewhat on the negative side of UFO encounters. Some of this work has been taken by a few to support their extreme notions that UFOs are "demonic." Vallee postulated that UFOs act as a control mechanism to change our belief system. In *The Invisible College* Vallee posits the idea of a "control system." UFOs and related phenomena are "the means through which man's concepts are being rearranged." He goes on to say,

> When I speak of a control system for planet earth, I do not want my words to be misunderstood: I do not mean that some higher order of beings has locked us inside the constraints of a space-bound jail, closely monitored by psychic entities we might call angels or demons. I do not propose to redefine God. What I do mean is that mythology rules at a level of our social reality over which normal political and intellectual action has no power. (Vallee 1975: 205)

Chris has published several speculative papers that deal with what he calls "inconsistent" or Type II reality transformations (see, for example, Styles 2002: 7). These are the ones where different eyewitnesses perceive entirely different features at the same UFO event. One person may hear a deafening noise while another reports only silence. One witness sees entities while another only normal wildlife, etc. There is no conventional explanation that gives a satisfactory explanation for these occurrences if one accepts the veracity of the witnesses. Chris's work on these cases only included police reports where the cases received no publicity or public knowledge. They were very "pure." There was no financial gain or "ego rub" for those involved. Chris tracked witnesses down through the information in the reports. No one was looking for attention. In fact the various individuals often disagreed and "badmouthed" the others' interpretation of events. (Anyone with a further interest in these types of anomalies should read Chris's paper "UFOs and Reality Transformations" in the MUFON 2002 International UFO Symposium Proceedings and explore the work of Jacques Vallee.)

As the banter between Chris and me continued to unfold that memorable summer day, an interesting analogy took shape. I remarked that I was at a loss to understand why so many struggle with or resist opening their minds to the existence of a familiar concept such as the subtle realm. Chris and I are both from a Catholic background, so perhaps it was inevitable that we considered the discrepancy between the Roman Catholic and most Protestant interpretations of the sacrament of Communion. For Protestants, Communion is a symbol of Christ's sacrifice. For Roman Catholics, the Eucharist (a wafer, representing bread, and the wine) is actually transformed into the body and blood of Jesus Christ. In the Catholic faith it is considered both a sacrament and a miracle, not just a symbol. The theological term is "transubstantiation." There are in excess of one billion practicing Roman Catholics on Earth. To be a good Catholic requires one to disregard what the physical senses tell you about the apparent physical nature of the Eucharist; many devout Roman Catholics accept this tenant of faith. By comparison, Mack's concept of a subtle realm and Jacques Vallee's warnings of possible reality transformations and controlled witness perception ask little. Perhaps the spiritual aspects of a religious upbringing helps open us to concepts related to UFO contact. Science has chosen to focus on the material realm to the point of exclusion of all others. Science has chosen to concentrate only on that that can be measured, demonstrated, and repeated in the laboratory. And we are the poorer for it.

The next few weeks of early summer, 2009, kept us busy reviewing Dr. Mack's various publications and papers. It helped me to see the commonalities between the cases that Dr. Mack delved into and the personal stories of the witnesses and residents of Nova Scotia's southwestern shore throughout the duration of what we now thought of as the "twenty year picnic" of an extended alien presence.

Dr. John Mack

My interaction with Dr. John Mack through his Program for Extraordinary Experience Research (PEER) in the mid to late 1990s was a memorable time at an interesting place. It offered me a unique view of the unfolding UFO phenomenon. Patients who were attracted to John Mack were generally talented yet typical, certainly perplexed, experiencers who trusted his impeccable credentials in such a delicate and mysterious matter. Many had heard of him through the media and connected to the fact that he focused on the transformative aspects of encounters. Through his patients, Mack came to see the big picture of the environmental crisis and the evolution of human spiritual nature at the centre of the phenomenon.

Mack's therapy, his ability to listen, and his quality of bearing witness attracted a high percentage of experiencers who were or would eventually become healers—body and light workers and shamanic practitioners. Many were highly successful and had adopted holistic frameworks around their businesses. They were seemingly ordinary people who developed a rich spiritual life and advanced perceptions after mind-bending interactions with higher beings. This transformation was a testament to Mack's skill and success as a therapist. He was able to aid his clients in understanding their experiences.

John Mack was born in New York on October 4, 1929. He was a clinical psychiatrist, a writer, and a professor at Harvard Medical School. He was primarily a psychiatrist but often bridged psychology and philosophy in his practice. He promoted an intellectual understanding of the psychology of the materialist world view that has in turn contributed to a further understanding of adolescent suicide, war, nuclear proliferation, and ecocide. Dr. Mack's research significantly enhanced the fields of psychiatry and transpersonal psychology. He worked tirelessly throughout his professional and personal life to promote world and individual peace.

At the beginning of Mack's journey into this unknown territory, his childhood friend Thomas Kuhn, the author of one of the standard History of Science textbooks, *The Structure of Scientific Revolutions*, encouraged him to accept and use his own findings to work with experiencers and to avoid traps of language and its dualities. Dr. Mack's seminal book, *Abduction*, was published in 1994 by Bantam Books, who gave it heavy promotion. *Abduction* was an instant success and made the New York Times Best Seller List, making John Mack a sudden celebrity, of sorts. In 1994 and 1995 he did numerous appearances on television talk shows, which included network favourites such as *Oprah* and *Larry King Live*. The mainstream print media often criticized Mack's work with a negative or sarcastic tone, but there was really not much they could say that stood up to his intellectual standard.

Mack's credentials and research were basically impeccable but did not serve to insulate him from attack. Before long he would manage to attract the ire of some academic colleagues, most notably some key members of the Harvard establishment. They became aware of the public's interest and the media attention Dr. Mack had garnered and resented that his work was affiliated with their university. A senior associate dean for academic affairs handed Mack a letter and told him there had been concerns about what he was doing.

A committee was being formed to investigate Dr. Mack's work. The dean, who was a friend, told Mack, "John, if you had just said that you'd found a new psychiatric condition that we didn't know the cause of you'd have been fine, but it's because you said that we might have to think of reality being different that you got yourself into trouble" (Chiten 2003). Mack realized that the dean was coming from the assumption that reality is fixed and anything else is deviance or heresy.

So began Mack's fifteen-month Harvard entanglement. The case would involve celebrity lawyers such as Daniel Sheehan, who had worked on the defence of Steven Greer's Disclosure Project and the Iran–Contra congressional investigation. Another legal heavyweight was Harvard Law School's Alan Dershowitz, who skillfully defended Mack. At one point, Dershowitz rhetorically asked the Harvard administration, "So angels yes, aliens no?" (Ibid.).

In "Defining Academic Freedom," an editorial published in the June 30, 1995 issue of *The Harvard Crimson*, Dershowitz wrote:

> If Dr. Mack had taught at the Divinity School, it is unlikely that any investigation [into his work] would be tolerated.... The paradigm of the scientific method is not the only criteria for evaluating academic undertakings. This is certainly true in the formative, exploratory phases in the development of an idea. If Sigmund Freud, Karl Marx or Martin Buber had been required to satisfy a committee before they could continue their research, the world might have been deprived of significant insights. (Dershowitz 1995)

Although he had previously described the investigation as "Kafkaesque," after the debacle John Mack said, "in some ways they dealt with me fairly. I could have gotten much worse. I don't think they wanted to get rid of me, just distance themselves from me, so they wouldn't have to be held accountable for what I was saying" (Hind 2005). As BBC Radio reported in 2005, "It was the first time in Harvard's history that a tenured professor was subjected to such an investigation" (Ibid.). In time, John Mack's methods withstood scrutiny and peer review. He was censured for some minor methodological errors but was completely vindicated after the investigation. The Harvard Medical School committee suggested he work with other academics who did not share his views. This form of peer review would eventually yield interesting results. The peer review multidisciplinary working group began in April 1999. Harvard issued a statement that the Dean of Medicine had "reaffirmed Dr. Mack's academic freedom to study what he wishes and to state his opinions without impediment. Dr. Mack remains a member in good standing of the Harvard Faculty of Medicine."[1]

The director of the nearby McLean Butler Mental Hospital sat in on the first four years of Dr. Mack's regression (light relaxation hypnosis) sessions; the clients' memories obviously existed without using hypnosis, but the technique aided recall. It was quickly demonstrated that mental illness was not responsible for the UFO contact experiences. John Mack bore witness to, listened to, and stood up for an important group of marginalized people.

While the nasty backlash against Dr. Mack presented by mainstream media and by some in the Harvard administration had largely passed by the time I began my position at PEER, to me it is all memorable. A reporter once secretly infiltrated the project, posing as an abductee, in an attempt to discredit Dr. Mack. I also remember when Mack wrote a cutting editorial piece about Hollywood and the public's attitude toward UFOs and aliens for the *New York Times* in the summer of 1996 when the film *Independence Day* was released. Soon after that, Mack defended experiencers against *New York Times* allegations that sleep paralysis—a condition where people waking or falling asleep are unable to move and may experience terrifying visions—was the likely explanation of the abduction phenomenon. As Dr. Mack pointed out, "They weren't asleep when it happened!" (Chiten 2003).

The impact of Mack's work has yet to be fully realized. He was ahead of his time, but he was not alone with his findings, as was made clear at the Abduction Study Conference he co-chaired at MIT in Cambridge, Massachusetts, from June 13–17, 1992, where leading researchers from around the world "came out of the closet" and presented their findings. It was a watershed moment for UFO research and defined an era of UFO reality.

CHAPTER 11: SHAG HARBOUR'S SUBTLE REALM

In almost every way, Phil Hoyle's case of the experiencer Paul, discussed in chapter 10, correlates with the research conducted by Dr. Mack. The essential nature of Paul's experience begins with his incredulous awareness of the UFO phenomenon in his life. In time it developed into a full range of physical and psychic effects that proved both personally devastating and transformative. The environmental connections, personal transformation, and trauma identified in Mack's studies were all present in Paul's case. Paul, like other experiencers, had been led to a deeper appreciation of our situation as humans within the vast universe of both inner and outer space.

John Mack's and Jacques Vallee's work are examples of modern comprehensive cross-cultural ufology. Both men have progressive theories. They have taken our knowledge beyond the traditional extraterrestrial hypothesis (ETH). They concluded that the ETH did not account for all the available evidence. While not wholly abandoning the ETH they focused more effort on addressing the scientific quandary that still challenges our thinking about who we are and what is real and what our relationship can be with the earth and the cosmos.

Our ontology—the philosophical and metaphysical study of how we understand the nature of existence—defines and therefore limits our understanding, as does the hard-wired circuitry of our perception. The mechanisms by which we perceive energy and our actual cognitive function both play a role here. Our understanding of higher perceptions and of the more subtle realms may in fact have become withered. It may be on the verge of becoming a vestigial structure of our psyche. If subtle contact is going on how would we sense it? The subconscious may be affected by contact, but all too often we habitually ignore, deny, or distort it. Sometimes we do seem to join into some sort of union, contact with the other, with the alien. It would be so useful to know how much perceptual content is generated by the human mind itself and how much is derived from our environment or from the UFO encounter. And just how much do the mind and our physical senses separate us from a phenomenon that we may be fundamentally connected to from the inside, via consciousness? These boundaries may be dissolved if the mind is not ultimately separated from what it observes.

As a culture we are comfortable with turning over our most fundamental questions to science for answers. However, the scientific method of investigation is a filter, altering our understanding according to our preconceptions before we even look at a UFO case. If a UFO crash occurred in the Victorian age it would have been seen as far too important to hand over to a bunch of "stodgy" scientists. The people would demand to know "what really happened."

Science can severely limit our interpretation of reality. Mack and Vallee each essentially declared the end of science as the be-all and end-all of our understanding of life in the universe, defining the possible limits of reality. This theme is central to both Vallee's and Mack's body of work. Both these men subscribed to the belief that traditional modes of modelling the universe are still as valid as they have always been. Yet we cannot ignore new methodologies in attempting to grapple with the UFO phenomenon. After all, we need more than mere materialistic, simplistic answers if we are to feel satisfied and grounded in our deepest understanding of who and what we are. And that is the problem with science, the truth changes over time. Science does not supply the anchor of certainty that traditional belief systems have long provided.

The Smith Brothers Case

There is a UFO case from the Shag Harbour area that gives us a practical example of the pitfalls and shortcomings of UFO research when it is limited to an approach of "pure" science and police techniques of investigation. On November 25, 1970—over three years after the 1967 Shag Harbour Incident—two local fishermen, Eugene and Lawrence Smith, were driving west along Highway 3 approaching the village of Shag Harbour. The brothers were searching for a missing child, and UFOs were the last thing on their mind. (As recounted in chapter 1, Lawrence Smith was one of the original witnesses of the 1967 Shag Harbour Incident.)

It was about 9:20 pm, dark and foggy. Suddenly, at a point between the two turn-offs to the Bear Point Road, a series of seven orange lights appeared above the roadway in front of the car. The lights were about eighteen inches in diameter. Although the car had been travelling at 45 mph, it suddenly stalled and "stopped on its own," as if it had entered an invisible gelatin barrier. Lawrence first thought that a tractor trailer had flipped and was straddling the highway. When the car came to a halt the two men could see that there were only lights, which remained for thirty seconds then disappeared. The radio quit. There was also a sensation of pressure within the vehicle when the lights were present.

The Smith brothers started the vehicle and immediately proceeded to the nearby local RCMP detachment where they reported their experience. The RCMP conducted an investigation that unearthed more witnesses. A seven page report resulted. Interestingly, the investigation triggered direct and immediate military interest with intervention from a NORAD colonel. Chapter 12 deals with the Smith brothers' encounter at length; our concern here is the effect that the incident had on Lawrence and Eugene Smith and their families.

As Lawrence Smith said in an interview with Chris Styles,

> There was my life before that day and my life after that day. It was like I suddenly felt that everything I knew, everything that I was told, was wrong. Everything was strange afterwards and strange things continued to happen. It was like living with a poltergeist. If I was not a man of faith I would have never gotten through it.[2]

Lawrence felt that he could not discuss his concerns with his doctor, his pastor, or his family. His questions went unasked and unanswered. Beyond faith, Lawrence and Eugene Smith had to rely on strength of character and homespun wisdom to get them through an intense "Oz factor" effect. For the rest of his life, Lawrence Smith drove several extra miles to avoid the spot on Highway 3 where he and Eugene had had their sighting.

Lawrence Smith felt that folklore and spirituality gave him more context and continuity than science did to explain what happened to him. He believed in such superstitions and psychic inclinations as "forerunners" and elemental spirits. Lawrence's world was not about opposites and conflicts. It had become a place where one lives with uncertainty and mystery within a shell of context provided by simple faith, acceptance, and tradition.

Scientists like David Suzuki have shown that we can understand our universe through the lens of science while also being sensitive to other new or traditional types of knowledge. This scientific tolerance is about opening our understanding to new ideas as opposed to a mere gathering of data.

The RCMP, the government, and the military—with their investigations based on "science"—all told Lawrence and the other people of Shag Harbour "we didn't find anything," so they had no choice but to move on. The night of the incident, Lawrence Smith went home, made a sandwich, and tried to get on with life as before, but that proved impossible. A Native, shamanic, or psychic perspective could have given Lawrence some tools, perhaps even have shown him how this event may have provided great meaning to his life. Native tradition, for example, provides a traditional way of understanding the "star visitors," who are "the ancestors." This framework does not differentiate between physical and spiritual manifestations, but addresses them as ancient and sacred. Science does not address important issues related to spirituality and consciousness, things that are more subtle and less concrete, things that are not replicable in a laboratory. This failure of science is the whole problem; it is what Dr. Mack was concerned about. Even if the government admitted to knowing that UFOs exist, Washington or Ottawa would likely be incapable of providing meaningful answers beyond the admission itself. By contrast, Native folklore or UFO research or even local folklore, for example, could provide some context for Smith's experience. Science, academia, the military, and government all have struggled or neglected to deal with the issue of UFOs and UFO contact genuinely or publicly.

The Smith encounter received no publicity. Luckily, Chris met with the witnesses, because if a researcher or layman read only the "dry" RCMP report, he or she might miss the life altering impact that would prove to be the various eyewitnesses' collective legacy.

A transmission of information occurs during some UFO encounters, which does not necessarily involve direct overt physical contact with alien entities, though these communications are often accompanied by physical displays and demonstrations, as is the case with the Smith encounter. The transmission of information can even happen if the UFO event is merely a distant sighting or when there is no vehicle present; a telepathic or psychic connection is established with the witness. Some experiencers have reported feeling that they were in communion with the occupants of a craft or even with the craft itself. In other instances large amounts of data are passed along in a sort of "telepathic download."

These interactions often carry significant emotional baggage for the human receiver in the form of missing time and "Oz factor" side effects. The person needs time to adjust and accept the sudden information overload that is conveyed, as is demonstrated in the contacts of Paul H. Some experiencers, like Lawrence Smith, will interpret their encounters in a negative way, both profound and disturbing. Others express their concern that they will likely never be lucky enough to have a repeat encounter. And still others feel something akin to ambivalence mixed with awe. When investigators probe the state of mind of such witnesses, the experiencers often state that they would not want their children to have to endure such an ordeal.

Could the light display witnessed by the Smith brothers, which included one light in the "constellation" blinking out, have been a message or symbol? A symbolic display is often induced in these kinds of sightings that involve a "soft" or implied UFO. Witnesses of such events sometimes report visions or telepathic communications. In fact Lawrence and Eugene Smith reported that their lives were inundated with strange psychic occurrences after the November 1970 incident on Highway 3. So what could the message be? What can one say that would have any cross-cultural meaning that doesn't involve language?

We Are Here

The UFO phenomenon sometimes suggests that "they" have been our nearly invisible neighbours for quite some time. And there are also suggestions that we behave like violent, selfish children and unworthy tenants of our little blue planet. Overall, much of the phenomenon behaves as if "they" are humanity's overseers, observing us from a distance, keeping tabs on our levels of progress and destruction, like anxious but ancient relatives.

Chris once told me that he feels that some UFO experiences are simple messages. They don't involve dialogue and they only disseminate one-way information. Books and television broadcasts also act as useful or informative one-way messages as do the manmade constructions known as inukshuks. The Inuit people of the Canadian High Arctic often leave inukshuks behind when abandoning a temporary campsite. It tells those who follow that someone else was there before them. The land may be barren but it is not *terra incognita*.

Chris's "Inukshuk Theory" suggests that some transient "soft" UFO sightings and light phenomena encounters, where a craft is absent, may be a simple message of sorts. Like the Inuit's inukshuk constructions, theses types of UFO sightings could be saying, "We are here." It would be a way of delivering that simple fact in a way that does not leave behind an artifact or alien technology that could "contaminate" the receiver's culture. Such a technique of communication would even honour the prime directive of the fictional United Federation of Planets in the television series, *Star Trek*—not to interfere with the internal development of alien civilizations. Our planet's history of empires and their damage to "absorbed" nations should tell us that such considerations are not merely intellectual exercises. A conscientious star-faring species would likely have such concerns unless they were simply empire builders and viewed us and our little blue planet as an untapped resource. It would be a mistake and pointless to assign human motivations to the actions of any alien group. Perhaps their mission and motivations would be uniquely their own. All we can say is that to come all this way there must be a reason, a profound connection. The point is that the mere fact they show themselves to us has started a process of the erosion of the old rational materialistic paradigm. To me this is the function of the communication, "We are here."

Mack and the Subtle Realm

Dr. Mack was worried that focusing too much on the search for scientific proof and utilizing traditional scientific methods could be a distraction from learning from the experience. His approach was refreshing because he observed the patterns of the evidence as a scientist, but he did so non-dualistically, in that he went beyond simply categorizing them as either real or unreal. Mack's theories introduced a blended reality view and an approach based on what he referred to as the unassuming or not-knowing mind. It required acceptance that we don't know everything and that our realities are not entirely rigid; it's necessary to suspend belief or disbelief in order to include information that is anecdotal yet vital.

Similarly, Mack pointed out that the UFO experience is in fact part of a broad class of anomalous phenomena ranging from crop circles to miracles and Marian apparitions that seem to involve a "crossing over" or blending into a more "subtle realm." This "crossing over" effect is key to what makes such contacts a transpersonal experience.

Mack explained how the phenomenon popularly called UFO and alien contact, which includes alien abductions, seems to be, in his words, "a spiritual outreach program for the spiritually impaired." It offers us a new way of knowing, or not-knowing, beyond our projections when we approach it with the Buddhist notion of emptiness, a mind that is open and devoid of preconceptions. In order to unify the dualism so prevalent in humanity today, we must see beyond our separateness so that we can integrate polarities into the whole. A true appreciation of the sacredness of all nature, both material and spiritual, is what we gain from the intervention of this phenomenon.

Understanding can be gained from UFO researchers like Vallee and Mack who remind us that strange vehicles and creatures from other worlds are not uncommon in other cultures. In fact it is uniquely our modern Western world that insists upon a world view that only allows for the cold hard facts of a science that can be repeated in a laboratory setting to determine what is possible, thereby limiting our understanding. Science so dominates our modern society that we have little understanding of or room for a spiritual realm, subtle or otherwise, as part of our reality.

In the past several hundred years under our modern Western culture's materialistic map of reality we have divorced spirit from nature. What used to be known as gods, spirits, or earth spirits came to reside only in a far-away and hypothetical place. The division of sky and earth has become the division of spirit and humanity. The idea of versions of our human bodies that are less dense, bodies that are more ethereal or subtle, is common in other cultures. Ancient cultures like Egypt and Tibet have a vast cosmology where other planes of density are filled with energy bodies, spirits, deities, and many varieties of beings, linked with earthly and unearthly virtues and realms. In these cultures, the concept of a vast spectrum of states of beings—embodied, disembodied, or invisible and formless—is no big deal.

Other scientists, philosophers, and peers of Dr. Mack shared his ideas on the destructiveness of the anti-spiritual, Western, materialist world view. Tulane University philosopher Michael Zimmerman was a colleague of Mack's who also spoke out against anthropocentric rationalism and humanism and our culture's dominant world view, dictated ultimately by our academic elites. This world view was one of a dead universe with certain humans on earth at its evolutionary peak. Zimmerman also examined the social and psychological roots of popular resistance to those who study the UFO phenomenon.

Mack's pleas for the environment were also echoed by Rick Tarnas, author of *The Passions of the Western Mind*. Tarnas, like Mack, says that the history of Western philosophy and science has been focused on the dominance and control of nature so that we need not be terrified of it. The UFO contact phenomenon, as the beginning of an encounter with the unknown, challenges that focus and the wisdom of our control over nature. Our need to control nature is destructive. Mack suggested that the psychological forces behind this need are rooted in the tendency of the human mind to perceive through the lenses of dualistic thinking and materialism. Dualistic thinking is a tendency to judge the world in extremes, opposites, resulting in what Mack termed "a polarity of separateness." Perhaps Mack said it best in his paper "The UFO Phenomenon: What Does It Mean for the Expansion of Human Consciousness?"

> We have extended our notions of separateness to such a degree that we experience ourselves as completely divorced from nature, including other human beings. The consequence of this extreme separation is the exploitation of nature, the treatment of Earth as a thing which we have the right to use, and even destroy, for our purposes. We have also separated ourselves from one another to

the degree that we can commit or risk genocide relatively casually. We do not include the other as part of ourselves. (Mack 1992: 3–5)

In this paper, presented at the International Transpersonal Association conference in Prague in June 1992, Mack posits that this philosophy or world view, characterized by the "extreme development and exaggeration of dualism and materialism," may have arisen from the feeling of "helplessness before the Black Death and other diseases, of man's terror of the natural world and the need to master and dominate it." Mack feels this world view "has become incompatible with the survival of life on this planet." It is "species arrogance, a monumental hubris." He writes, "We are now faced with a different set of circumstances, requiring a new psychology and a different science, whose epistemology is not restricted to sensory, empirical ways of knowing." Further,

> We have lost our relationship to nature, including our own human nature,…and with it the sense of the sacred, which, almost by definition, means a deep connection with nature, a reverence for the natural world as the highest expression of God's work. (Bryan 1995)

Seduced by the Subtle Realm: The Fairfax Encounter

So, what is it actually like to have contact with the denizens of the subtle realm? Dr. Mack has stated that an altered state of consciousness is typically a prerequisite for contact. Sometimes a person who takes on extraordinary tasks can set himself up for just such a state of mind. The case of Englishman John Fairfax is a fascinating example of how the subtle realm can manifest itself much like a process of seduction.

On May 5, 1969, John Fairfax was rowing a boat solo across the Atlantic Ocean. He was at a point about half-way between the equator and Nova Scotia. It was evening when John Fairfax spotted a UFO amongst the stars that he was using as navigational aids. It became clear that the UFO was not an astronomical object when it remained visible as the adjacent star field was obscured by broken cloud cover. This observation was bolstered by some unusual flight characteristics. What happened next is best told in Fairfax's own words.

Something happened that I do not consciously remember anything about other than a feeling that my body was floating in a void, or rather, that I no longer had a body, as my whole being seemed to be struggling against a terrific, mental esoteric force that I was willing to give myself up to. To say yes, to go away, to abandon myself…it was so vivid and yet so vague, vague. All I remember is the struggle, the resistance and saying, "No, no. No!" And then, at the last possible moment, when I was about to give in, I snapped out of it. The cigarette had burned, its entire ash completely unmoved, until it reached my fingers and then the burn had brought me back to my senses. I found myself absolutely bathed in sweat and by the look and feel of them, my fingers must have been burning for quite a while before I had noticed. After that the UFOs went east again and what happened then is in my log. (Fairfax 1972)

UFO experiences, such as that of John Fairfax, often involve an alteration of consciousness that allows one to be receptive to the subtle realm contacts that can lead to change and growth in our outlooks. In the case of John Fairfax the change was subtle. There was nothing profoundly new about his views on "life, the universe and everything." After his experience Fairfax was simply open to the UFO reality whereas before his sighting he was a strong skeptic of anything deemed paranormal.

Mythology Manifests Metaphor
The UFO experience is life changing. Positive or negative, for better or worse, those who have been touched by the subtle and not so subtle realm of UFO contact become a breed apart. Abductees and experiencers often feel that they have bonded with "the others." Some become absorbed with past life recall, communications with transcendent beings, and the guidance they received when discorporate. In the spirit realm, one's spirit or subtle body is capable of interacting with ET beings, also in light form. This is identifiable with stages of the death process and comparable to out-of-body experience, near death experience, and after life communications—alive between lives. The out-of-body state has been compared to the Buddhist concept of being in a Bardo state when one has a life between incarnate lives. Like ET and UFO encounters, NDE experiences are personally transformative and may be seen collectively as harbingers of the next stage in the evolution of human consciousness.

Although Dr. Mack's patients experienced interactions with aliens, it was not unusual to have encounters with orbs of light or even just a sense of presence. Some of these deceptively "low key" types of cases, and some that cannot be easily categorized, were touched upon in earlier chapters. In both types of encounters the intensity and side effects suffered seem to be proportional to the proximity of the witness to the apparent or perceived location of the phenomena. Dr. Mack found virtually no difference in the degree of trauma experienced by those whose UFO encounters were more psychic in nature and those involved in "nuts and bolts" incidents.

Mack outlines four aspects associated with the trauma of UFO encounters that can be applied to the cases outlined in this book. First, the physical shock; second, the resulting isolation from loved ones and society in general; third, ontological shock (everything you know might be wrong); and fourth, the loss of control and self-determination. In time, those traumatized may interpret the past differently. If the initial contact occurred in early childhood, the encounters are often forgotten, only to be recalled later as play friends that could be familiar, benign, or even protective in nature. The relationship between experiencers and "the others" moves beyond victimization and eventually involves consciousness altering information of transpersonal meaning, universal love, and connectedness. Ultimately, according to Mack, the aliens are recognized as intermediate entities that act as a go-between with the primordial source of creation.

Dr. John Mack twice met with the Dalai Lama. The Dalai Lama indicated to Mack that some extraterrestrials emanate from the "formless realm," which is distinguished among the subtle realms. As Mack explained, their conversation ranged well beyond the usual speculations of whether ETs were real or not real, good or bad.

> The Dalai Lama once pointed out that the devastation of our planet's ecology was destroying not only the habitat of plants and animals but the realms in which the spirits reside as well. Perhaps this has left them [extraterrestrial beings] no choice but to manifest in our world, to appear to us in the only language that remains to us, the language of the physical world.... Perhaps our own consciousness has become so atrophied that we are simply unable, on our own, to be open to the spirit world. (Mack 1994: 418)

CHAPTER 11: SHAG HARBOUR'S SUBTLE REALM

John Mack's Legacy

On the evening of September 27, 2004, Dr. John Mack died in London, England, after he was struck down by a drunk driver one week short of his seventy-fifth birthday. It was a tragic and senseless end to a life of remarkable accomplishment. He was not just a psychiatrist, Harvard professor, and Pulitzer Prize-winning biographer. He was also considered to be the leading authority on the spiritual and transformational effects of alien encounter experiences. Perhaps John Mack's greatest contribution was in validating the reality of UFO experiencers. Although his upbringing was as an atheistic clinical scientist of German-Jewish heritage, his world view would transform from the scientific to the metaphysical. His body of work and several research foundations that bear his name live on and continue to influence the fields of psychology, spiritual writing, UFO research, and enlightenment.

Chapter 11 Endnotes

1. Harvard's Dean of Medicine quoted in "John Edward Mack," <en.wikipedia.org/wiki/John_Edward_Mack>.
2. Lawrence Smith, interview by Chris Styles, May 7, 1994.

An aerial view of CFS Shelburne looking south towards Government Point, the site of theShelburne UFO operation, and open sea.

Milton Crowell took this photo of his son eating an ice-cream cone while watching Canadian navy divers and RCMP search the shore near Moss Plant on October 7, 1967. The Crowell's were driving when they heard CBC radio news announce that officials were searching the Shag Harbour area for a UFO, so they decided to visit the area. When they asked the RCMP what they were looking for, the RCMP officer replied "a flying saucer".

Father Michael Walter Burke-Gaffney.

Father Michael Walter Burke-Gaffney was born in Dublin, Ireland on December 17, 1896. He studied engineering and worked as an engineer for the War Office in London, England in 1917. He studied theology in Ireland and France and then served in the Air Ministry. In 1920 he came to Canada and joined the Jesuits, was naturalized and ordained. He earned a Master's Degree and Doctorate of Astronomy from Georgetown in 1935. At Saint Mary's University he was the Dean of Engineering and Dean of Science, and taught Astronomy until 1965 when he became professor emeritus and quietly began investigating UFO sightings for the RCMP and DND. He died in 1979 and his personal papers are located in the SMU archives.

Shag Harbour fisherman & truck driver Norm Smith was an eyewitness to October 4th, 1967's UFO Incident. Smith attempted, unsuccessfully, to sample the strange yellow foam floating at the impact site with a dip net.

Ralph Loewinger was the first officer aboard cargo flight PAN-AM 160, a Boeing 707 flying between New York and London, England on October 2nd 1967. At approximately 23:00 hours EST, just off the coast of Shag Harbour at 33,000 feet in the air, Loewinger and crew had a near collision with a UFO identical to the one seen in Shag Harbour 48 hours later.

Major Victor Wishart Eldridge enlisted in the Royal Canadian Air Force from January of 1941 until May of 1971. He served on the Yarmouth Town Council for 18 years and was a stringer for the local newspapers. He was Executive Officer at CFS Barrington at Baccaro during the time of the Shag Harbour and Shelburne Incidents. He monitored the Maritime UFO situation for aspects of the Canadian and the American governments. He passed away at the age of 90 in 2012.

Dr. Maurice (Mace) Coffey. Mace Coffey was a search and rescue expert, scientific researcher of arctic studies and a self styled parapsychologist. At the time of the Shag Harbour Incident Coffey was Maritime Command's Scientific Adviser, hand picked by Commander Rex Guy. He was in charge of the underwater search conducted by Maritime Command for DND HQ's "Air Desk".

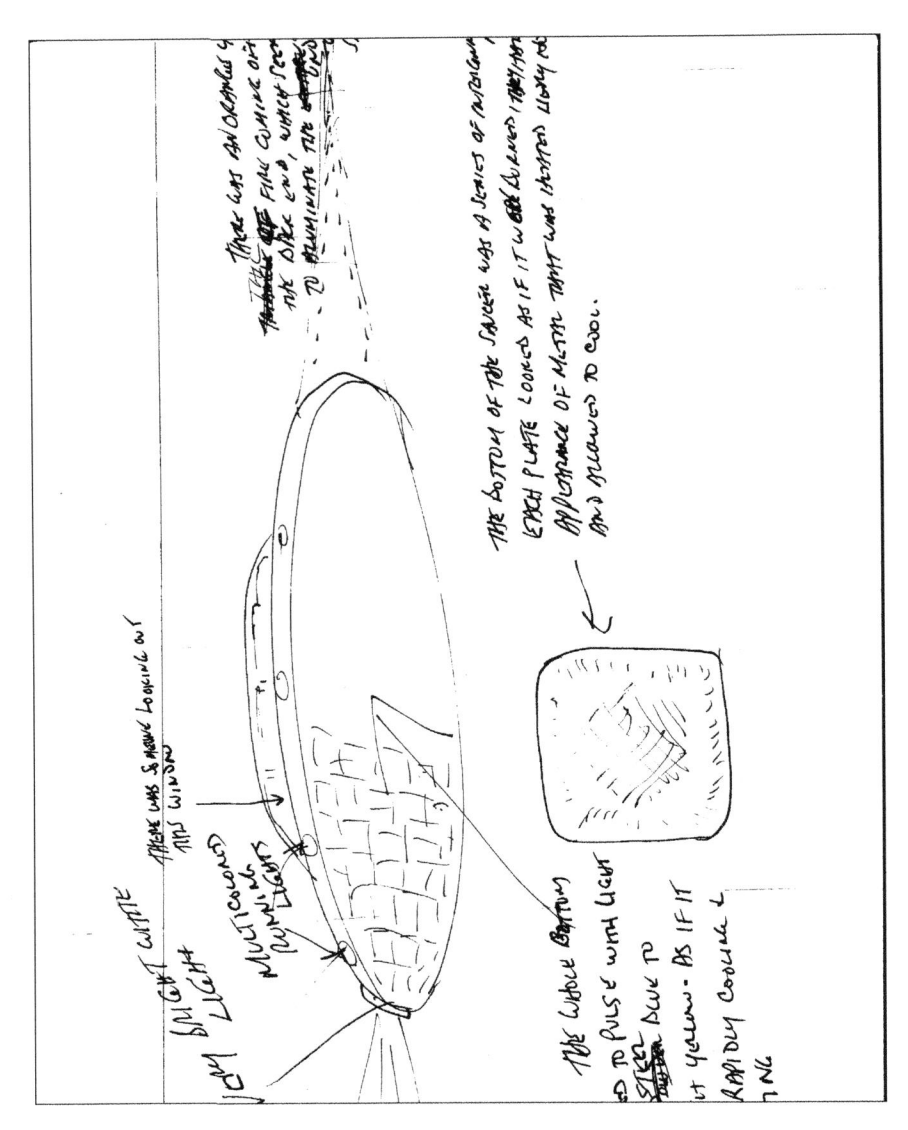

One of two drawings by Wayne Outhouse of his close-up sighting of a UFO near Shag Harbour.

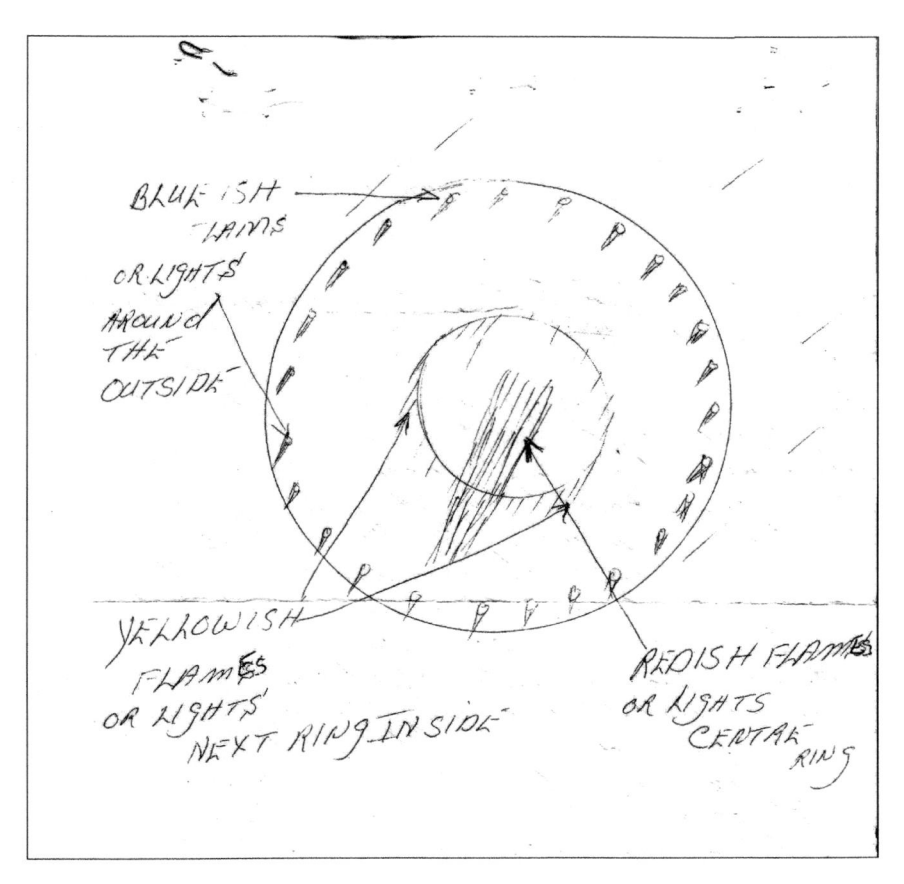

Wayne Outhouse witnessed a classic disk and not just a pattern of lights that imply a saucer. His report indicates a scorched bottom and fire coming out the back of the craft, which corroborates details reported by several other eyewitnesses. In his written report regarding the night of October 4, 1967 in Shelburne County, Wayne describes a sudden acceleration that is beyond that of any conventional aircraft. After that maneuver, the UFO is joined by several others. Wayne, along with several friends watch the subsequent "darting about display" for some time through binoculars. His report also states that there was someone looking out of the window on the top of the craft.

Bob Stevens' depiction of the UFO he witnessed from the back seat of his parents car in the early 1970's while travelling between Bridgewater and Halifax. This is an example of the three-sectioned craft with the "tea-strainer" middle which was commonly seen in Nova Scotia from the 1960's to the early 1980's- the "twenty year picnic."

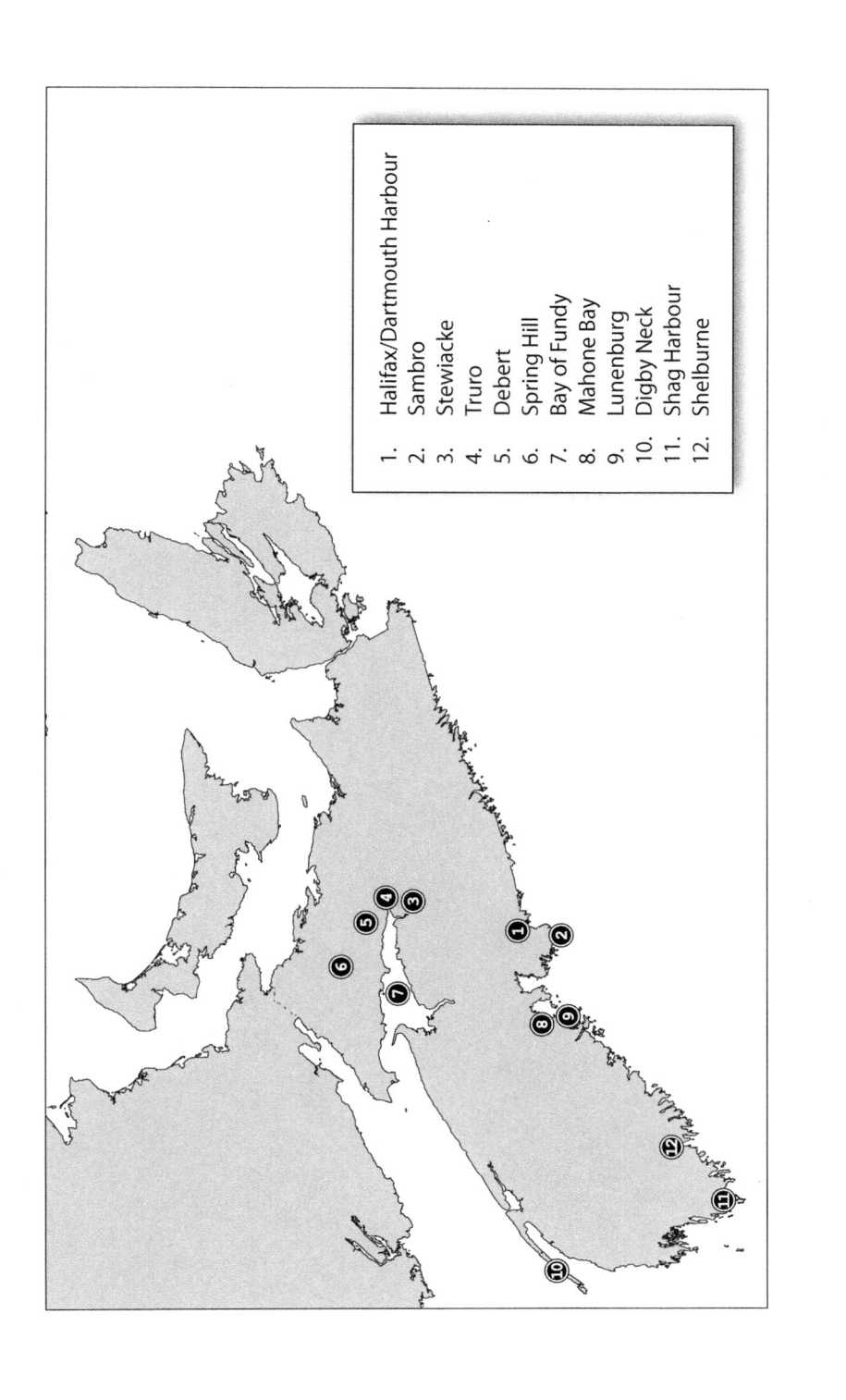

1. Halifax/Dartmouth Harbour
2. Sambro
3. Stewiacke
4. Truro
5. Debert
6. Spring Hill
7. Bay of Fundy
8. Mahone Bay
9. Lunenburg
10. Digby Neck
11. Shag Harbour
12. Shelburne

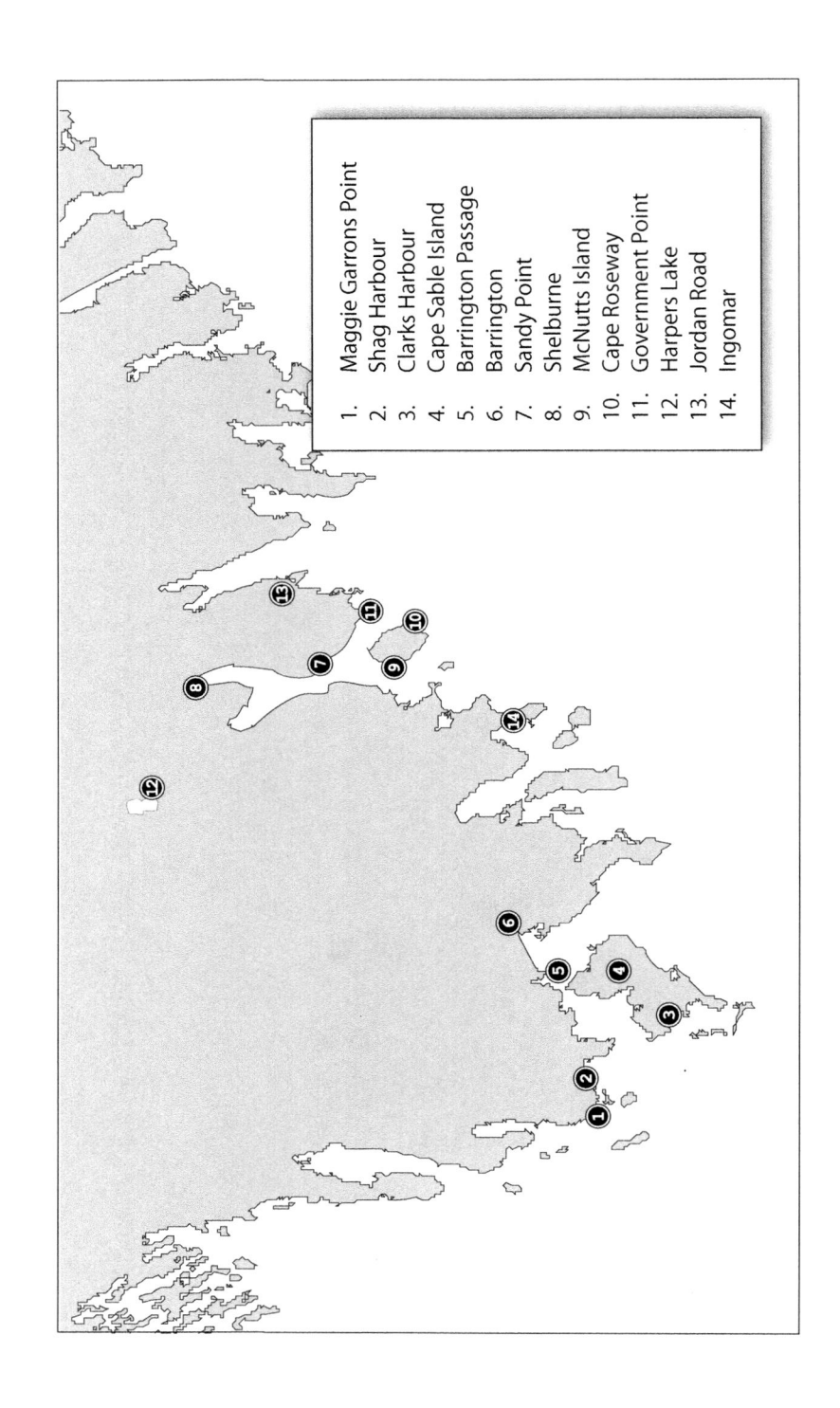

1. Maggie Garrons Point
2. Shag Harbour
3. Clarks Harbour
4. Cape Sable Island
5. Barrington Passage
6. Barrington
7. Sandy Point
8. Shelburne
9. McNutts Island
10. Cape Roseway
11. Government Point
12. Harpers Lake
13. Jordan Road
14. Ingomar

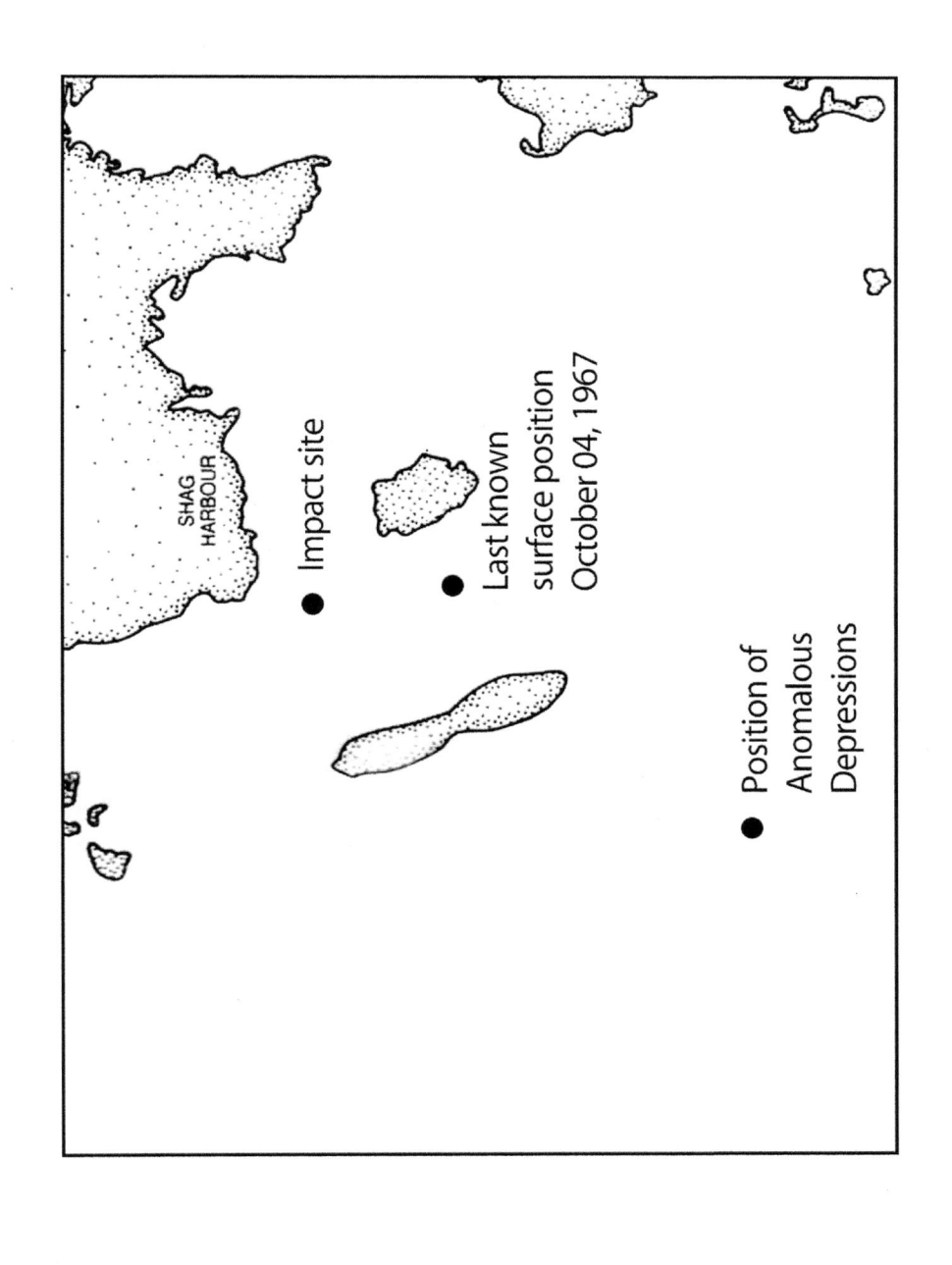

- Impact site
- Last known surface position October 04, 1967
- Position of Anomalous Depressions

SHAG HARBOUR

SECTION 3

INSIGHT

Chapter 12: The Smith Encounter
Chris Styles

"Be still, and know that I am."
– Psalm 46: 10

"When will the kingdom come? It will not come by watching for it. It will not be said, Look here! or Look there! Rather the Father's kingdom is spread out upon the earth. Men don't see it."
– Verse 113, Gospel of Thomas

To the minds of most people who ponder the UFO phenomenon, the central question is, just what is it and where does it come from? In North America the vast majority of those who feel that we are not alone believe that most unidentified UFOs represent intrusions of technologically advanced alien civilizations. That premise is known as the Extraterrestrial Hypothesis or ETH, and it is the dominant view held by the lion's share of North American ufologists. However in Europe, Asia, and the Third World, ufology blends seamlessly into other paranormal fields and even folklore. Point of origin theories range from other dimensions and time travel to having the UFO phenomenon wholly internalized as part of an emerging collective unconscious.

As early as 1993 I was finding the ETH to be deficient when it came to explaining the frequent and profound psychic component of many UFO cases. The growing number of potentially connected UFO incidents from the October 4, 1967 "Night of the UFOs" was proving especially troublesome. And then one special case came to my attention that brought about a personal epiphany. In the spring of 1994 I was compelled to change my view not only of the Shag Harbour Incident and the so-called "Night of the UFOs" but even my understanding of UFO reality. Once again, such an influential case was to be found within the modern history of Shag Harbour, Nova Scotia.

I first became aware of what has become known as "The Smith Encounter" in September of 1992. Veteran UFO researcher Stanton Friedman and I had arranged to meet face to face for the first time in the lobby of Halifax's Lord Nelson Hotel. Stanton was in Halifax to present a private lecture at Dalhousie University, and he brought a large cardboard box of unsorted Canadian UFO documents that he thought might be helpful to me in my fledgling Shag Harbour investigation. That hodgepodge of documents was part of a bulk release from the National Archives of Canada that he received as a response to an earlier access request. Although the seven page RCMP report about a November 25, 1970 UFO incident would later surface in the National Archive's RG 77 collection, this was my first introduction to it. It fascinated me from the moment I first read about it. The first two amazing pages appear below, completely unedited.

ROYAL CANADIAN MOUNTED POLICE - GENDARMERIE ROYALE

DU CANADA

Unidentified Flying Object, Bear Point, Shelburne, Co. NS

November 25, 1970

1. At approximately 9:50 pm this date while on patrol at Barrington Passage, NS, I was contacted by Lawrence Charles Smith of Lower Shag Harbour, Shelburne Co., NS. Smith was accompanied by his brother Manus Eugene Smith of the same address and they stated that they had seen lights in the sky at Bear Point, Shelburne Co., NS.

2. They stated that they had seen lights in the sky at Bear Point approximately 30 to 50 feet in the air. These lights were described as being 20 inches in diameter and were reddish-orange in colour.

CHAPTER 12: THE SMITH ENCOUNTER

The two witnesses stated that the lights disappeared without moving. The duration of the sighting was described by the witnesses as approximately 20 to 30 seconds. They stated that the tape player in the car had stopped and that the car had stopped on its own when it had been travelling 45 mph. They stated that the second light from the left had gone out at least once and had lit up again at least once.

3. An immediate patrol was made to the scene with the Smith brothers. They explained the position of these lights and how they had been driving normally along the highway towards their homes when the sighting occurred. Nothing could be seen at the place of the sighting that was out of the ordinary; the area is thickly wooded. I was at the scene for approximately 30 minutes and after a thorough search I left.

November 26, 1970

1. At approximately 9:15 AM, on this date Col. Rushton, CO at CFS Barrington at Bacarro, Shelburne Co., NS, called and asked if our office had any reports of UFO sightings on the previous night. He was advised that there had been. During a short telephone conversation he revealed that one of his men had seen a UFO the previous evening and from comparing notes it appeared that the sighting had been very similar to that of the Smith brothers. Col. Rushton stated that he wished to see me after I had completed my investigation concerning the UFO.

2. Lawrence Charles Smith and Manus Eugene Smith, of Lower Shag Harbour, NS, were interviewed separately concerning the sighting. They related to me how they had seen the lights as described in paragraph # 2, statements attached. Diagram of Lawrence Charles Smith's version of the sighting is attached.

3. Patrol was made to CFS Barrington and the sighting was discussed with Col. Rushton. He was supplied with the names of the witnesses already interviewed. Col. Rushton stated that a UFO sighting had been made by one of the men under his command, Corporal Timothy Nielson.

4. Cpl. Timothy Daniel Nielson, of Baccaro, Shelburne Co. NS, was interviewed concerning the sighting and he stated that he sighted the lights at approximately 9:40 pm at Smithville, Shelburne Co., NS. Nielson's account of the sighting was very similar to that of the Smith brothers. He stated that he saw 4 reddish-orange lights stretched out in the sky in a straight line. These lights were in a northwest direction from him at the time of the sighting. He stated that the most southerly light was about 20 degrees above the horizon. He stated that the lights were about 18 inches in diameter and were perfectly round with no light reflecting off of them. His girlfriend, June Smith and her mother were with him at the time of the sighting. Statement of Nielson attached.

5. Cathlene Mary Smith and Carol June Smith were interviewed at

CHAPTER 12: THE SMITH ENCOUNTER

their home at Smithville, Shelburne Co., NS, and they related how they had seen the lights in the sky. Their account of the sighting compared with that of Nielson but they also stated that the lights were about 300 to 400 feet away and that one of the centre lights had gone out and came back on again. The height of the lights would have been just over the tree line. The duration of the sighting was approximately 30 seconds. Cathlene Smith stated that the lights had disappeared by gradually sinking below the trees, statements attached.

6. Message was forwarded to Halifax sub/division as per instructions.

7. With regard to the reliability of the witnesses, I can say that I have known the Smith brothers for approximately 5 months. Lawrence Charles Smith is not superstitious and does not believe in common superstitions. I have known Lawrence Smith in as much as we have gone on fishing and duck hunting trips together. Approximately 9:00 pm, 25 Nov. 70, I met with the Smith brothers at Barrington, NS. They were looking for Manus Smith's daughter who had left home after school without saying where she was going. This would have been approximately 40 minutes prior to the sighting, and both men were perfectly normal and had not been drinking. I feel that the Smith brothers are reliable in this instance. As for Cpl. Nielson, I can say that Col. Rushton had no reason to disbelieve him. I do not feel that persons like Cathlene and June Smith are persons who make up stories. It is just a coincidence that two of the

witnesses in each sighting had the surname Smith. There is no blood relation.

8. These sightings were made at two points approximately 20 miles apart in a straight line. The sighting at Bear Point, Shelburne Co., NS, would have been 20 degrees north from due west from the sighting at Smithville, NS.[1]

Stanton Friedman's initial observation of Cst. Ralph Keeping's RCMP report focused on the absolute consistency of the size estimates of the reddish-orange lights by all of the witnesses at both locations. The veteran UFO researcher and nuclear physicist was also quick to point out that it is not every day that a NORAD Commanding Officer calls the local RCMP to inquire about UFO sightings. While being impressed by those same two facts, there were other features of the RCMP report that I found even more compelling. I was amazed that the RCMP was willing to turn over a civilian report at the request of the military. Just what was the RCMP's policy? Why did Col. Rushton want the police report so badly? Who else was privy to the data? Let's not forget that CFS Barrington was, at the time, a NORAD radar facility under shared Canadian and American command. Eight years earlier, in 1962, it was a US-controlled base on Canadian soil. I had always doubted witness reports of American military personnel rolling into Canadian territory to carry out UFO investigations and witness interrogations, but I was beginning to wonder about the potential validity of such claims. A decade would pass before I got the definitive answer to all of the above questions when, in 2003, the RCMP archivist would release a full copy of its "Space Object Contingency Plan" to me. The unique story of that drawn out "paper chase" is covered in the next chapter. However, the full ufological significance of the Smith brothers' UFO incident on Highway 3 would become suddenly apparent during a dramatic face-to-face interview with Lawrence Smith on May 7, 1994.

During the early nineties I spent a great many weekends driving to the Shag Harbour area to knock on doors and track down eyewitnesses. It was a stimulating time filled with endless leads and stories. I have great memories of overwhelming hospitality received at so many homes and workplaces all over Nova Scotia's southwestern shore. Not every one of those weekend sojourns

CHAPTER 12: THE SMITH ENCOUNTER

had a strict itinerary. Time was given to making friends, patting wet dogs on porches, and to letting the enchantment of the area seep into my bones. And it was on one of those rambling unhurried jaunts in the spring of 1994 that I finally found the unintentionally elusive Lawrence Smith.

On previous trips I had found several Lawrence Smiths, but none of them proved to be the Lawrence Smith in question. Smith is quite a common name in Shelburne County. Eventually, though, persistence, the process of elimination, and a hot tip and free phone call from the General Store led me to Lawrence Charles Smith's warm home and kitchen at Upper Clyde's River.

Upon arrival at Lawrence's house I was welcomed and led into the large warm kitchen, as was Eileen Joyce, a well-known blues singer on the east coast and longtime friend, who had come along for the ride that day. Lawrence's wife, Molly, brought a large carafe of coffee to the table and was puttering about the kitchen. Lawrence remarked that 1967 had been a truly odd year and that he would forever remember the night that he had been woken to help the RCMP search for what at the time was thought to be a downed aircraft and later a flying saucer. I then told him that I would love to listen to his recollections of the search effort but that I really wanted to talk about his November 25, 1970 UFO experience first. My stated preference seemed to shock Lawrence. He had assumed when I called from the store that I wanted to discuss the UFO crash of October 4, 1967. Of course I did, but I also wanted to get into the puzzling and largely unknown events from three years after. He didn't expect and wasn't prepared for that eventuality. The first thing he did was ask Molly to leave us alone. When she left the kitchen Lawrence closed a large solid wood door that sealed off the room from the rest of the house. He wheeled around to face me and asked, "How the hell do you know about that? I haven't told anyone outside of the family, and we rarely speak of it. I have tried to forget about it."

"I've read the Mountie report."

Lawrence looked stunned. "It's public?" he asked.

"Yes. RCMP UFO reports typically are in Canada. National Archives has it preserved in several of its heritage collections." This seemed quite unsettling to Lawrence. He looked physically ill.

"Do you have a copy?"

"Yes, but I would sooner talk to you first, before reading it. You see, we try to avoid contaminating—"

Lawrence cut me off with a demand. "I want to see it now, or this interview is over."

It was clear that his demand was firm, so I shifted to "Plan B" and handed him a photocopy of Ralph Keeping's seven page RCMP report. I wasn't terribly concerned about not doing the interview by the books, but I was beginning to fear that Lawrence was about to pull the plug. He read every word of the report before looking up and staring me down. I began a rambling soliloquy about what I was trying to accomplish with my Shag Harbour investigation, but once again Lawrence interrupted me.

"Are you from the government?"

"No." It occurred to me at that point that Eileen's and my choice of black clothing was an unfortunate fashion faux pas even though we bore little resemblance to any "men in black" that I have run across in my research.

"Do you understand what happened to me?"

"No."

Lawrence's eyes seemed to acknowledge and approve of my honesty on that simple fact. He seemed to cut some slack for someone who wasn't afraid to say, "I don't know." For the first time I felt that I might salvage the interview and that Lawrence might open up to me. However, as I spoke that simple "no" to Lawrence's question, I confess that I had never felt so useless or pathetic. I had nothing to offer except questions and theories. I resolved at that moment to somehow correct that and to put off beating myself up until later.

"You've seen it, haven't you."

"Yes." At this point the manual had gone out the window along with the silly unwritten rule that a UFO researcher isn't suppose to see UFOs…or admit it. But it was at that precise point that Lawrence opened up and began to speak. What he had to say changed the whole disposition of Ralph Keeping's seven page tome.

Lawrence never knew about Timothy Nielson's simultaneous UFO sighting. He never knew that the details of his and Eugene's experience had been passed on to a NORAD colonel and eventually to NORAD headquarters. Such is the way of the RCMP. Although Lawrence and Ralph Keeping still had a personal friendship and hunted together, the Mountie never divulged the fact that there were other similar UFO sightings that night with multiple witnesses. The fact that all of the witnesses were deeply disturbed by their experience caused them to keep it quiet, sharing it only with close family. As a result, none of those involved in the two separate sightings ever became aware of the other experiencers' stories.

Lawrence would come to hold Ralph Keeping's silence against him, and it affected their friendship for the rest of his days. He was disturbed to learn that

CHAPTER 12: THE SMITH ENCOUNTER

others had experienced what he and his brother had back in 1970 and that they too had been affected negatively. Many times—during several follow-up interviews and even casual social encounters and conversations at his camp on the Clyde River—Lawrence told me that there was his life before November 25, 1970, and his life after. Lawrence and his brother would always drive the loop of the Bear Point Road, which added miles to any trip, so as to avoid passing over the eerie spot on old Highway 3 where their disturbing encounter occurred. The two brothers maintained this habit for the rest of their lives. Once while at his camp on the Upper Clyde River, Lawrence told me that it was only his faith that kept him together over the years. At times Lawrence regretted that I had "stirred things up" and had forced him to ponder and re-examine something he would have preferred to forget. Sometimes Lawrence didn't want to talk to me at all but would later seem relieved that I understood his mixed feelings on such a personal and traumatic experience. He would sometimes say, "You, I know what you want. You want answers, but it will take more than that to put my life right." And the sad truth was that I had no answers for Lawrence.

I really liked Lawrence Smith and always felt a real sense of empathy for his plight. I was sad to hear of his untimely death when he succumbed to a lengthy illness. I do think that Ralph Keeping's words in his unique UFO report sums it up when he says, "I think that Lawrence Smith is not the kind of man to make up stories." But I would add he sure had some interesting ones to tell.

The remainder of 1994 and 1995 would reveal even further insight into the mysterious UFO incident of November 25, 1970, when the personal memories and observations of Cst. Ralph Keeping and Colonel Calvin Rushton were added to the mix. Ralph Keeping visited Shag Harbour and Shelburne in 1995 to do an interview for a syndicated US television show about the paranormal called *Strange Universe*, which did a short treatment about the Smith brothers' mysterious encounter with the tiny lights on Highway 3. At some point during the down time between shooting, Ralph Keeping told UFO researcher Don Ledger, my co-author on *Dark Object*, that he had conducted a little homespun experiment with Lawrence that did not get mentioned in his RCMP UFO report. Keeping placed Lawrence Smith on the back floor of his police cruiser and covered him with a heavy opaque blanket. It did not seem to matter how confusing a route the Mountie drove toward the spot of the Smith brothers' puzzling encounter, Lawrence seemed to sense when he was in close proximity to the exact spot where the November 25 sighting had taken place. Lawrence's uncanny ability was put to the test numerous times and seemed consistent and reliable. After Don informed me about Ralph Keeping's "little experiment" I quizzed Lawrence Smith himself about it. He told me that no amount of backtracking or diversion prevented his detection of what he thought of as "ground zero."[2] Lawrence asked me if I knew what it all meant. I did not. I could only tell him that it must mean something.

The UFO sighting of Lawrence and Eugene Smith and Timothy Nielson and company would prove to be a huge influence on my interpretation and understanding of not just the Shag Harbour Incident and the ongoing "flap" in southwestern Nova Scotia, but the UFO phenomenon itself. My first impression was that more than any other UFO case with which I had any personal contact, this one had to be true and of unconventional origin. No one involved had made an effort to seek publicity. All of the witnesses were reluctant to share their story with anyone beyond close family or trusted authority figures. Neither of the two separate witness pools had any knowledge of each other. (Timothy Nielson's girlfriend and mother bore the surname Smith but were no blood relation to the Smith brothers of Shag Harbour.) And no one expected me to come a knocking twenty-four years later.

Chapter 12 Endnotes

1. RCMP UFO File 70-400-18, RG 77, pages 1–7.
2. Author's notes from personal interviews with eyewitness.

Chapter 13: In Search of "Mace Coffee"
Chris Styles

"There is no shortage of good days. It is good lives that are hard to come by."
– Annie Dillard

"When one admits that nothing is certain one must, I think, also admit that some things are much more certain than others."
– Bertrand Russell

Right from the start and throughout the nineties the central questions for me regarding the Shag Harbour Incident would be quite simply:

1. What was the UFO?
2. Where did it come from and what was its mission?
3. What happened to it after impact?

By the mid nineties these unanswered questions remained in the forefront of my mind and provided a large portion of the motivation needed to continue researching the Shag Harbour Incident, but other concerns were beginning to distract me with an ever increasing priority. I began to wonder about the influence of the various personalities involved in the handling of the case. A close examination of communications at the time of the incident, between the Air Desk, the Department of National Defence (DND) Maritime Command, and the National Research Council (NRC), reveals that UFO cases such as the Shag Harbour crash and the Michalak case had become a political "hot potato" in Ottawa.[1] The military "brass" and the politicians were far more concerned about who was seen to be responsible for UFO investigations than about any real issues, such as whether the UFO phenomenon actually represented an extraterrestrial penetration of our skies and defence systems.

A new character entered the picture in 1995. He would prove to be both elusive and mysterious. I felt that getting to "know" him would be essential to a greater understanding of the Shag Harbour Incident, especially Maritime Command's 1967 underwater search effort. I needed to know just what kind of man DND would trust for advice when searching for a crashed UFO and just what kind of advice he had to offer. I had to get to know "Mace Coffee."

In 1995 I received a phone call from Jan Aldridge, a US-based UFO researcher who created and directs Project 1947, a voluminous and heroic effort to compile anything and everything in print that any media source has ever produced on the topic of unidentified flying objects. Jan Aldridge called to say that he'd found an old "Preliminary Report" of the Aerial Phenomena Research Organization (APRO) that dealt with the Shag Harbour Incident. He thought that it might prove significant. Aldridge had discovered the APRO report while researching the files of former UFO researcher John Brent Musgrave (Styles 1996: 33). He immediately posted it to me.

Jan Aldridge's intuition proved correct. The APRO Preliminary Report would be a key source of previously unknown facts. It displays a level of detail not found in the press clippings or even many of the archived military documents. It is there, on page three of the APRO report, that Dr. Maurice "Mace" Coffey's name first appears, though with an erroneous spelling. The uncredited writer of the APRO report (believed to be William F. Dawson, former APRO member from Dartmouth, Nova Scotia, and former head of the Royal Astronomical Society) recorded the words of the Officer of the Watch for Maritime Command.

> He [Fl. Lt. Fox] further indicated that his unit was in charge of the case and any recovered artifacts would be turned over to Mr. "Mace" Coffee [sic], the unit's scientific consultant, who could be reached through CANMARCOM [Canadian Maritime Command]. If anything of extreme interest was found, it would be turned over to the National Research Establishment.[2]

So, who was this man with the somewhat unusual name? What kind of scientist was he? And why was he uniquely qualified in the view of Maritime Command and the National Research Establishment to be personally entrusted to receive possible artifacts of extraterrestrial origin?

My quest to know the real "Mace Coffee" began, as has so often been the case with my Shag Harbour research, with an afternoon visit to the reference room of the Halifax Public Library. Once there I grabbed a 1967 copy of

CHAPTER 13: IN SEARCH OF "MACE COFFEE"

Might's City Directory for Halifax and Dartmouth. I would discover that in 1967 Dr. Maurice Coffey had had a Dartmouth street address and a listed phone number. The directory listed his job as scientific consultant for DND. I scribbled down the phone number and checked to see if it could still be found within the current phone directory. It turned out that the 1967 phone number was still active in 1995 and still linked to the same street address; however, it was now listed under the name Sylvia Coffey.

As soon as I arrived back at my Dartmouth apartment I dialed the phone number hoping to reach Mace Coffey. That phone call took a turn that I did not anticipate and would deliver a double dose of both disappointment and embarrassment and one of the greatest "teaser" answers of any interview regarding my research of the Shag Harbour Incident. My call was answered by the husky, pleasant voice of Mace's oldest daughter, Marsha Coffey. That awkward but memorable conversation unfolded something like this.

"Hello?"

"Hello, I'm hoping to speak with Mace Coffey. Would he be in?"

"I'm sorry but my father has been dead for over twenty years. Who is this?"

"My name is Chris Styles. I'm sorry, I didn't know. Mace's name came up as part of a research project that I'm working on, and I would have loved to have chatted with him about his career. Would you happen to be Sylvia Coffey?"

"Again, I'm sorry. My name is Marsha Coffey. I'm afraid that my mother died three days ago."

"I am so sorry. Listen, I'll let you go. I didn't know and certainly would not have called had I known. I'll call back in a few weeks and perhaps ask if there is anyone you might direct me to who could help me with my research. It can wait."

"It's okay. What is your research about?"

"Have you ever heard about the Shag Harbour UFO crash back in 1967?"

"No. Was my dad involved with it in some way?"

"I believe so. I'll explain when I call back in a few weeks."

"Well just make sure that you do. It sounds very interesting. Arrangements and things should be largely out of the way after next week."

"Sure. Just one very quick question before I let you go. It's been gnawing at me. Just what was your father's job with the navy all about? What was his specialty?"

"He was a parapsychologist."

"Wow. Ah…OK. Ah, goodbye."

Saying good bye to Marsha Coffey at that moment was a hard promise to keep, but what else could I do if I was to maintain any semblance of respect and decency considering Marsha's then recent loss? So Mace Coffey was a parapsychologist. Why did the Royal Canadian Navy need a parapsychologist in 1967 and why would he be the scientific consultant of choice when tasked with the mission of searching for a crashed UFO? Marsha's all too brief answer had certainly fired my imagination. I now had a new quest for answers spurring me on.

Some weeks later Marsha and I chatted again both on the phone and later face to face. Marsha's initial answer about her dad's career with DND would prove to be more than a little incomplete. You see, Mace Coffey was a scientist who specialized in the development of new search and rescue techniques. He was also an expert in High Arctic survival techniques, government organization, and yes, parapsychology. Perhaps Dr. Coffey's most precious skill was his ability to find missing things, especially where others had failed.

With Marsha's kind help I was able to locate a number of former colleagues and family friends who helped me to understand this complex man who had enjoyed an eclectic career as a scientist with the Defence Research Board and a consultant with Maritime Command. Marsha also provided me with a copy of the memorial dedication that is displayed over Maurice Francis Coffey's final resting place, which lies in the Canadian High Arctic, on Beechy Island, a few yards away from the final resting place of four seamen who had searched for the missing members of the Franklin Expedition. That dedication appears below and gives an overview of a life that had a powerful impact on those around him.

Mace Coffey
In honour of the memory of Dr. Maurice Francis Coffey, Ph.D., born in Moncton, NB, January 5, 1919, died April 22, 1975, in Kuala Lampur, Malaysia. This cairn contains the mortal remains of Maurice Francis (Mace) Coffey, scientist, man of letters, inventor, adventurer, humanitarian, and recipient of the Centennial Medal bestowed in 1967 by the Government of Canada in recognition of his contributions to this country.

On these bleak and lonely shores Maurice Francis Coffey lies in honour. It is at this place that the first trace was found of the probable fate of Sir John Franklin, who sailed from Britain in May 1845, on his Majesty's service to complete the discovery of the Northwest Passage. In the years to come Beechy Island was to become the base of operation for one of the most massive and expensive search

CHAPTER 13: IN SEARCH OF "MACE COFFEE"

and rescue operations ever mounted in the history of man. To explorers and historians worldwide this sweep of desolate beach is a shrine no less revered than Westminster Abbey to kings, princes, and men of distinction.

Maurice Francis Coffey does not lie alone here. Scant yards away are the graves of four gallant seamen, few among scores who gave their lives in search of Sir John and the crews under his command on his Majesty's ships *Erebus* and *Terror*. No honour would be more richly deserved for Dr. Coffey in his role as scientist and scientific advisor for the Canadian Armed Forces and has done [sic] much by personal experiment, invention, and ingenuity for long periods in the icy grip of Canada's Arctic winters. Aided only by a small band of Inuit to make our inhospitable Arctic a safer place for those who have need or desire to travel its treacherous icy waste. For his endeavours he became a worldwide expert on Arctic survival and search and rescue.

In the later months of 1974, Dr. Coffey, who by academic training was a specialist in government organization and dynamics, while on leave for preparation for an overseas assignment, gave freely of his time and talent to bring about the reorganization of the executive and senior level of the administrative government of the Northwest Territories in order to formulate an administrative structure in preparation for increased political autonomy handed to these territories by the Government of Canada. Dr. Coffey could perhaps have used that time to rest from the rigours of accomplishments past. Rather he chose to work late into the night, almost unceasingly for three months to meet its legitimate changes when they came about.

Dr. Coffey left Canada in February 1975 to undertake a special assignment in Malaysia for the Department of External Affairs. His intention, once his work in Malaysia was finished, was to return to the North where he planned to continue his inspired work towards the well being of the Northwest Territories and the people who make the North their home, but it was not to be. Maurice Francis Coffey died from the effect of an overtaxed heart in a land far distant from his friends and the land that he loved so well. Despite his mental brilliance, Dr. Coffey had about him the air of simplicity, incisiveness, humour, and humility that distinguish mere talent from genius.

While grieving his passing with great regret let it be known that Maurice Francis Coffey would not look upon departure from this life as a foe to be fought but rather as a unique and inevitable adventure beyond the realm of those that he has left behind. It is then, in recognition of this great man, that the mortal remains of Maurice Francis Coffey rest with brave men who helped bring this North into being, and in consequence this plaque is erected by the Commission of the Northwest Territories and her people by Dr. Coffey's beloved wife Sylvia and their children Marsha, Marlene, and Joanne. "To leave behind in this life a legacy of knowledge and understanding is not to die but to live forever in the heart, the mind, and memory of mankind." Anonymous, September 10, 1975

In the years since I began my research into the Shag Harbour Incident, I have spoken at various events where I met people who had personally known Mace Coffey. Invariably, those who approached me to pass on their recollections of him were lost for words sufficient to describe just how they had valued making his acquaintance. The result was that over time an image emerged. I felt that I was coming to know the man. I knew that he didn't drive a car. He walked to work every day and believed that cars would soon fall out of public favour. Many times I heard assurances that Mace was a believer in the extraterrestrial hypothesis. This was "all good action," but I wasn't learning the things that I really needed. What I needed to know was what the good doctor thought and felt about the Shag Harbour Incident.

Over the years, many attempts to locate a detailed or final report on the Shag Harbour Incident had come up dry. In the fall of 2004 I decided to cast a wider net. I decided to look in archives for anything bearing Dr. Coffey's name. The Operational Research Division of DND came through on November 23, 2004, with the following response from one A. Bradfield, Director General of Operations Research (DGOR).

> Dear Mr. Styles;
> You recently called the library of the Operational Research Division of DND asking if we held any documents written by Dr. Maurice (Mace) Coffey. We checked our holdings and found some. A list is attached which names the reports.
>
> These old reports relate mainly to the analysis of problems in search and rescue and group decision making. They have been superseded by developments since that time.
>
> A. Bradfield
> DGOR

I requested copies of all of the reports listed on the attachment. A couple of the reports gave considerable insight into the mind of the man who advised DND as to how to find a downed "flying saucer."

Former DRB scientist Jason Greenblatt had been a colleague of Mace Coffey. In a telephone interview he claimed to not remember anything of the Shag Harbour Incident but expressed the opinion that "Mace would have been the man for the job if you were looking for something missing" and that "being

CHAPTER 13: IN SEARCH OF "MACE COFFEE"

the consummate professional, Mace would have treated the search for a crashed UFO as the search for any target." I wasn't sure that I agreed with that second opinion expressed by Dr. Greenblatt, but I knew that Mace Coffey's 1971 paper, "Search Concepts 1971," was telling me how he might go about searching for a UFO—or "target," if you prefer.

Coffey's paper explains that a number of target qualities are important to search theory. In fact there are four basic categories of target. The Shag Harbour UFO would have been considered a category four target, which is one that is both "mobile and evasive." The next important consideration is thrust. All targets have thrust. This can range from zero or exhausted thrust (downed aircraft or human casualties) to intended or imposed thrust, again ranging from zero to the operational limit. Imposed thrust is normally dictated by a) mission, b) environmental constraints or environmental impingements, and c) strategic decisions. Thrust and subsequent vectoring might be intermittent. If sensors do not detect the target, more observational data should be collected and utilized (Coffey 1971: 5).

Utilizing the above listed and other principles in Dr. Coffey's 1971 paper we can categorize the data on hand in October 1967 in Shag Harbour. That data would include known facts such as "Bacarro radar negative" and Cst. Ron Pond's field glass observations of the UFO "apparently moving toward open sea faster than the ebbing tide." Observations of the UFO's bottom on fire when over Seal Island and the Granby diver's statement, "We thought that it had lost an engine," would have been considered. A reconstructed model of events and raw military intelligence would have suggested the following to Coffey:

> a. The UFO was mobile and evasive.
> b. The UFO exhibited a diminished ability to impose thrust (both aerodynamically and hydrodynamically). It was reduced to something between zero and the operational limit of the UFO.
> c. Like most targets the UFO would likely continue along its original course vector.

I believe that these few determinations would have likely been Mace Coffey's initial assessment, until sonar and other sensor data regarding course and vector changes suggested the possibility of a rendezvous off of Shelburne County's Government Point with a second submerged USO.

It was at this point in my attempt to forensically reconstruct the logic chain that Mace Coffey might have employed in the Shag Harbour underwater search that I caught an unexpected break. A chance encounter with Marsha Coffey resulted in another follow-up conversation about Mace in which she just happened to mention "Commander Rex Guy, Dad's former boss, who is still around and, I think, retired in the Valley. You should talk to him." It was a great suggestion; talking with Cmdr. Rex Guy would prove to be a much needed breath of fresh air.

Commander Rex Guy

It turned out that Rex Guy was not simply a boss but the former commanding officer of Maritime Command at the time of the Shag Harbour Incident in 1967. He was not forthcoming with all the answers that I would have liked regarding the incident, but he was more than capable and willing to answer anything as to the question of why Mace Coffey was the guy to consult with on the Shag Harbour search.

In two lengthy telephone conversations Rex Guy explained that Mace Coffey was Maritime Command's scientific consultant in 1967 as a result of Guy's personal request to have him fill that position. "It was one of my conditions for accepting the posting as CO," he told me. "There was no one like him. I had him seconded from the Defence Research Board for five years. They set up an office close enough to mine that I could reach out of the doorway near my desk and grab him by the neck when I needed him. If you were looking for something that was difficult to find or out and out evasive he was your man,"

"How so?" I asked.

"If you had a Soviet sub that we'd lost track of in pursuit, I'd have Mace peruse the charts and make his best guess as to where to have the surface ships hold station to wait 'em out. Invariably, Mace would sprawl the charts on my desk and tap a location and declare, "There, he's down there.""

Rex Guy went on to explain, "He would always bet me a case of Scotch. Sounds good, but he was always right. I don't remember ever getting so much as a taste."

I then asked Rex Guy if he remembered the Shag Harbour Incident.

"Yes. That was the UFO that splashed into Shag Harbour. It was there. I guess that even the Mounties seen it."

"Was it the one that got away?"

"Yes, we didn't find it. Mace did his best, but we didn't come up with it. It bothered him greatly. He felt that it was the real deal, you know, something actually extraterrestrial. He wanted to keep looking, but there were limits. You had to justify the dollars spent."

"So the 'nil results' press release was accurate? There was no evidence?"

"We knew that it was there. I can't tell you anything more than that. I took no personal interest in these things if it wasn't a strict military target. You probably find that odd, but Mace and I were opposites when it came to that stuff."

"Didn't Mace owe you a case of Scotch at the termination of the search for the Shag Harbour UFO?"

Rex Guy chuckled. "No. The deal didn't apply to UFOs."

I asked Cmdr. Guy about the purported Shelburne operation off of Government Point, but he gave no answer. Posing the question a second time brought no response. I decided to skip back to the more open topic of the night of the UFOs before the trail and the conversation turned cold.

I told Rex Guy that as a twelve-year-old I had seen a UFO on the same night as the Shag Harbour Incident, on the Dartmouth Cove waterfront. By the time of our conversation I knew that Mace Coffey's family home had been situated at 48 Hazelhurst Street and that the backyard of the property and the rear windows afford a panoramic view of Dartmouth Cove. I wondered aloud, as I often had, if Mace had been home that eventful evening. I did not expect an answer, but in fact I got two.

"Yes, he was home that night. He saw the UFO in Dartmouth. I guess that it was quite near to his place. He was quite excited when he walked to work the next morning and found that we had been asked to search for the UFO in Shag Harbour, the day after he had had a UFO sighting."

It put a chill in my spine. It was the kind of personal detail I never expected to get. It also meant that somewhere in the vicinity of 10:40 pm, on the night of October 4, 1967, when I had run to the Dartmouth Cove waterfront to be amazed and terrified at the sight of a large spherical UFO hovering and tracing the shoreline, less than three hundred feet away Dr. Maurice Coffey also stood, at the time unknown to me, and had taken in the spectacle from his own backyard. It was a memory that I was more than willing to share. I have no doubt that the experience would have stayed with Mace Coffey as it has with me. Somehow that UFO sighting and the Shag Harbour Incident have always seemed like yesterday to me.

There was no more data to be wrung out of my memorable conversation with former Maritime Command CO Rex Guy, but there was an interesting final story from the retired naval officer regarding the passing of Mace Coffey. At the time of Dr. Coffey's untimely and unexpected death, Rex Guy and his wife resided in Admiralty House in Halifax. Mrs. Guy was awakened on the night of April 22, 1975, by hear the sound of Mace walking with his dog through the halls of Admiralty House. She immediately woke her husband and said that she believed that Mace had just passed away.[3] On the other side of the planet, at Kuala Lampur, Mace died on that very day, just as the canine forerunner had predicted.

There was a statement in Mace Coffey's paper, "Search Concepts 1971" that especially intrigued me. It was in a section titled "The Human Input in Search." In it, Dr. Coffey states,

> The human input in search can be exploited on several levels: a.) The non-expert may introduce the pure hunch or guess as to what happened and where the target is. This can range from the person who dreams of the incident to staff involved who are not familiar with the circumstances, but who feel a compulsion, hunch or impulse. (Coffey 1971: 13)

Doesn't sound very scientific, does it? That unusual idea from Coffey's 1971 research paper figured prominently one year later, in a famous 1972 Canadian search and rescue operation, directed by Mace Coffey. It would demonstrate his willingness to consider and use both the conventional and unconventional to achieve success when searching for a missing target, in this case missing humans.

Mace Coffey and SAR Hartwell

Readers of sufficient years might remember the story of Martin Hartwell, a Canadian bush pilot. On November 8, 1972, Hartwell piloted a charter flight to fly from Cambridge Bay to Yellowknife, Northwest Territories. He had three passengers: a pregnant Inuk woman; a twelve-year-old boy, David Kootook, who was suffering from an acute appendicitis; and Judy Hill, an attending nurse. On the way to Yellowknife the plane encountered a fierce storm and crashed into a hillside near Lake Hota. The plane was a couple hundred miles off track and not where one would expect to find it. Hartwell had a huge

CHAPTER 13: IN SEARCH OF "MACE COFFEE"

reputation as a great pilot. That fact combined with the reality that the plane had gone down off course contributed to the eventual cancellation of the initial search effort after several days. It was thought that perhaps the plane had punched down through thin ice that later refroze.

Judy Hill and the pregnant woman were killed upon impact. Hartwell and the boy survived the crash, but the pilot's legs were broken. The two managed to survive for several weeks, largely due to David Kootook's efforts to gather firewood and by removing flesh from the body of Judy Hill to sustain the two survivors.

A second search was carried out that lasted thirty-one days. Hartwell was found alive. David Kootook had died the day before. Hartwell always refused to discuss his story with journalists and blocked any attempt to portray the story on film. The 2003 motion picture *The Snow Walker* is loosely based on Hartwell's story. In 1998 a ship was named after David Kootook to honour his effort to save Martin Hartwell from starvation and hypothermia.

What is not generally known about the search and rescue operation known as "SAR Hartwell" is this. The second search and rescue effort used a new technique for the first time. It was one developed by Mace Coffey for the Canadian Armed Forces and the Rand Corporation. It was known as the Delphi Concept and differed greatly from previous methods such as Data 0, which was employed in the first search effort for Hartwell. The Delphi Concept would have the team leader consult with search and rescue experts and those with local knowledge of conditions. None of those giving ideas were allowed to confer with or influence each other. Though SAR Hartwell was a successful operation in the end, no one involved other than Dr. Coffey believed that it would find anyone alive. But Mace had a special reason to hold out hope. In fact it was the only reason that there was a second attempt to find Hartwell and company at all. And it was all based on "such stuff as dreams are made of."

Martin Hartwell had a fiancée. Her father was a math professor at Wolfville, Nova Scotia's Acadia University. Prof. Haley was a personal friend of Mace Coffey. Haley brought his daughter to Mace and got her to tell her story. You see, she had a dream that Martin Hartwell was still alive. The girl insisted that it was in fact more than a dream. She believed that she was somehow psychically connected with Hartwell. She gave details of the others deaths. She claimed that Hartwell seemed unaware of her insight and did not know for sure what his location was, but she knew he was alive.

Coffey and Haley believed the girl and used their mutual influence to lobby DND into carrying out a second attempt to find Hartwell. Prof. Haley complained before the media that money was wasted on many pointless training missions. He argued that we should continue to search for Hartwell, which would constitute real training and would justify the huge cost to DND and the Canadian taxpayer. Coffey argued to his superiors that it would be a great first test of the Delphi Concept. The two academics got their way, and the rest, as they say, is history, albeit unusual history. Interestingly, in Coffey's final report to DND on SAR Hartwell, there is no mention of the dream, his belief in it, or even the human input in search.

A Believer

In the world of UFOs and cases like the Shag Harbour Incident it is sometimes more interesting to consider the words of experts that are purposely not committed to paper as opposed to those that are. This can be tormenting to UFO researchers, but it is a fact of life. Typically spoken words are rarely or never repeated and slip into the dustbin of history. Countless times I've read the DND telex that instructs the HMCS *Granby* divers to restrict themselves to verbal updates only regarding their underwater search for Shag Harbour's UFO[4] and wondered, why?

Two words are omitted from this chapter: the name of Mace Coffey's former Defence Research Board colleague who spoke to me, on condition of anonymity, about what Mace believed about the UFO phenomenon. Here is a partial overview of what Dr. Coffey considered possible.

The function and abilities of the human collective unconscious mind are not well understood. In fact many within and outside of the scientific community doubt its existence in terms of a functional common mindscape. Mace Coffey felt that Carl Jung's concept of a collective unconsciousness had to be considered as valid. He also believed that an alien collective unconsciousness might be capable of communication and mental direction of other sentient species. In fact he considered that this might account for many (but not all) abduction scenarios, miracles, and unexplained permanent disappearances. In contrast, the best efforts of humans to tap into the power of the collective unconscious have been limited to the possibility of communicating vague concepts or very general impressions.

Mace Coffey was sympathetic to the concept that with the Kenneth Arnold sighting and the Roswell Incident in the summer of 1947—considered by most ufologists to mark the dawn of the modern UFO age—our collective unconscious had a CE–5 encounter (i.e., non physical contact and interaction) with an extraterrestrial super consciousness and that this coincided with a series

CHAPTER 13: IN SEARCH OF "MACE COFFEE"

of physical visits by extraterrestrials. As a side effect of this, our collective unconscious became self-aware, overstimulated, and hyperactive. Apparently, our collective unconscious was not sufficiently developed to acknowledge, appreciate, or even tolerate first contact without suffering numerous side effects. In fact it could be said that our collective unconscious was suffering from a bad case of what ufologists refer to as the "Oz factor," a psychological condition fairly well portrayed by the Richard Dreyfus character in the motion picture *Close Encounters of the Third Kind*.

Coffey believed that some UFO encounters represent true physical events, some do not. He felt that many were a blend of the two. To Mace a great deal of the UFO data seemed to indicate that an unknown directed intelligence was behind the phenomena.[5]

In case you suspect that an admiring colleague has expanded upon or embellished Mace's view of the UFO phenomenon as outlined in the previous paragraphs, consider his daughter Marsha's recollections of her dad. "My father was a believer. He often told me that he knew that we are not alone. Told me never to doubt it. He sometimes apologized for not being able to explain the reasons behind his absolute certainty."

Perhaps Mace's certainty was the result of access to secrets that few of us are privileged to know, a fringe benefit of an eclectic and productive scientific career. Perhaps it was as simple as "seeing is believing" after a brush with the UFO phenomenon in his own backyard.

Chapter 13 Endnotes

1. Hon. Leo Cadieux, Minister of Defence, in a letter to Hon. C.M. Drury, Minister of Industry, dated Nov. 1967, released to the author by DND Directorate of History.
2. APRO Preliminary Report RE: Shag Harbour Incident, page 3.
3. Author's notes from interview with Rex Guy, fall 2004.
4. DND telex from Maritime Command to *Granby* Divers, 061913Z, Oct. 67, RG 77.
5. Author's notes from anonymous interview with DRB science colleague of Mace Coffey.

Chapter 14: The Master Plan
Chris Styles

"Its invisibility, and the mystery which was attached to it, made this organization doubly terrible. It appeared to be omniscient and omnipotent, and yet it was neither seen nor heard."
– Sir Arthur Conan Doyle, A Study in Scarlet

"There are no better secrets kept than the secrets that everyone guesses."
– George Bernard Shaw

How does one go about finding a crashed UFO? Are their set rules or procedures to follow? And who is ultimately in charge? From the beginning I expected that the Shag Harbour Incident would provide insight into the workings of the various agencies that typically show up and take charge of a potential UFO crash site. What I didn't expect was that accessing the RCMP's UFO retrieval policy would prove more challenging than the recovery of any of its actual UFO investigation reports. The seeds of that decade long paper chase were sown after I stumbled my way into an unscheduled conversation with an on duty RCMP staffer at the Halifax RCMP "Info Centre."

In the mid nineties the RCMP had an information centre located on the waterfront of the east side of Halifax's prestigious Northwest Arm neighbourhood. The facility was housed within a historic Victorian mansion. It served as a staging office for both staffing deployment and postings. Only a small iron plaque affixed to a stone pillar at the beginning of a long serpentine driveway gave any clue as to the heritage property's special function.

One hot summer day in 1993, I deviated from a planned stroll so as to satisfy my curiosity as to why the RCMP held such a beautiful residential property. Upon entering the building I was met by a large oak desk that blocked the hallway beyond. Behind it sat Cpl. Richard, a pleasant and helpful sixty-ish career officer. Cpl. Richard quickly explained to me that the "Info Centre" functioned as an assignment and job posting office for the force and that prior to the 1980s it had served as a residence for single male RCMP staff. Before I could say goodbye, Cpl. Richard recognized me from the few local television appearances I'd made that dealt with my efforts to reopen the Shag Harbour investigation. This initiated a rather lengthy discussion regarding the history of UFO activity in Nova Scotia.

Cpl. Richard proceeded to tell me that in the late 1960s and the first half of the 1970s there were frequent periods when the RCMP was swamped with UFO sightings throughout the province. He remembered that in 1966 and 1967 they were sometimes kept running, night after night, from one UFO event to another. Most of the UFO sightings seemed to represent unusual observations from credible witnesses and could not be explained. Sometimes this pattern would continue for several consecutive shifts. He also recounted an investigation of a mysterious impact site on the top of Debert Mountain in November 1966.

I decided to ask Cpl. Richard straight up what the rules were. Did the RCMP have a policy to deal with UFO situations? Logic alone dictated that they must. After all, the RCMP had a UFO form, the HQ-400-Q5 form; I had seen many completed examples that dealt with every known aspect of the UFO phenomenon. And Cpl. Richard, who stood before me, could be considered a veteran "UFO first responder."

"The Space Object Plan. Yeah, that's what it's called." Cpl. Richard was close. The RCMP's plan for dealing with security concerns connected with the entry of unknown objects (UFOs) or any manmade object that comes down to the surface of the earth from space is actually known as "The Space Object Contingency Plan" or by its more alluring label "The Master Plan." Full access to that elusive and enlightening document would only occur after a lengthy and frustrating ten-year paper chase.

Richard went on to explain that The Space Object Contingency Plan wasn't something that members of the force trained on extensively but that it was a manual that sat in H Division, the RCMP's provincial headquarters in Halifax, and other regional headquarters. It could be referenced for clarification on how to proceed with a problem like the Shag Harbour Incident. The Master Plan would also serve as the guide throughout the 1970s for the re-entries of several threats of terrestrial origin such as the debris field left behind by the January 24, 1978 crash of the Soviet nuclear RORSAT satellite Cosmos 954 in the Canadian High Arctic and the potential threat that America's Skylab posed before its eventual re-entry half a world away over New South Wales, Australia.

CHAPTER 14: THE MASTER PLAN

I made several direct attempts with both the National Archives of Canada and the RCMP archivist to get a full copy of the Space Object Contingency Plan but to no avail. It either could not be found, or they did not know what it was that I was talking about. In Canada the chances of getting a previously unreleased document from an agency such as the RCMP diminish greatly without the specific, correct file number. Essentially you are supposed to know what you're looking for and be able to tell the archivist exactly where to retrieve that information. Understandably, agencies cannot make the effort to find every whim of every curious Canadian, especially when many researchers are not even certain what it is they are looking for. And I must say that when I get a file number or a collection box number from another source, such as correspondence that records such data, the chances of retrieving said document rise dramatically. Without any such location aids, the chances hover just above zero.

I also tried to get some insight into the contents of The Master Plan through unofficial sources. When approached by former police members after speaking engagements, I would always broach the issue of the elusive plan. Many retired RCMP officers were aware that there was one. Some claimed to be familiar with a portion of its contents. But no one I spoke with had actually handled or read it. The various tidbits of information had always been disseminated by a superior officer, who had checked with headquarters as the need arose for some Master Plan wisdom. Most fellow UFO researchers doubted that I would ever get access to the genuine article. A few offered to introduce me to former staffers who could "tell me all about it." Needless to say, that would have failed to meet my needs. I needed an official release. I wanted to see if the rules had been adhered to in the Shag Harbour search. And I needed to know just what the working relationship was between Canadian and US authorities. Throughout the nineties I had heard numerous tales from UFO eyewitnesses of US military personnel being allowed free access to Canadian UFO landing and impact sites. Were these claims true? Was this level of purported international cooperation in the field an acknowledgment of the reality of UFO crash scenarios? Many of these questions would eventually be answered in 2003 when I finally caught a break with the powers that be.

In September of 2002 I received a letter from RCMP historian Margaret Evans. That letter concerned two RCMP UFO reports that I had been seeking and informed me that I might find what I was looking for from a formal request directed toward the RCMP archivist. However, by the time that access request had been processed, the two reports had been transferred to the National Archives in Ottawa. I was slightly "miffed" about this outcome as I had placed a follow-up call in which an archival assistant suggested that the reports were not due to be transferred. As is usually the case in such written responses, the November 5 letter from the RCMP archivist provided contact information for someone I could call to discuss any special concerns regarding my access request. I decided to call Cpl. Lise Lachance.

Cpl. Lachance was not able to shed much light on why the UFO files in question had been transferred ahead of schedule to National Archives or explain why a junior staffer had assured me that they would not be moved in the near future. Typically, RCMP UFO files sit in their originating detachment of investigation for the first year. After a year has elapsed the reports are transferred to the RCMP archives in Ottawa. There they will be held for the next three years, at which time they are handed over to the National Archives for preservation in a permanent public collection. Their process of reviewing and cataloguing documents can take several years or more.

Cpl. Lachance went on to say that it was unfortunate, but they had just cleaned out their files and there were in fact no UFO reports in their collection. She claimed to be quite certain of this and said the only documents left were old policy documents that went way back to the 1950s, such as the Space Object Contingency Plan.

I snapped to attention in my old office chair. "That's it!" I said. "That's what I was looking for!"

After a brief pause Cpl. Lachance responded with, "No. No it isn't. I have your access request before me, and quite clearly that's not what you asked for. You were—"

"I didn't know what it was called, but that's what I want." I confess that my "explanation" sounded lame even to myself as I interrupted Cpl. Lachance's more than reasonable response.

"Well I can't forward a copy to you based on this request. I just can't. You will have to send in a new request."

"Of course. Could you please give me the correct file number for the Space Object Plan?" This was the moment of truth, I hoped.

"I guess so. Sure. You'll have to hold. The copy that I was looking at earlier in the week is up the hallway in another room."

"That would be great." Due to my flat rate calling plan and the sudden promise of fruition in my ten year on again, off again search, I was willing to wait until moss grew on my north side, if need be. I clearly remember hearing

CHAPTER 14: THE MASTER PLAN

Cpl. Lachance's heels click up the hallway after she set the phone down. When she returned with the file number, I had her repeat it several times just to be sure. I didn't want to leave anything to chance. I immediately filled out a bright green Access to Information form that I retrieved from my file cabinet and grabbed another five dollar money order for Canada's Receiver General. In the business of UFO research, persistence pays off. And sometimes you don't get what you were looking for. Sometimes you get something better. I was both excited and hopeful on my walk to the mailbox.

Two days later I received a phone call from the chief archivist for the RCMP. He told me that my request contained a file number that did not make any sense. I assured him that it must be correct as it had been given to me in my phone conversation with Cpl. Lachance, and I had her repeat it more than once.

"I see. I will have to look into it and get back to you." The chief archivist's strong tone and French-Canadian accent sounded most serious. True to his word he called me back the next day and said that he now understood what I wanted. He went on to explain that my request could not be handled in the usual time frame that one expects under the *Access to Information Act*. This was due to the fact that its release would require letters of permission from the federal government, all ten provinces, the territories, and the US government. Apparently the American permission would be most necessary as the document revealed details of how our agencies worked with a foreign power. The RCMP archivist went on to say that this would take some time and that I would have to be patient. I assured him that that sounded reasonable. I could be patient if I could see that progress was being made. I went on to suggest that if I received periodic updates by phone that I could show patience with the process and that there would be no need to file a complaint with Canada's Information Commissioner.

Once again, the RCMP archivist was true to his word and called a few times to keep me up to date on progress with receiving the necessary letters of permission. There seemed to be no special order or sense of priority as to how the responses made their way to Ottawa. Finally, on October 8, 2003, I received a copy of The Master Plan: The Space Object Contingency Plan. My formal Access to Information request had been posted on May 2, 2003. My fondest memory of the whole process was the slight embarrassment caused by The Space Object Contingency Plan's alternate title, "The Master Plan." Cpl. Lise Lachance described the choice of words as "unfortunate." I countered with the concern that it was going to take considerable reassurance on my part when presenting a lecture that I was not making these things up or embellishing the documents in any way.

So what does The Master Plan have to say about UFOs in Canada? The short but misleading answer would be nothing. The term UFO is never used. However, when one considers the multiple verbal reassurances from retired and current RCMP staff that these are the rules regarding UFOs and crashes of unknown objects from space, then The Master Plan has plenty to say and is a must read for any Canadian UFO researcher.

The forty-eight page manual explains such things as: who is in charge at an impact site (the RCMP is until Canadian Armed Forces arrive, at which point they become the lead agency); how far upwind to keep personnel if there is a threat of radiation (500 feet); and who decides to remove deceased casualties (the senior RCMP officer that is on site).[1]

The plan also explains that it is a duty of the RCMP to escort any bona fide US official to the impact site at their request. And the document contains scripted answers for difficult media questions. It is clear that much of the policy is there to deal with mishaps such as that of the errant Soviet nuclear spy satellite, Cosmos 954. Much of the procedures are what you would expect, but it is still useful to have those things acknowledged and clear. The few things that are unexpected, such as the extremely slack open door policy for US officials,[2] explains much about their purported presence and ease of movement when following up Canadian military and police UFO investigations.

So does the Space Object Contingency Plan tell us anything about the Shag Harbour Incident? I believe that it explains where the Air Desk and Maritime Command's search went "off of the rails." It basically comes down to the immediate and persistent US involvement, which was not a "two way street." The Master Plan simply helped portray US personnel and authorities as citizens above suspicion.

Consider all of the following: At the time of the Shag Harbour Incident the US navy was flying a high altitude air photo reconnaissance mission in the Shag Harbour area; within the hour NORAD launched a thirty-five minute Strategic Air Command (SAC) operation over the area;[3] the two nearby NORAD bases—CFS Barrington at Bacarro and CFS Shelburne—were 50 per cent staffed by US military personnel; there were no missing aircraft, but US search and rescue aircraft were entering our airspace at will according to an electronic intelligence (ELINT) officer who flew grid search patterns that night; Bon Portage lightkeeper Ervin Banks claims to have discovered an unusual cylinder on the shore of Bon Portage Island in the early morning daylight hours of October 5, 1967, and he claims to have packaged it and turned it over to US authorities under the orders of a superior officer of the Canadian Coast Guard service (see chapter 15); there are credible claims of a second simultaneous search for a submerged UFO in the waters off of Shelburne County's Government Point, and that purported operation is not reflected in the Canadian archival record although an unrelated RCMP X-file mentions the Shelburne operation; and the Air Desk's former staffer, Squadron Leader William Bain, conceded to me in a face-to-face interview that Ottawa could have been "stick handled" by American authorities regarding the Shag Harbour Incident.

I will conclude by saying that I believe the US authorities treated the provisions and protocols of The Master Plan as "fluid." They interpreted the plan within the framework of what could be best described as situation ethics with the application of rules and regulations on a case by case basis. The end justified the means as far as the American authorities were concerned, and results, if any, were rarely shared with Canada.

Chapter 14 Endnotes

1. From the 1950s RCMP policy document, The Space Object Contingency Plan (AKA "The Master Plan"), page 44.
2. Ibid.: 47.
3. APRO Preliminary Report RE: Shag Harbour Incident, page 5.

Chapter 15: The Cover-up?
Chris Styles

"A neurosis is a secret that you don't know that you are keeping."
– Kenneth Tynan

"Three may keep a secret, if two of them are dead."
– Ben Franklin

There are many aspects to my investigation of the Shag Harbour Incident. One of the most rewarding and yet frustrating is what I think of as "the paper chase." Dealing with the various archives and authoritarian agencies can prove tedious, frustrating, but occasionally quite rewarding. For the most part staff members at these archives and agencies are quite professional and fair in their attempts to locate and release copies of primary documents. However, I am forced to note one exception to this overall positive experience.

The Coast Guard and I got off on a bad footing right from the start. In the first week of October 1993, I phoned the Dartmouth office. I called to inquire about the possibility of accessing any log entries regarding the efforts of Coast Guard Cutter (CGC) 101 to help locate the object responsible for the Shag Harbour Incident back in October 1967. My call was put through to the Regional Director, Larry Wilson.

Larry Wilson was quick to say that the Coast Guard might have preserved the ship's log book. Mr. Wilson then asked why I had an interest in accessing such a record. I explained that I was investigating the Shag Harbour UFO crash. Immediately, Larry Wilson countered with, "I don't believe that I have to respond to or be a part of that. I'm sorry, goodbye." He hung up. However, my first Coast Guard encounter was not to remain that "short and sweet."

Ten minutes later Larry Wilson called me back. I was at my desk, typing a letter of complaint to Canada's Information Commissioner about Mr. Wilson's curt response to my telephone inquiry. Mr. Wilson apologized with the explanation that, "You must understand that we don't get many requests for information. I guess that I can have someone retrieve that information for you if we in fact have it. I've been told that indeed we have to. Once again, I am sorry for my initial refusal."

I asked Mr. Wilson if he would require a formal access to information request, but he assured me that that would not be necessary. I took him at his word and decided to wait for the reply.

Since I had "broken the ice" with the Coast Guard I also decided to put in a written request the very next day for the lighthouse logs from October 1967 for the formerly manned lighthouse on McNutt Island. That particular lighthouse faces CFS Shelburne and was under the direct control of the Coast Guard at the time of the Shag Harbour Incident. The Cape Roseway lighthouse, as it is known by the locals, would have afforded an excellent view of the purported naval operations just off of Shelburne County's Government Point. The request for the lighthouse logs was passed on to Mr. Dave Smith, regional superintendent of the Coast Guard.

Dave Smith's response arrived first. In a letter dated October 25, 1993, he stated, "I regret to inform you that our attempts to locate the information you requested concerning Cape Roseway have been futile. We cannot locate the light station logs from that time frame."[1] In a subsequent phone conversation Mr. Smith suggested that perhaps the light station logs were transferred to Ottawa and that they might be held at the National Archives. Follow-up requests to National Archives also failed to find any trace of the Cape Roseway logs. Years later I made several attempts to have other Coast Guard staffers search the Coast Guard's Burnside warehouse for any trace of the logs, but to no avail.

Over the years since that initial 1993 request for the Cape Roseway logs I have not had success in retrieving any of the pertinent light station records from any of the nearby lighthouses that may have witnessed any known UFO event. The Coast Guard's consistent outcome of "nil results" for all of my requests also holds true for the Shag Harbour Incident itself. The entries of former lightkeeper Ervin Banks have never been found. Mr. Banks was the keeper on duty the night of October 4, 1967. I believe that some of the public statements made by Banks over the years may explain the Coast Guard's failed document searches and poor record keeping, but his claims regarding events on the night of October 4, 1967, and the lack of subsequent documentation are not without controversy.

CHAPTER 15: THE COVER-UP?

Back in 1995, while in the Shag Harbour area shooting the *Sightings* episodes for Paramount Television, I attempted to interview Ervin Banks about the night of October 4, 1967, in the hope of getting his recollections of what was happening on Bon Portage Island during and after the UFO crash. Ervin Banks told me that he was asleep at the time of the incident. He did not see the UFO in the air or on the water. Shortly afterwards he was awakened by a phone call from the Coast Guard and was asked to do a patrol of the shoreline. Nothing out of the ordinary was found and later the next morning he searched the shoreline again and once again found nothing unusual. This was all that Ervin Banks claimed to know when interviewed in 1995. In the fall of 2001 his story would change dramatically.

Ervin Banks's Story

In October 2001 the Chapel Hill Historical Society organized a book signing event for *Dark Object*, which had been released in March of that year. The event was held at Evelyn Richardson Memorial School in Shag Harbour. There were a number of brief oral presentations scheduled for the event from the various eyewitnesses and from my co-author Don Ledger and myself. One new name was a late addition, Ervin Banks. He had never presented before and asked if he could be added to the program. Doug Shand, the event coordinator and MC, had no idea what Ervin had to present but agreed to list him anyway. After all, he had been the lightkeeper on duty on the night of October 4, 1967. Shortly before the program began that evening, Doug Shand asked me about the possibility of new evidence being given by the former lightkeeper, but I was unaware on any new revelations. As far as I knew Ervin Banks had witnessed nothing significant and was not privy to any special inside information, leaks, or rumours from the Coast Guard "brass."

When it came time for Ervin Banks to speak he explained to the audience how he had been asleep in bed when the UFO struck the waters of The Sound. He went on to say that the Coast Guard and the RCMP phoned to request that he check the shoreline of Bon Portage for the possibility of debris or wreckage. Ervin did so and found nothing unusual to report. Ervin Banks then went on to claim that when he checked the shoreline a second time, shortly after first light, he found an unusual metal cylinder. It was small and could be held in one's arms. It appeared to be damaged and had a profusion of exposed wires and electronics. Ervin also stated that the cylinder was covered with strange writing and gave off a terrible smell.

I stood up from my seat, situated toward the back of the packed school auditorium. Before I had a chance to interrupt, Ervin Banks addressed me from the stage.

"I know what you're going to say. When you spoke to me back in 1995 I held all this from you. I'm sorry but people have been talking in the community, and some in my family feel that I should tell what I know. I understand that it sounds bad, but I worked for the government and had a lot to consider."

"If you lied to me then why should we believe you now?" My question was direct. I felt it was necessary and justified since Ervin Banks had just become the first person who had been involved with the Shag Harbour Incident to alter his testimony. He simply repeated his concerns regarding his family and pension and asked for our collective understanding. I sat back down and decided to hold off until the scheduled question and answer time to probe Ervin further. It was the polite thing to do, and he deserved to have the rest of his story heard. As we were about to find out, Ervin had more to tell.

Ervin Banks went on to explain that when he discovered the mysterious cylinder he called his superiors at the Coast Guard to see what he should do. According to Banks, he was given instructions on how to package the cylinder and then was told to ferry it over to the Prospect Wharf and hand it over to an American military officer. The Bon Portage lightkeeper did as instructed. Banks said the US military officer was someone that had been flown in from Virginia and was not one of the local US personnel that made up half of the manpower at the two nearest military bases.

When Ervin Banks finished his talk I asked him if he would reveal who it was that took possession of the cylinder, but he refused to say. I then asked him who it was at the Coast Guard that had instructed him as to what to do, but again he refused to answer.

The evenings' program continued and the unanswered questions remained just that for the night. I approached Ervin Banks as soon as he left the stage and let him know that I would get the answers I needed no matter how long it took. I was far from through with the Shag Harbour Incident, and I was far from through with the Coast Guard.

It would be wrong to make Ervin Banks the villain in this story. If Ervin's second version of events is both valid and accurate, then the fault lies with "the brass" and the erroneous interpretation and implementation of policies and systems that were in place at the time of the search if October 4 and 5, 1967. The Coast Guard was most certainly not supposed to hand over any important artifacts to US military personnel. According to William F. Dawson's APRO

CHAPTER 15: THE COVER-UP?

Preliminary Investigation Report and my own interviews with retired Squadron Leader William Bain of the Canadian Forces Air Desk and retired commander Rex Guy of Maritime Command, any findings were to be reported to the Rescue Co-ordination Centre in Halifax and any artifacts were to be turned over to Dr. Maurice Coffey at Maritime Command.[2] The Coast Guard had been made aware of these policies by both Maritime Command and the Air Desk in Ottawa. Any questions from the public or the media were to be handled through the watch officer at Maritime Command. Ultimately, artifacts were supposed to be transported to and become the property of the Defence Research Board facility located at Grove Street in Dartmouth. All of the aforementioned procedures were in compliance with the RCMP's Space Object Contingency Plan, which clearly states that DND would be the lead agency once they were on the scene.[3]

In fact, William Bain admitted that the Americans responded immediately (they were responding to NORAD radar detection of a "bogey" entering the atmosphere from space and landing near Shag Harbour[4]) and that they may have left Ottawa out of the loop on any findings. He said that this was "possible" and that he could "see why my data would lead you to think it likely."

In October 2008 the Shag Harbour Incident Society sponsored a UFO festival in the community of Barrington. Graham Simms and I were both present for the event; in fact I gave the opening talk, "Updates on the Shag Harbour Incident." Ervin Banks sat in the audience and asked a couple of questions during the fifteen-minute Q & A period following my presentation. While answering his queries I pointed out to those in attendance that Ervin Banks was as the lightkeeper at Bon Portage in October 1967. Once again I invited Mr. Banks to name his contact person at the Coast Guard and the US military officer that took possession of the "mysterious cylinder," but once again he refused. I then stated that I was still searching for the missing light station logs and that there was a degree of new hope since I now understood—thanks to a tip from Halifax radio personality Chris Mills who is involved with the Lighthouse Preservation Society—that the missing logs were in all likelihood never kept in Dartmouth but in the Saint John, New Brunswick, office of the Coast Guard.

Ervin laughed aloud and said, "That won't help you. I was ordered not to make any entry, and I did not." And therein lies the whole problem with Ervin's story. It remains just that, a story. There are no other witnesses of record and no documentation, and it was a radical change of testimony from Ervin's first interview. The Coast Guard has not taken a stance on the validity of Ervin's details. Even though Ervin Banks has made his claims on camera in an internationally broadcast US feature documentary (*UFO Files: Canada's Roswell*), the Coast Guard does not feel compelled to respond. Ervin's story remains one man's recollections. With the spotty record keeping and the "fog of bureaucracy," the Coast Guard remains silent and makes no comment. That said, in 2008 Coast Guard staffer Bill Parker told me that he personally had packed the Bon Portage lighthouse records of 1967 and had shipped them off to the National Archives in Ottawa from the Saint John office some fifteen years earlier. As of the time of writing this book, the National Archives had not yet cataloged the lighthouse records into an available collection.

Could Ervin Banks's claims be true? Yes. But I cannot say that they are. And just what could it have been that Ervin recovered from the shoreline of Bon Portage? I doubt that it was an artifact of extraterrestrial origin. His composite description from several statements would lead me to believe that the "mysterious cylinder" was likely a passive sonar buoy used in the search effort on the first night. However, it could have been a very important buoy that recorded crucial information about Shag Harbour's "dark object."

A Dog's Breakfast

The ongoing saga of the missing light station logs does not hold the record for the most frustrating document search with the Canadian Coast Guard. That distinction would definitely be claimed by the ongoing comedy of errors that began the day before the light station log request. Remember my October 1993 phone conversation with Coast Guard Regional Director Larry Wilson? The brief account given earlier in this chapter of my request for the CGC 101 log entries looks like a "save situation" with a happy ending; following my very negative initial reception from Larry Wilson, he called right back with a change of attitude about my document request, apologized, and ultimately located and sent photocopies of what I had requested. And that's where and when the trouble began.

By the time of that initial phone call in October 1993, I had already accessed and studied a large amount of military and RCMP documents regarding the Shag Harbour Incident. No aircraft were ever reported missing throughout the period of the underwater search. Although the incident was initially reported by the local eyewitnesses as the apparent crash of an aircraft or simply as lights descending rapidly toward the water, by the morning of October 5, 1967, all the other primary source records of the military and

CHAPTER 15: THE COVER-UP?

RCMP refer to the search as the search for a crashed UFO. The only exception is the CGC 101 log, which was unexpectedly lean on details. And there was another problem. The times recorded in the CGC 101 logs were wrong by four hours if one accepts that they were meant to be taken as Greenwich Mean Time (GMT) as was written. Another curious feature was that the photocopy appeared to be of a page from a long narrow spiral notebook and not from the pages of a bound ledger as one might expect. All of the aforementioned details and anomalies made me question the authenticity of what the Coast Guard had sent.

I contacted Larry Wilson again in the last week of October 1993 to see if arrangements could be made to see the original log book, a right that one has under the *Access to Information Act*. Once again Wilson seemed to want to be helpful. He said that it would take a few weeks to retrieve the book and set up a time to meet with Yves Leclerc, who would bring the book to me. I thanked Larry Wilson and awaited the call to make arrangements to meet Yves Leclerc, but before that call came something unexpected happened.

I was driving back to Halifax from Shag Harbour and decided to take a right turn onto the causeway at Barrington that goes across to Cape Sable Island. It was my hope to catch skipper Ronnie Newell between rescue calls at the Clark's Harbour life station where CGC 101 was stationed. Newell was the skipper aboard CGC 101 on the night of October 4, 1967, and twenty-six years later had yet to retire. We had never met and I was dying to interview him.

When I arrived at the life station, Ronnie Newell had CGC 101 out on a minor rescue for a boat with a fouled propeller. I decided to wait, and the staff made me a cup of tea. As I wandered around the room taking in the sights and sounds, I noticed a huge oak bookcase with glass doors. From the dates on the covers of the books inside, it appeared that the bookcase held the total collection of log books going back to 1966, the beginning of service for the station. So there was the book I wanted to handle.

When CGC 101 pulled into the wharf I went outside to greet Newell. He shook my hand but never made eye contact. He kept looking at the boards in the wharf and shuffled his feet. It was rather awkward. He was quite certain that there was nothing to the Shag Harbour Incident and assured me that there was no such thing as UFOs but then said that they were also looking for one back then near Port Mouton. He said that he heard later that, "someone had shot a flare." When I asked to see the log book and told him that Larry Wilson was making arrangements to get it to me, he flat out refused to consider my request. I showed him a letter from Wilson and offered to pay for the phone call, but Ronnie Newell would not be persuaded. I then showed Ronnie Newell the photocopy that Larry Wilson had sent me. I asked him if that was his handwriting, and he said no. Newell said that a hand on the boat did the logs and that his name was Elliot Worthing. He didn't work there anymore and did not live in the area. Clearly I had to find Elliot, but the pleasure of that interview was still a few years off into the future.

A few weeks after my visit to Clark's Harbour I finally got to handle the ringed notebook that served as the ship's log. I had to meet with Yves Leclerc in a Tim Horton's coffee shop. Like Ronnie Newell, Leclerc felt compelled to inform me that there was no such thing as UFOs. That informal examination of the notebook over a cup of coffee did little to answer the questions left behind by the sparse entries and the errors. Not only did some of the answers lie in the future, but as I would discover so did many more questions.

Since my impromptu meeting with Ronnie Newell in October 1993, there is now a new boat and a new life station in Clark's Harbour. Ronnie Newell is retired, and the logbooks have since been moved to a warehouse in Burnside Industrial Park where, according to the Coast Guard, they have been "lost" for some time.

During the filming of Mike MacDonald's documentary, *The Shag Harbour UFO Incident*, in 2000 I discovered that I could not locate a hard copy or scan of the CGC 101 photocopy sent to me in 1993 by Larry Wilson. I attempted to get another copy from the Coast Guard, but they claimed that all of the logbooks were lost. I was assured that any further searching would be futile. In spite of that dire prediction I attempted to get another copy from the Coast Guard whenever I became aware of relevant staff replacements, but to no avail. I still kept trying even after I found my missing copy. That may seem wasteful or redundant, but sometimes when you don't find what you are looking for you actually discover something better. Persistence pays off.

On October 4, 2007, precisely forty years to the day after the Shag Harbour Incident, I finally tracked down Elliot Worthing, who had long ago left the employ of the Coast Guard and was enjoying his retirement in Newfoundland. He had not heard of all the attention the Shag Harbour Incident had received since 1993. He seemed eager to help, so I posted a copy of Larry Wilson's response and the photocopy of the CGC 101 logs. A few days later Elliot assured me that it was his handwriting but could shed little light on the mistakes. He explained that the Clark's Harbour Lifesaving Station had been thrown together in 1966 and that no training was given. The Coast

CHAPTER 15: THE COVER-UP?

Guard simply hired dependable local people with basic marine knowledge and little to no fear of navigating in terrible weather. That was it in a nutshell. Elliot was given the task of writing the logs because he had "good penmanship and the most schooling."

Unlike the career Coast Guard men who seemed so negative toward the possibility that the Shag Harbour Incident was some aspect of the UFO phenomenon, Elliot felt that there was always something "solidly weird" to the case. He said that he got that strong impression from the navy divers when CGC 101 acted as a diving tender for the first few days of operations. He remembers the *Granby* divers being quite serious and very quiet when they brought up "things put into a metal box that they did not want us to see." In our October 4, 2007 telephone interview, Elliot elaborated.

> I know that there was something within because I helped the men bring it over the side and it certainly weighed more than if it were just a box flooded with water and it certainly weighed more than when it went down.

With the help of Shag Harbour fisherman Norm Smith, I was able to track down the other hand on the boat that night, Leslie Smith. Leslie feels of like mind about the whole incident and well remembers that they kept radio silence on board CGC 101 throughout the night of October 4 and the early morning hours of October 5, 1967, which was most unusual and not normal procedure. Like Elliot, Leslie Smith remembered the ringed notebook, which he described as "pathetic." He went on to state that the first few years of the lifesaving service was marked by poor equipment and no training. One had to beg and fight for every little improvement and sometimes even the necessities were scarce. Only the vessel itself was sound and well maintained.

At that point in my investigation, in October 2007, I accepted the input of Elliot Worthing and Leslie Smith and was generally satisfied by their explanation of poor record keeping. After all, the tradition of losing records at the Coast Guard seemed to be alive and well. Record keeping just did not seem to be a priority.... And then a funny thing happened on the way to Boston.

In mid October 2007, I was about to leave for a UFO conference in Boston where I was booked to present an illustrated lecture on Shag Harbour, when I did a last minute check of my email. There was a message from Shag Harbour's postmistress, Cindy Nickerson, who heads up the non-profit Shag

Harbour Incident Society. The message stated that Cmdr. Graham Smith of the Coast Guard had dropped off the actual ship's log from CGC 101 and that it would be on display at the Shag Harbour UFO museum for some time. I groaned when I read the message. I thought it odd that the last interim regional director had been unable to find the logbook in spite of what he called "an exhaustive search," but now it just suddenly rematerialized and was donated to the Shag Harbour museum for the public to enjoy.

Cindy had attached two scans that I did not bother to open until I returned from Boston. When I did open them, I was astounded by what I saw. There was a scan of a set of log entries that differed significantly from the photocopy sent to me by Larry Wilson in 1993. I knew it from first glance. This new version, which I immediately felt was the genuine article, held more detail and made greater sense. The first thing I did was phone Cindy Nickerson and tell her to scan the whole book because the Coast Guard was going to repossess it as soon as I contacted them with my complaint.

On October 17, 2007, I phoned the Coast Guard's Dartmouth headquarters and was connected with its new regional director, Nancy Raybert. I asked her how many logbooks their vessels had. She, of course, said "one." After hearing that reassurance I told her what my concern was regarding the apparent case of two sets of log entries for CGC 101 from October 1967. She promised to assign someone to look into the matter.

The next morning, from 10:00 to 11:00 AM, I spoke on the phone with Captain Tony Potts about the CGC 101 logbook situation. Tony Potts is a career officer with the Coast Guard. He has commanded some of its big ice breakers. Potts seemed somewhat familiar with and interested in the Shag Harbour Incident. He asked all the right questions and promised to get right to it. And he did.

That same day I was out of my apartment from noon until about 4:00 pm. When I checked my email I discovered that Captain Potts had sent a message at 3:56 pm. It reads as follows:

> Chris
> Spoke to Graham Smith, the Commanding Officer in Clark's Harbour this week. He has the logbook from the museum once again in his possession. This logbook which contains about one and a half years of information was discovered with all the other station logbooks during the move to the new station in

CHAPTER 15: THE COVER-UP?

2001. Because of the history it was retained at the station and the other logbooks were archived in Burnside.

Looking at the two documents and the amount of discrepancies for all incidents I cannot speculate which is the original document. I would assume that the one found by Graham is the original. I had first thought one was a rough onboard logbook and that the one with better penmanship was the official log. I really don't know. It doesn't appear this was an attempt to cover up anything.

Regards, Tony

This was the swiftest response I had ever received throughout my history of requests with the Coast Guard. Unsure of where to turn next I decided to go to what should be "the source," Elliot Worthing. I posted a copy of the 1993 photocopy and the 2007 logbook found by Cmdr. Graham Smith in the hopes that Elliot could state which one was his handwriting and therefore which version was genuine. When I spoke to him on the phone before posting the samples, he assured me that only one logbook was kept aboard CGC 101.

A week later I phoned Elliot and asked what his opinion was. He said, "You're not going to like it. I think that they are both mine. I don't remember writing a second version, but I think they are both written by me."

Elliot was right. I didn't like it. It raised more questions for which there would be no answer. And if he did not remember writing a second copy he therefore could not give any explanation as to why there would be so many discrepancies between the two versions. Unlike the DND and RCMP records from the time of the Shag Harbour Incident, the term UFO is never used in the CGC 101 log entries. One entry actually reads, "Resumed search for aircraft, or ?" Interestingly, even the "or ?" was edited out in the version released to me by Larry Wilson in 1993. In fact one whole entry is entirely missing. At least when the National Archives removes material under Access to Information regulations they add a yellow sticker that states, "This is a sanitized file," and a staffer signs and dates it.

In his email, Tony Potts says, "It doesn't appear that this is an attempt to cover up anything." I don't know what it is. I'll leave it up to the reader to decide. As one retired Coast Guard staffer put it to me after reading an early draft of this chapter, "I could believe anything about the place. The whole time I worked there things were always as mixed up as a dog's breakfast."

Chapter 15 Endnotes

1. Letter to the author from Canadian Coast Guard, CMA 8010-282, Oct. 25, 1993.
2. APRO Preliminary Report RE: Shag Harbour Incident.
3. From the 1950s RCMP policy document, The Space Object Contingency Plan (AKA "The Master Plan"), page 44.
4. This information was told to the author by a former radar tech and by a weapons tech, both of whom served at CFS Barrington.

Chapter 16: In The Middle of the Air
Chris Styles

"The beginning of knowledge is the discovery of something that we do not understand."
– Frank Herbert

"The most exciting phrase to hear in science, the one that heralds new discoveries, is not 'Eureka!' but 'That's funny!'"
- Isaac Asimov

Ever since I began my research into the Shag Harbour Incident back in 1992 I have repeatedly enjoyed the reassuring feeling that I chose a winner as a point of focus on which to devote the bulk of my own personal UFO research effort. The Shag Harbour Incident has shown considerable resilience against the pitfalls that plague many other classic UFO crash scenarios. Even the plethora of abrasive career skeptics has preferred to avoid "that which they cannot easily explain or explain away." But that does not mean that the Shag Harbour Incident and the October 4, 1967 night of the UFOs have entirely escaped the torment of having the odd "fly in the ointment."

Noted British ufologist Jenny Randles has pointed out that in purported UFO crash scenarios no one ever seems to both see the UFO in flight and then track the object to its final landing or crash site. This curious feature would also appear to hold true for the Shag Harbour Incident. However, some of the initial eyewitnesses, who were driving along Highway 3 on the night of October 4, 1967, only lost sight of the descending UFO for a few seconds as it dipped below the treeline. When their vehicles advanced to a point where the road ran closer to the shoreline, those witnesses regained sight of the UFO, apparently floating on the surface of the water. With such a brief interval, the chain of evidence is hardly suspect. The strange dome-shaped yellow glow that drifted in the ebbing tide was the obvious consequence of the descending sixty-foot wide set of flashing lights seen seconds before their impact with the water's surface.

Personally, one of the concerns I have with most UFO crash scenarios and landing cases is that they tend to become large, unruly "passion plays" that fall victim to the desire of both UFO researchers and the public for "runaway inclusiveness." Lines of connection are often drawn between events and features where more accurately there should be a dotted line or no line at all. Ufologists are often coaxed over the edge of this slippery slope by overzealous editors, TV producers, and excitable fans to provide a case with a little more spin and sizzle.

The Shag Harbour Incident occurred around 11:20 pm AST on October 4, 1967. Numerous other UFO sightings were reported that night in the skies over Nova Scotia and throughout eastern Canada. Some of the other UFO sightings reported on the so-called "night of the UFOs" had a definite connection to the Shag Harbour Incident. Some did not. Some of those sightings have been shown not to be UFO events at all, and some others were mere coincidences of witness misinterpretation. One of those amazing coincidences is the curious and fascinating story of Air Canada Flight 305.

Air Canada Flight 305
At 7:15 pm EST (8:15 AST) on October 4, 1967, Air Canada Flight 305 was flying westbound at 12,000 feet above layered cloud along V-300, forty-five miles east of St. Jean, Quebec. The aircraft was piloted by Captain Guy Charbonneau and First Officer Bob Ralph. Captain Charbonneau noticed an unusual set of lights twenty degrees above the horizon south of the aircraft's position. At first it appeared as a large white light followed by six smaller ones. While the two men continued to watch the display, the large white light changed into a large red fireball. The fireball turned to violet and then light blue. This sequence actually repeated at 7:19 and at 7:21 EST. By 7:35 EST a large blue pear-shaped cloud was seen to be drifting east. The changes left the two airmen with the impression that what they had witnessed was the result of large violent explosions high up in the atmosphere. The two men were puzzled and concerned by what they saw and maintained communication with the airport in Montreal to report their ongoing observations. A formal UFO report was filed when Flight 305 landed.[1] That UFO report would eventually make its way to the civilian UFO groups of the day such as the National Investigations Committee of Aerial Phenomena (NICAP), APRO, the Condon Committee's UFO study for the USAF, and the RCAF's Air Desk and finally to the National Archives of Canada.

CHAPTER 16: IN THE MIDDLE OF THE AIR

In 1993, while searching for Shag Harbour files, I found copies of the Flight 305 documents among the National Archives's RG 77 collection. As a UFO researcher I found the story interesting. Pilot sightings always are. Their training and responsibilities serve as an excellent filter. When an airline or military pilot reports seeing a UFO, you can be fairly sure that he or she saw something quite strange, but that doesn't automatically mean that the sighting was the observation of a genuine UFO or alien space craft. What it does mean is that the sighting is unlikely to be a misinterpretation of common conventional objects or phenomena such as birds, aircraft, or the northern lights. But sometimes the skies are home to unusual or rare objects of manmade origin, and such would ultimately prove to be the case for the Air Canada Flight 305 sighting of October 4, 1967.

I found the Flight 305 sighting interesting right from the start,,but what did it have to do with the crash of the mysterious sixty-foot UFO into the waters of Shag Harbour on the night of the UFOs? The explosive light phenomenon seen while the aircraft flew over St. Jean, Quebec, bore no resemblance to what was witnessed in Shag Harbour or most of the other UFO sightings over Nova Scotia and the Gulf of Maine on the night of October 4, 1967. However, there was some similarity between what Flight 305 saw and what was photographed by Wilfred Eisnor in Lunenburg some two hours before the crash in Shag Harbour. Interestingly, Mr. Eisnor was looking south at roughly the same time that Flight 305 was looking in the same direction. Eisnor took a five-minute time exposure with his trusty Pentax Spotmatic camera, and Flight 305 filed an official UFO report. It is clear from the witness details of both sightings that the objects responsible were quite far away from the observers. Most of the other UFOs sighted over Nova Scotia on the night of October 4, 1967, were in close proximity to the witnesses. Such was the case in Shag Harbour where the UFO was a mere 200 to 300 yards off shore when it first hit the water. In another sighting, two glowing spheres hovered and "danced" at low altitude over the herring seiner *Quadra Isle*, which was positioned near Brier Island at the mouth of the Bay of Fundy (Ledger and Styles 2001: 21–22).

Because Flight 305 appeared to see a very distant phenomenon and was at the time flying hundreds of miles west of the Maritimes I did not consider it to be directly connected with the Shag Harbour Incident. That is why I did not include it in earlier published papers on the Shag Harbour Incident, such as my MUFON 1996 International UFO Symposium presentation titled "Shag Harbour in Perspective." Many UFO sightings from the "night of the UFOs" are mentioned in that paper, as are subsequent Shag Harbour UFO events, some from as much as three years later, but I decided against including anything about Air Canada Flight 305. But as the nineties unfolded I would discover that others felt quite differently about the value of the St. Jean, Quebec, sighting.

Television and UFO research mix together about as well as water and oil. It is just the "nature of the beast." Each specialty has very different needs. Over the years I have been fortunate enough to collaborate with several directors, both in Canada and in the US, who tried as best they could to accurately portray just what happened in Shag Harbour on the night of October 4, 1967. A couple of the feature documentaries involved directors and producers who could be considered "believers," and they were often willing to listen to my advice and grant considerable concessions to keep me happy. Even so, there were always some differences with certain "grey" cases, and Air Canada Flight 305 would prove to be one of them.

To the TV producers and book publishers Air Canada Flight 305 was just too good to pass up. It offered a chance to do re-enactments, broaden the area of "local interest" in the Shag Harbour Incident, and add the credibility of a pilot sighting. I would counter these arguments by quoting the *Sesame Street* ditty, "One of these things is not like they other," but they would usually hear none of it. The TV people would counter that all would be made clear with the magic of editing and voice-over. The sighting by Air Canada Flight 305 was part of the "night of the UFOs" with no direct connection to the Shag Harbour Incident. Inevitably, the voice-over script and editing would fail to adequately highlight that distinction when the productions aired.

In all fairness, though, I can say in defence of the TV people that in no case was this editorial difference of opinion ever a purposeful attempt at deception. I remember that during the post-production phase of the US History Channel's feature, *UFO Files: Canada's Roswell*, the director demanded to see and have copies of all of the National Archive of Canada's Flight 305 documents before including it in the final cut. An unsuccessful attempt was made to locate either Guy Charbonneau or Bob Ralph to further vet the case. Further documentation was sought and obtained from the files of NICAP, APRO, and the Condon Committee. Ironically, the truth behind the cause of Air Canada Flight 305's UFO sighting would be found a mere two years after the 2006 broadcast of *Canada's Roswell*.

The year 2008 would prove to be a banner year for gaining further insight into the Shag Harbour Incident. The Air Canada Flight 305 sighting would be identified and lose its status as a UFO sighting, but before the year was over, a

CHAPTER 16: IN THE MIDDLE OF THE AIR

new aircraft encounter would make itself known, and unlike Flight 305 this one would prove relevant and connected to the Shag Harbour Incident and the corresponding flap of UFO sightings. It would all begin with an email from veteran UFO researcher Stanton Friedman.

In the early summer of 2008 Stanton Friedman forwarded an email to me and to fellow Canadian UFO researcher Don Ledger. It was from someone who claimed to have important information regarding the Shag Harbour Incident. The original email address gave no clue as to who its author was or what the information entailed; it turned out to be from Air Canada Flight 305 co-pilot Bob Ralph.

A friend of Bob's had watched *Canada's Roswell* and had made the connection that the UFO sighting being re-enacted over St. Jean, Quebec, was none other than that of his friend, Bob Ralph. He consequently brought it to the former pilot's attention. Ralph's adult son subsequently helped put his father in touch with Stanton Friedman via email; Stanton forwarded his message to Don and me.

Several phone conversations took place over the next few days between myself, Bob Ralph, and Don Ledger. Before long a different interpretation began to emerge of what was responsible for the UFO sighting of Air Canada Flight 305. Like myself, Don Ledger and Bob Ralph had seen photos of glowing noble gases that had been vented high into the atmosphere by test rockets. I had just viewed a very similar photo that I ran across the day before in an attractive, large format coffee-table book about UFOs. Such experiments were a frequent occurrence throughout the 1960s. They were usually done as part of an ongoing study of cosmic rays. The final stage of the rocket boosters would often include an elaborate pinhole camera that would record the subsequent light display given by the irradiated noble gases that were released into the high atmosphere. I did some basic checking in several online databases and sure enough, there was just such a launch on October 4, 1967, from Wallops Island off the coast of Virginia, which would allow the payload to be in the right altitude and position to account for the sighting from Air Canada Flight 305 on the night in question. It seemed to fit like a glove. The explanation was even accepted by Bob Ralph. Don also felt that it was the best explanation, and I know that he had harboured doubts for some time about both Air Canada Flight 305 and the Wilfred Eisnor photo. So decades later a UFO became an IFO.

In UFO research errors tend to get passed down the line again and again. Flight 305 is a good example. Someone like myself accepts the reports and correspondence in the files as generally accurate. The data is used, speculated upon, and interpreted, which typically serves to preserve or even magnify the errors of recording and transcription. Again, I hadn't bothered to vet the data further because it was from official sources and not central to my main topic of interest, the Shag Harbour Incident.

It turns out that there were numerous errors recorded within the Flight 305 files. According to Bob Ralph, even the flight direction was wrong. The Air Canada Vickers Viscount prop-driven aircraft was travelling west to east out of Toronto. What I found most interesting after interviewing Bob Ralph was the details that were not included in the "dry" aviation reports, which concerned themselves with the many flight details such as altitude, true ground speed, etc. One of the most amazing revelations was that the air crew asked air traffic control in Montreal if they knew for sure that New York was still there! The men in the cockpit wondered if what they were seeing was in fact the first flashes of World War III from over the horizon.[2] I guess the pilot's rush to interpret the anomalous phenomenon could be seen in retrospect as Cold War hysteria.

The Air Canada Flight 305 sighting was not a UFO event. It is, however, a unique sliver of Canadian history and a lesson for UFO researchers everywhere. Question everything. Get out of the armchair. Check with the original source or witness whenever possible.

On August 15, 2008, I presented an update on the Shag Harbour Incident in the nearby town of Barrington Passage at their annual UFO festival. I was one of several speakers including Stanton Friedman and Don Ledger. During my presentation I explained the new understanding of Air Canada Flight 305 and how it should no longer be considered part of "the night of the UFOs." Afterwards a few attendees expressed regret about Flight 305 becoming an IFO. I reminded them of how I had always had "mixed feelings" about its previous inclusion. But those who raised the point regretted giving up the value of professional witnesses like pilots, even if Flight 305's observations had no direct connection to the core case in Shag Harbour. They felt that the added credibility of a pilot strengthened the argument that such a wild and busy night of UFO activity had actually occurred back on October 4, 1967.

Those Shag Harbour Incident enthusiasts who were disappointed at the loss of Air Canada Flight 305 from the roll call of "the night of the UFOs" did not have long to wait for a "remedy" for their disappointment. The sudden appearance of that unexpected remedy would again prove that the Shag Harbour Incident has depth, credibility, and staying power. Once again, the

CHAPTER 16: IN THE MIDDLE OF THE AIR

Shag Harbour Incident would become an active case thanks to dramatic new evidence in the form of pilot testimony, and this time that evidence would prove quite closely linked to the UFO case in Shag Harbour. And once again this new chapter in the case would commence with a forwarded email from veteran UFO researcher Stanton Friedman.

Pan Am Flight 160

On September 29, 2008, I received a forwarded message from Stanton that informed me of a retired Pan Am captain who claimed to have important information about the Shag Harbour Incident. The source of that tip was Butch Sigmund Witkowski, who serves as both Chief Investigator and State Section Director for the Mutual UFO Network (MUFON) in the state of Pennsylvania. The message explained that the retired pilot was Ralph Loewinger and that he had met with the MUFON representative on an unrelated matter. Mr. Witkowski, who wears many hats, was doing an investigation for the American specialty cable network FEARnet about hauntings along Bloody Spring Road, located in Pennsylvania's Berks County. Ralph Loewinger owns a summer home on Bloody Spring Road and was interviewed during the FEARnet shoot. After the interview the MUFON rep asked Loewinger if he had had any unexplained UFO sightings during his career as a pilot. Without hesitation the pilot responded with, "One. In October of 1967."

Apparently, the video equipment was set up once again and with the help of one Craig Telesha, Butch Witkowski recorded the pilot's testimony and made sure that the data ended up in MUFON's case management system (CMS) database. After that task was out of the way Butch thought it prudent to contact Friedman in case there was still a local investigator involved, and of course Stanton forwarded everything on to Don Ledger and me because of our ongoing involvement with the Shag Harbour Incident. I wasted no time in contacting Ralph Loewinger by telephone.

When I first phoned the Loewingers at their Pennsylvania summer home the call was answered by Ralph's wife who stated, "He's out in the yard. Just hang on, he really is looking forward to talking to you." When Ralph got to the phone I asked him to basically tell me his story, and I would ask questions afterwards. It felt to me like that moment when a private pilot has the blocks pulled out from the wheels of his small single engine aircraft.

Ralph Loewinger began by explaining that in October 1967 he worked for Pan Am aboard a weekly cargo flight that shuttled between New York and

London. That regular run was designated Pan Am Flight 160. The aircraft was a Boeing 707. At the time, Ralph was a young first officer paired with a more experienced captain by the name of Curt Olsen, who is now deceased. Loewinger recalled departing about the usual time, which he estimated to be about 2300 EST. The flight was uneventful from takeoff until at least half-way across the waters of the Gulf of Maine. Ralph guessed that would put the aircraft somewhere around sixty to ninety minutes into their scheduled flight. Their altitude would be somewhere between 29,000 to 33,000 feet and slowly climbing. The freighter's airspeed would be in the range of 480 knots. Visibility was unlimited. The atmosphere was completely transparent. The moon had already set. Ralph could discern the lights of fishing boats that were at least fifty miles or more in the distance.[3]

At a point estimated by Loewinger to be about one hundred miles out from the Shag Harbour area, the crew noticed a set of four to six lights ahead of their flight position. The lights were in a stacked formation and appeared to be banking to the left but were slowly drifting to the right, relative to the nose of Flight 160. The formation of lights also seemed to be slowly descending and settling into the same altitude as the cargo heavy 707. Ralph Loewinger remembered initially thinking that it must be a plane showing all lights. However, that assumption made even less sense when a new light came on that shone with an intensity beyond that of any conventional aircraft known to the pilot. It was also apparent that the Pan Am jet was getting closer to the anomalous light formation.[4]

Olsen called Boston and asked if they were showing any traffic near them. Boston did not show anything near Pan Am Flight 160 except for a Strategic Air Command (SAC) refuelling mission forty miles away, and that was behind their position. Captain Olsen called Boston a second time and asked them to check again. Neither the plane's onboard radar nor the land-based system in Boston "painted" anything near Pan Am Flight 160. It was apparent that 160 was still closing on the strange set of lights. There was a brief discussion in the cockpit about coming out of auto pilot "just in case." Ralph Loewinger said that he remembered leaning on the yoke ready for Curt Olsen's decision when suddenly the UFO drifted to the right of the jet's nose and then shot away at high speed. The whole incident spanned less than six minutes. The crew was stunned by the rapid acceleration manoeuvre. Boston radioed back asking if they wanted to file a UFO report, but Captain Olsen decided against it.[5]

As soon as Ralph Loewinger finished his initial telling of the story I asked him in which direction the UFO had headed when it left the area near Pan Am

CHAPTER 16: IN THE MIDDLE OF THE AIR

Flight 160. His response was simply, "Up and away. Like nothing that I had ever seen." My next question was about his certainty of the date. He admitted that it was "soft." It could have been the third, fourth, or fifth of October. He clearly remembered hearing media reports about the crash of a UFO into Shag Harbour when he returned from overseas. It had to be the same week. Ralph then told me that in his winter home in Florida there was a copy of his flight log. He would be there in three weeks.

Three weeks later we had our second conversation. It turned out that Pan Am Flight 160, a Boeing 707 (300-C) with tail number 446, had been scheduled to fly from JFK New York to London Heathrow on October 2, 1967, at 2200 EST. The actual block time departure—when the blocks were pulled away from the wheels of the aircraft—was recorded as 0338 GMT October 3, 1967. So, some forty-eight hours before the locals in Shag Harbour saw a sixty-foot set of flashing lights plunge into the waters of The Sound, a Pan Am commercial cargo jet would play chicken with a very similar set of mysterious lights at 33,000 feet in the same area. The men who were crowded together in the cockpit of Flight 160 had an unobstructed, lengthy view of the UFO. And as I would soon discover, some of the crew were treated to a few extra details.

At the conclusion of my second conversation with Ralph Loewinger he offered me a few possible phone numbers for Michael Littlepage, who served as the flight engineer on board the October 2, 1967 flight of Pan Am 160. Ralph encouraged me to make the call. As he put it, "Michael is a little younger and always had a great memory. Besides, he wasn't as busy as me and Curt were at the time of the incident, and I believe that he managed to get a better look at the lights. You should call him." It turned out to be great advice.

The list of phone numbers for Michael Littlepage spanned North America from the Caribbean to the Colorado Rockies. My persistence eventually got me connected with a feeble cell phone signal that dropped out and died just as Michael Littlepage was descending a peak on a Colorado highway. Eventually, he arrived at a location with a dependable land line, and I was treated to a truly "electric" interview as the former flight engineer of Pan Am Flight 160 put me "in the cockpit."

Michael Littlepage agreed with most of the facts as presented in my earlier interviews with Ralph Loewinger; however, wherever the former First Officer gave a range of details, such as four to six lights, Littlepage would state that it was definitely just four lights. Four to six minutes was described as about five minutes. Though both men agreed on many key details of the UFO sighting, there were two major differences between their respective stories.

The first was that former flight engineer Michael Littlepage remembered that there was a second flight crew on board Pan Am Flight 160 that was being ferried back to London.[6] Littlepage went in back of the aircraft and woke the sleeping men who all came forward and crowded into the 707's cockpit to take in the spectacle. That put no less than six professional witnesses in the "best seats in the house." In a third interview with Ralph Loewinger he did recall the second flight crew mentioned by Michael Littlepage and was surprised that that fact had slipped his memory. In fact he later remembered details that would aid in the search for the additional witnesses.

Another discrepancy, which is probably wholly attributable to the fact that Littlepage was not directly involved with the piloting of the aircraft and therefore was able to get out of his seat during the incident, is his much more detailed description of the UFO itself. At times during the spectacle he cupped his hands to the airplane's windshield in an attempt to discern whatever airframe features he could. In fact, at the point when the 707 was within its closest proximity to the UFO, the flight engineer did discern something most revealing about the nature of the anomalous lights. And he remains adamant about that on the spot interpretation over forty years later. Michael Littlepage believes that the four amber hued lights, which he and Ralph Loewinger described as, "not giving off any real illumination," were in fact internal lighting. He could discern no details, but he is convinced that he could see into the UFO. Littlepage estimates that at that point the 707 was a mere half mile behind the UFO and flying at the same altitude and heading, that is, in exactly the same direction.[7] That distance is much too close for safety or comfort but proved a bonus situation for chance observation.

That brings me to the second big difference between Ralph Loewinger's previous interviews and the testimony of Michael Littlepage. In a word, fear. There was fear in the cockpit. Not panic or dread but a dependable, healthy, and logically derived at state of mind, compartmentalized and being employed in that cool reserved way that seems a special skill honed by well trained pilots. They were too damn close to the UFO. There was fear in the cockpit and Michael Littlepage wasn't afraid to admit it. He also wasn't afraid to voice his concerns to the outwardly cool Captain Curt Olsen. Several times Michael Littlepage urged the captain to consider coming out of autopilot. What if the UFO slowed further or pulled an unexpected manoeuvre or shed a piece of debris? It would be game over for Flight 160. They all knew it.

After five minutes elapsed and the distance between the 707 and the UFO continued to shorten Captain Curt Olsen decided to act. Just as he grabbed the

CHAPTER 16: IN THE MIDDLE OF THE AIR

yoke and prepared to give the order to come out of autopilot, the UFO began to rapidly pull away from the aircraft. When it reached about three miles out it drifted to the right of the nose and shot upwards at a forty-five degree angle and accelerated at such a pace that Michael Littlepage estimates it was likely up and out of the atmosphere within ten seconds.[8]

The extra flight crew that had been disturbed from their sleep stayed awake all night. The cockpit discussed the UFO sighting all the way across the Atlantic to London. A few days later, when stories of the Shag Harbour Incident were heard around the globe, they figured that they had had a "sneak preview." None of the flight crew aboard Pan Am Flight 160 would witness another UFO event throughout their lengthy careers. But then again, none of them needed to. Seeing is believing.

It is unfortunate that Curt Olsen decided against an official UFO report. It is, however, most fortunate that over forty-one years later the actual names of Curt Olsen, Ralph Loewinger, and Michael Littlepage can be used to tell these former airmen's amazing adventure. During the telephone interviews I could hear the awe and apprehension in the voices of the two airmen as they recounted their mysterious UFO encounter of so long ago. It was so reminiscent of the tone I'd heard back in 1993 when first interviewing the eyewitnesses to the October 4, 1967 UFO crash in Shag Harbour. And let's not forget that that UFO incident played out less than forty-eight hours later. Was it the same craft? Could it have been the second UFO claimed to be lying two days later on the seabed off of Shelburne County's Government Point?

The unique emotional inflection that I have heard, over the years, in the voices of so many UFO eyewitnesses may not constitute hard evidence, but I have come to expect its familiar cadence when looking into any solid UFO case that holds up under close scrutiny. And for me it makes all the nuisance and pitfalls of volunteer civilian UFO research worthwhile. There is no better payday.

The story of Pan Am Flight 160 brings this update on the Shag Harbour Incident to a close. Collectively the Shag Harbour Incident and the plethora of other UFO events have tantalized, teased, and woven themselves into the fabric and lives of many communities in Atlantic Canada. But how wide a net should we cast in our quest for meaning and connection? For some reason I've always considered the quest "an indulgence," one that I had little time for. However, my latest research partner and co-author, Graham Simms, has proven much more difficult to ignore or squelch. As a result of his questions and perspective I feel that my appreciation of the UFO phenomenon has been enriched and reinvigorated.

UFOs may indeed be "real"; they are also relevant. For those whose lives have been touched by this enduring phenomenon, UFOs can prove most demanding but also worthy of our attention.

CHAPTER 16: IN THE MIDDLE OF THE AIR

Chapter 16 Endnotes

1. NRC UFO file, N67-403, RG 77.
2. Author's notes from July 9, 2008 telephone interview with Bob Ralph, retired co-pilot of Air Canada Flight 305.
3. Signed witness statement of Ralph Lowinger, retired co-pilot of Pan Am Flight 160 regarding a UFO encounter on October 6, 1967, while flying over the Gulf of Maine.
4. Ibid.
5. Ibid.
6. Author's notes from telephone interview with Michael Littlepage, retired flight engineer for Pan Am Flight 160.
7. Ibid.
8. Ibid.

Reflections
Chris Styles

"In these matters the only certainty is that nothing is certain."
– Pliny the Elder (23–79 AD)

"Doubt is not a pleasant condition, but certainty is absurd."
– Voltaire

For more than sixty years UFOs have mystified and sometimes tormented countless eyewitnesses and experiencers. Science has been allowed by governments and the public at large to deny the questions and issues presented by the UFO phenomenon. And yet many governments continue to stockpile the evidence, often to clutch it tightly for reasons of "national security" that could be more accurately thought of as reasons of "national insecurity." The result is an information vacuum that demands to be filled, and there is a willing group of hoaxers, charlatans, con men, and debunkers who labour and prosper as they attempt to satisfy the public's need to know. In the information age it is open season on believers and doubters alike, and we are all the losers in this cruel game of semantics and pseudo logic.

In spite of this bleak overview I see both hope and light. I believe that things could change rapidly if sufficient numbers of us began to ask the right questions and considered all of the possible answers including the likelihood of multiple and seemingly contradictory conclusions.

A true comprehension of the UFO phenomenon may prove to be like an aesthetic truth (e.g., God mad man in his own image; man made God in his own image) in which the opposite interpretation may prove an equally valid consideration. That kind of duality is always disappointing if not abhorrent to our Western outlook. So what are some of the "right questions"?

A list of some essential problems that must be tackled to effectively approach the UFO phenomenon should include:
1. Would we even recognize alien "contact" if it were not painful or obvious?

2. How would such an event be chronicled prior to the information age?

3. Why does science avoid such an issue of public concern? How do they get away with it, especially given the fact that such a large amount of research is publicly funded? In contrast, a police officer cannot refuse to investigate the purported crash of a mysterious object. An air traffic controller cannot ignore an unidentified target in his controlled air space.

4. Why do the majority of mythologists and social scientists ignore the UFO phenomenon? Are they blind to the obvious physical and psychic duality of this enduring mystery and the implications that it holds for their fields? Men such as psychoanalyst Carl Jung, mythologist Joseph Campbell, and psychiatrist John Mack were exceptions.

5. What are the feasible possibilities of other life systems that do not involve organic chemistry, DNA, or even matter? (It is interesting to note the wide-ranging possibilities and definitions considered by NASA's "Origins Program." Shouldn't consideration of such possibilities be mirrored in UFO research?)

6. My last point is not a question but an observation on ourselves and a necessary area for change. We need to shed the belief that if something can be done it will be done—somewhere, sometime, by someone. Mankind is just not that dutiful or ambitious. Some examples would include the fact that there has not been a manned lunar mission in decades, and no one is planning a double supersonic transportation system to replace the loss of Concord service. And consider that no one in the modern world could get backing for a space mission or construction project that would take a century or more to complete. Today humanity just doesn't have the mindset for endeavours that lack immediate payoff. In the 1500s stunning cathedrals were built that sometimes took two hundred years to complete. The individuals who designed them and commenced the work knew that they would not live to see the fruition of their efforts. There are no plans to send a manned mission to the outer solar system or a generational ship to a nearby star system. NASA has shelved plans to produce a booster to replace the loss of the space shuttle. All of the aforementioned could be accomplished with existing technology, but nothing is being done. And no government is tackling the UFO problem with the resources that it requires and deserves. UFOs are just not an issue that wins votes. They only become important to those who experience their unscheduled, sporadic acquaintance.

It may seem moot to point out that there are probably as many divergent opinions and ideas about UFOs as there are people to consider them, but I believe that eventually all sides will forced into fundamental change. The strength of those who resist the evidence will be eroded away when science allows itself to truly grapple with the data. Surely behaviourists will have to concede that not every eyewitness, police officer, airline pilot, and astronomer who ever witnessed a UFO is mistaken.

Several scientists have suggested, over the years, that UFO advocates should call attention to a single case, so strong that it could stand up to scientific scrutiny and be established as a real extraordinary event. I am not sure that that is the best approach, but I am comfortable with it. I am not sure what science is supposed to conclude or do next with the declared extraordinary event. However, I believe that the Shag Harbour Incident could fit the bill. I don't believe that it is the only possible candidate, but it is probably one of the safest potential UFO cases that could be nominated for such consideration. Here's why.

Something happened on the night of October 4, 1967. The eyewitnesses know this. The three RCMP officers and the other authorities who were there and who saw the UFO on the water know this. Many UFO skeptics, including the late debunker Phillip Klass, have quietly conceded to me that something extraordinary happened on that odd fall night so many years ago. The remaining eyewitnesses have moved on with their lives as best they could. Most of the skeptics have chosen to ignore the challenging UFO cases like Shag Harbour. Most of the active and serious UFO community busies itself with the latest point of origin theory or research gossip. And yet, the Shag Harbour Incident remains a mystery. It has steadily gained notoriety and consideration since I began to investigate the case back in 1992. The Shag Harbour Incident has refused to evaporate. No one has recanted their essential testimony. New witnesses and interpretations have appeared and enhanced our understanding of the case.

The incident has even secured its place as a part of Canadian history. The Library and Archives Canada website has an entry on the Shag Harbour Incident (lac-bac.gc.ca/ufo/002029-1500.01-e.html) where visitors can also see an archived UFO Report. Significantly, the principal entry says, "Both the RCMP and locals had rushed to the shore of the harbour, but what they encountered there was far from a conventional aircraft." That page concludes with the further determination that, "The Department of National Defence has identified this sighting as unsolved."

Those statements are consistent, several decades later, with the initial impressions of the investigating agencies. Perhaps most notable is the third paragraph in a DND memorandum that has been preserved at the Library and

Archives and at DND's Directorate of History. It reads, "The Rescue Coordination Centre conducted a preliminary investigation and discounted the possibilities that the sighting was produced by an aircraft, flares, floats or any other known objects." This why I continue to point out that the Shag Harbour incident remains the only UFO crash scenario that is supported in that interpretation, by government documents, that are freely available and without controversy as to their origin or authenticity. To my mind, the Shag Harbour Incident remains one of the most compelling arguments for acceptance of UFO reality.

Chris Styles
April 2013

Reflections
Graham Simms

The pursuit of the UFO phenomenon is both relevant and important in several ways. On the practical side, gaining access to and understanding of the advanced technology of these essentially free-energy devices, which I believe have been hoarded by the military and private contractors, will certainly help our environmental and energy crises. On a more profound level, the unfolding of our understanding of the UFO phenomenon will expand our scientific and spiritual knowledge of ourselves, of life, and of the universe. We will arrive at a greater knowledge of who we are individually and collectively, that we are part of something bigger than ourselves. This brings meaning and even compassion to our lives, which in turn instigate growth toward a greater society. This is an incredibly practical side effect of exploring the UFO phenomenon.

When we come from the anthropocentric perspective that we on Earth are the only intelligent life in the universe, an acceptance of the existence of the UFO phenomenon evolves our view to one where we see that intelligent life in the universe is actually flourishing. Further, acceptance that UFOs do indeed exist can bring us to the view that while we are not alone in the universe, life is rare and precious. By contrast, contemporary culture is destructive and takes life for granted. This is reminiscent of the classic 1951 film *The Day the Earth Stood Still*, in which a UFO lands in America, and its occupants inform people that our planet is one of only a handful in this galaxy supporting intelligent life; therefore, we will not be allowed to destroy the ecosystem. Our spiritual development has not kept pace with our rapid development of technology, so we misuse technology, threatening our very survival.

Behind the secrecy and denial of UFOs, the truth is that they exist, and I believe that we can handle the truth. UFOs are the crack through which the light will shine that will illuminate our true past, that is, earth's historical connection to the rest of space and beings from other worlds. I believe that we have, in fact, evolved with the help of ETs. Understanding that connection will also illuminate our present situation on Earth and frame our future as we explore this solar system and the rest of space. Disciplines like archaeology, which are based in this anthropocentric view, will expand and benefit from the revelation of intelligent life in the universe, especially if there are historic artifacts to be found within our solar system.

Acknowledging the ET presence is part of the growth of humanity. That acknowledgement and the associated spiritual and historical revelations are important and relevant to everyday life and to working toward creating a more enlightened society. In repositioning ourselves from the lonesome pinnacle of life in the universe, an individual and collective "ego death" will affect our view of the universe and infuse it with richness and awe. Hopefully it will advance our spiritual growth.

Chapter 9 discussed the local folklore concept of forerunners. The Shag Harbour Incident can be seen as a forerunner, an early forerunner to some future event. Does this forerunner foretell a happy event, or predict death? I suspect that if humanity can avoid the trajectory of death we have been on, the foretold future event will be contact en masse. I believe that in the face of possible Cold War annihilation, humanity released a psychological and spiritual cry for help. The universe's response to this plea was the subsequent increase in UFO activity seen in Nova Scotia and around the world. UFO sightings, crashes, and alien encounters are both literal and symbolic representations of contact with our higher selves. As with the treasure hunt at Oak Island, Nova Scotia, we are like a poor man who does not know that there is a great treasure directly under his own house. We just need to know it is there, then to decide to look and dig a little to find it. There are glimmers in the darkness. There is a much richer, greater reality available for us to take possession of. To accept this greater reality and the accompanying greater levels of consciousness is necessary to bring about the return of the golden age of humanity on earth. It is our birthright, and it already exists—we just need to acknowledge it.

What we call paranormal is normal, just as the supernatural is actually natural. It is a paranormal universe. Religion is paranormal. The concept of God can be called paranormal. Supernatural beings are common currency in the universe according to most world views. The argument of the materialistic world view versus the spiritual and the supernatural world view is overly simplistic and dualistic. These concepts transcend that duality, so the argument of one versus the other is moot or at least a waste of time. The physical, material world and the spiritual world of consciousness cannot in reality be separated by hard lines. They are ultimately one. Invisible lines in the form of words and concepts can only separate the one reality in our personal world views. And when that happens we are poorer for it.

REFLECTIONS

Just as several governments around the world have begun a trend to declassify UFO reports, the Catholic Church has recently opened up about their position on the matter of intelligent alien life. The Director of the Vatican's Observatory Fr. Jose Gabriel Funes, in an interview titled "The Alien is my Brother" with the official Vatican daily newspaper L'Osservatore Romano, said there is no contradiction between Catholic faith and belief in aliens. Monsignor Corrado Balducci, a long-time exorcist with the Archdiocese in Rome often spoke about the likelihood of extraterrestrial life, and that it was not demonic in nature. Similarly, it would be beneficial to the general public for western governments to release military witnesses from their oaths of secrecy, and to open up about their experience and knowledge of UFOs and intelligent alien life on earth and in the rest of the universe.

I believe the Unidentified Flying Objects witnessed at Shag Harbour and Shelburne were known to the US military. They knew what it was. They had been tracking this sort of activity for years, in space, in the sky, and underwater. I agree with retired *Chronicle-Herald* reporter Ray MacLeod that the US military acted as if they knew what it was that crashed. They were on the scene instantly, and they knew what to do, as if they had done it before. As MacLeod said to me, you don't stop a search like this, where something was known to enter the water, unless you know what it was or at least what happened to it. To me it is clear that the US military knew what it was and where it went. But I disagree that they knew what it was because it was one of their own advanced test craft. They knew what it was because they tracked it just as they had been tracking UFO activity in this area and around the world. This was an identified object. It was a crashed alien craft that was then repaired by another alien craft underwater, then both of them took off. This reality would be covered up, just as it always had been. I believe that it is possible that the powerful NORAD early warning system radar, emanating from the Pinetree Line at CFS Barrington in Baccaro, interfered with the UFOs in some way, disabling them.

What about hard evidence? Many witnesses stated that the bottom of the UFO seen coming down near Shag Harbour was ablaze, the bottom side of the disk radiating white and orange like metal in a forge. When it submerged itself in the harbour, the burning hot craft would likely have scorched and fused the sand or rocks on the bottom. This is almost certainly responsible for the indentations which BIO and David Cvet have identified in their investigations of the area just outside the last known location of the Shag Harbour UFO. Scientific analysis may be able to confirm if the depressions were made from high heat, or to provide more information about them. Another dive, this time to retrieve samples for this purpose is planned by David Cvet to take place just after this book goes to print. Could there be any other hard evidence?

The US military dominated the Canadian military, who sheepishly followed their lead when it came to the top secret aspects of the Shag Harbour and Shelburne incidents in which they needed Canadian cooperation. And otherwise the Americans kept the Canadian military out of the loop. But we shouldn't forget that the purported crashed UFO artifacts, film of the UFOs and aliens, "items of extreme interest" from the Shag Harbour and Shelburne efforts were taken directly to the Maritime headquarters of the Defence Research Board in Dartmouth. Consequently, we know the Canadian military scientific research establishment has continued to hide evidence of UFOs in relation to the Shag Harbour Incident and probably UFO reality beyond that. Although due to the military hierarchy it is possible that the American forces absconded with the evidence in this case. Certainly that is the case in regard to the smouldering artifact that lighthouse keeper Irving Banks found on the shores of Bon Portage (also known as Outer Island, one of the closest islands south-west of Shag Harbour) on October 5-6th, which he handed over to high ranking US Navy brass on the inexplicable suggestion of the Canadian Coast Guard. None of this hard evidence has ever been seen again.

It seems that the growth of humanity has been stunted somewhere along the line, cut off from the knowledge of truth. Has our evolution been held back by our own human nature or by overarching conspiracies? The good news is that if we have been deliberately held back, once we are released from the grips of the controllers, from ignorance, we can move forward. Despite the darkness, in fact because of it, there is hope.

I would like to see a new equivalent to the disbanded RCAF UFO Air Desk of the 1960s—a scientific group with academic and military affiliations devoted to studying UFOs and other anomalous paranormal phenomena. An elite and well funded group somewhat like that in the UK television drama *Torchwood*, one that works with yet is not beholden to government, police, or the United Nations. Except this would not be a covert group but would provide the fruits of their research to the public.

Consider the UFO phenomenon as a litmus test which measures our resistance to change. A test which measures our resistance to a more vast reality. Like 'The Emperor Has No Clothes', our fear of going against culturally conditioned norms, our fear of the unknown, and our fear of shattering our paradigms may unconsciously overwhelm our acceptance of reality as it actually is. Do we put down those who go against the grain, and do we blindly accept consensus as truth? If so, is it not a sign of cultural immaturity, and if we tolerate this is it not a sign that we are a society as oppressed as any in the past?

How we see and understand ourselves and our relationships with people, nations, problem-solving, science, and the universe are incomplete; we require a shift in thinking and actions in the direction of honesty, freedom, and completeness.

Graham Simms
April 2013

Epilogue: The Research Continues
David M. Cvet

Shag Harbour Rip Dive Report – July 20, 2009

The events and evidence surrounding the Shag Harbour Incident of October 1967 are compelling, resulting in a number of individuals, myself included, who actively continue research into the incident in the hope of uncovering more evidence and facts in support of this extraordinary event. In this spirit, I organized a dive expedition to the area known locally as the "Shag Harbour Rip," hoping to contribute to the ever growing body of evidence that supports the anomalous nature of the Shag Harbour Incident.

The purpose of the dive expedition was twofold:

1. to gather intelligence on the water, seabed, and diving conditions southwest of Outer Island in the Shag Harbour Rip

2. to attempt to qualify the anomalous sonar targets (i.e., readings) obtained by the ship *Navicula* during a bottom survey in 1988, which were located at 43 degrees 26 minutes 10 seconds N by 65 degrees 46 minutes 15 seconds W and initially interpreted and charted as "may not be boulders."

The targets were described as four depressions or mounds on the seabed, which were differentiated enough from the surrounding seabed to cause areas of high contrast on the sonar record. The reason for the interest in these sonar targets is that they reside on or near what may have been the path on which the "dark object" had vectored out of Shag Harbour on the evening of October 4, 1967, before purportedly altering course and turning northward, travelling toward Shelburne.

The dive was planned for 2:00 pm Monday, July 20, 2009, at the point of low tide during slack tide, thus reducing the depth of the dive and thereby increasing bottom time. The dive profile was based on the expectation that the bottom would be approximately 110 to 120 feet in depth. Bottom time at that depth, using standard dive tanks, allowed for ten minutes. We felt that the objectives of this preliminary dive could be satisfied within the allowed timeframe.

The team consisted of myself as lead diver, Laurie McGowan as underwater photographer, diver Freeland Reynolds, who stayed on the surface to assist and to handle radio communications, and videographer Rick Davis. The trip to the dive site onboard a 45-foot lobster boat piloted by Vincent Goreham took about thirty minutes. Upon arrival at the coordinates of the alleged anomalous sonar targets, we deployed a marker buoy. The weather was perfect for diving: a clear sky, calm waters (with rollers of approximately one metre), a slight breeze, and a surface temperature of 22°C.

Laurie and I entered the water up current from the marker and descended. To our surprise, the water was clouded with a greenish, brownish suspension that only allowed for two metres of visibility. However, the depth turned out to be only seventy to eighty feet, which allowed for twenty to thirty minutes of bottom time as opposed to the anticipated ten minutes.

Unfortunately, visibility did not improve at the bottom. There was a noticeable current, which took us toward the area marked by the surface buoy. The bottom temperature was 15°C. The ambient light was lower than expected due to the heavy suspension in the water, which we described as "pea soup."

Using compasses, we proceeded toward the marker buoy. The bottom was composed of random pebbles, primarily round or ellipsoid. Most were four to twenty centimetres in size. The bottom was also strewn with irregular rocks. Silt was evident between the rocks; it was easily stirred up by fin action. The bottom was populated by a variety of flora and fauna growing on or between the rocks. Scallops and lobsters were abundant. We were swimming literally inches off of the bottom, as the visibility was extremely poor and depth perception was difficult at best.

Enroute toward the marker, Laurie and I came across what appeared to be a slight depression. It was easily noticed because it was obviously different from its surroundings. The depression was gentle and appeared to be about fifteen to twenty feet in diameter. The bottom of the depression was covered in uniform pebbles that were four to six centimetres in size. This contrasted sharply with the surrounding area. We also observed that there was no flora or fauna in the depression. It was as if it had been cleared of debris and vegetation. After a few minutes exploring the depression, we continued toward the marker and soon discovered a second, similar depression that shared all of the same attributes as the first.

It is possible that the sonar on the *Navicula* detected these depressions. It is possible that we had in fact discovered two of the four sonar anomalies detected at the time of the 1988 survey. Due to the poor visibility and a lack of remaining bottom time we did not seek out the other two depressions. We surfaced and boarded the boat.

While the poor visibility of the water made our search for the anomalous sonar targets extremely challenging, we consider the dive a success. We gathered data on bathymetry, bottom conditions, and dive parameters. Such knowledge will prove useful in planning any future expeditions to the site. The discovery of the depressions, which may or may not be responsible for the original sonar returns, was a bonus. The sharp contrast of their inconsistent features is compelling and deserves further exploration and examination.

No doubt the poor visibility was the result of heavy rain over Nova Scotia throughout June and July. The rains introduced huge amounts of sediment and particulate that had remained in suspension. If a repeat dive were to happen in the future, I would suggest that it take place in the fall or winter, with the hope that the water would be much clearer.

The best approach would be to have highly sensitive equipment such as a sub-bottom profiler, multi-scan sonar, and a magnetometer to more accurately survey and confirm the targets prior to sending a diver down. A diver could then descend to inspect, observe, and procure samples. This would confirm whether the depressions do indeed account for the sonar returns of the 1988 *Navicula* cruise.

Given the unusual lack of flora on the seabed within the depression compared to the profusion of flora in the surrounding areas, it's hard not to at least consider a causal link to the UFO of the Shag Harbour Incident. It might prove useful to have dosimeters and other sensors to help determine if there are any other unusual characteristics within the depressions. Samples would also be useful, as would an excavation.

It is our desire to organize another expedition in which we would hope to confirm that the depressions we discovered are in fact one and the same as the anomalous sonar targets detected by the *Navicula* cruise of 1988. The purpose of the follow-up mission would be to collect sufficient measurements, data, and samples to ascertain the mechanism of origin for such a seabed feature, whether natural, anthropomorphic, or truly anomalous.

Acknowledgements
Chris Styles

The authors wish to express their sincere gratitude to the hundreds of people who contributed their stories and observations regarding the Shag Harbour Incident and the many other UFO sightings mentioned in this book.

We must acknowledge the efforts of those groups and individuals who helped advance the Shag Harbour case through the early years of its re-investigation: the Mutual UFO Network for publishing papers on the Shag Harbour Incident and other UFO sightings of southwestern Nova Scotia; the Fund for UFO Research for its financial support that helped get the case "out of the blocks"; Antonio Huneeus for writing articles in international publications such as *Borderland* and *FATE*; Kevin Randal for including the Shag Harbour Incident in his book *The Randle Report: UFOs in the '90s*. Kudos should also go out to those filmmakers who believed enough to produce quality feature documentaries. A short list would include Michael MacDonald (*The Shag Harbour Incident*), The History Channel's *Canada's Roswell* and *Incident at Shag Harbour* by Paul MacRae and Chris Grant. Many segmented treatments were broadcast within productions such as Paramount Television's syndicated show *Sightings*, A&E's *UFOs 2, Have We Been Visited?*, Paul Kimball's *Top 10 UFO Cases*, and numerous radio and podcast treatments including the *Hieronimus & Company: 21st Century Radio* and Whitley Strieber's *Dreamland*.

Specials thanks should go to Cindy Nickerson and the many dedicated volunteers of the Shag Harbour Incident Society who tirelessly promote the case, and the eyewitnesses like Laurie (Dicky) Wickens, Norm Smith, and David Kendricks who have helped spread the word.

Many people have contributed to the advancement of this case. It would not enjoy the recognition it enjoys without the contributions of people like Don Ledger, Jan Aldrich, and veteran UFO researcher / nuclear physicist Stanton Friedman.

A list of those who have helped over the years would have to include Marsha Coffey, the late RCN Commander Rex Guy, Captain Ralph Lowinger, Michael Littlepage, David Cvet, Gordon Fader, Bob Miller, Anette Tol, Ervin Banks, Bob MacDonald, Eugene Frisson, Walt Andrus, and Michael Strainic.

A very special thanks to those whose names might be missing by oversight and those whose names must remain unknown. Thank you for your stories, insights, encouragement, and criticisms.

Acknowledgements
Graham Simms

For her love, support, and confidence in me and this book, primary thanks to Janet Ainslie (Amy) Stewart.

For their help in the production of this book, thanks to the editor Marianne Ward, Ron Such, Chris Dean, Sean MacInnis,, David Cvet, George Simms, Nicola Parker, Bob Stevens, and Wayne Outhouse. Also Ray McLeod and Eugenia Macer-Story.

For their inspiration and help in understanding the nature of these phenomenon, thanks to the staff and directors from the Program for Extraordinary Experience Research (P.E.E.R.) and the John E. Mack Institute, especially John Mack, Dominique Callimanopulos, Leslie Hansen, Roberta Colasanti, Audrey O'Shaughnessy, Karen Wesolowski, Will Bueché, and Laurance Rockefeller; also Dan Winter, Terrence McKenna, Jeffery Hinchey, Dr. Richard Boylan, Paola Harris, Paul Kimball and Nick Redfern.

I also wish to thank my family, especially my parents, Dorothy and George Simms; my aunts, Elizabeth Simms and Lucy Broman; my sisters, Suzanne Langlais and Jordan MacIntyre; and my nephews, August, Malcom, and Duncan.

For their friendship and belief, thanks to Cathy Jones, Eleanor Jones-Hannon, Brad and Andrew Barr, Albert Wing, Hunter Toran, Liam Murphy, Adam Short, Paul Singh, Tariq Al-Omari, David Adekayode, John Huszagh, Matthew Webb, Onice Lopez, Kathryn Heckman, Navjeet Kaur Mackie, Genie Brighton and Anna Allocco.

Also thanks to Gesar Mukpo and the teachers of the Shambhala, Kagyu, and Nyingma traditions.

The Shag Harbour Incident remains an open and active UFO case. The search for even more hard evidence continues. If you had any involvement in this or other significant UFO cases, whether on the civilian, military, or government side, or if you know of anyone else involved, please contact the authors or publisher.

shagharbour@hotmail.com
grahamsimms22@hotmail.com
info@arcadiahousepub.com

AH Publishing
PO Box 36130 Spring Garden Road
Halifax, Nova Scotia, Canada
B3J 3S9

Chris Styles is an independent UFO researcher, who was the first to reinvestigate the Shag Harbour Incident since the demise of the original military and civilian effort. In 1995 he directed an inconclusive underwater search for physical evidence in the area. He has presented his theories and findings at various international UFO symposia. He has been featured both on camera and as a technical advisor in several feature UFO documentaries. In 2001 he co-authored, "Dark Object," a mass market paperback, with fellow UFO researcher Don Ledger. Styles continues to reexamine the Shag Harbour Incident and other classic UFO cases in Atlantic Canada with the hope of furthering our understanding of the UFO phenomena.

Graham Simms is a native Nova Scotian who has worked in print-media and journalism for twenty years. In 1996 he worked for Dr. John Mack's Program for Extraordinary Experience Research (PEER) at the Centre for Psychology and Social Change in Cambridge. He started Arcadia House Publishing in 2010.

Appendix

According to Steven Greer, who founded the Center for the Study of Extraterrestrial Intelligence (CSETI) and The Disclosure Project, which has brought the testimony of witnesses involved in the UFO cover-up to public light, there are five classifications to be assigned to close encounters.

CE-1: Close encounter of the first kind, a sighting of an extraterrestrial spacecraft within 500 feet.
CE-2: Close encounter of the second kind, which involves trace evidence of a landing or a radar lock-on.
CE-3: Close encounter of the third kind, the sighting of a life form, usually in association with a spacecraft.
CE-4: Close encounter of the fourth kind, which involves interaction with extraterrestrial (ET) beings, usually aboard a spacecraft.
CE-5: Close encounter of the fifth kind, produced through the conscious, voluntary, and proactive human-initiated or cooperative communication in a meeting with extraterrestrial biological entities and/or their spacecraft. CE-5 encounters are described as joint, bilateral contact events instead of unilateral contact events.

See more at siriusdisclosure.com/ce-5-initiative/materials/glossary-of-terms/

References

Bentley, David. 1967. "Shelburne UFO Comes Under Attack." *Halifax Chronicle-Herald*, October 18.

Birdsall, Graham W. (dir.). 2001. The Secret NASA Transmissions: "The Smoking Gun." Quest Publications International.

Bryan, C.D.B. 1995. Close Encounters of the Fourth Kind: A Reporter's Notebook on Alien Abduction, UFOs, and the Conference at M.I.T.. New York: Penguin.

Campagna, Palmiro. 2010. The UFO Files: The Canadian Connection Exposed. Toronto: Dundurn Group Ltd.

CBC News online. March 7, 2013. "Canadian government no longer investigating UFOs." <cbc.ca/news/canada/nova-scotia/story/2013/03/07/ns-ufo-investigation.html>.

Chiten, Laurel (dir.). 2003. *Touched*. Blind Dog Films.

Cleaver, A.V. 1957. "'Electro-Gravitics': What It Is—or Might Be." *Journal of British Interplanetary Society* 16 (2).

Coffey, Maurice. 1971. *Search Concepts 1971*. Ottawa: Department of National Defence.

Colombo, John Robert. 2004. *True Canadian UFO Stories*. Toronto: Prospero Books.

Condon, Edward U. 1969. Scientific Study of Unidentified Flying Objects. New York: Bantam.

Creighton, Helen. 1976. *Folklore of Lunenburg County, NS*. Ottawa: McGraw-Hill Ryerson Limited.

———. 1957. *Bluenose Ghosts*. Toronto: Ryerson Press.

Curtis, T. 1985. "Court Enters Twilight Zone and 3 Claim Attack by UFO." *The Oregonian*, September 17.

Dawson, William F. 1968. "UFO Down Under?" *FATE*, February.

Dershowitz, Allan. 1995. "Defining Academic Freedom." *The Harvard Crimson*, June 30.

Devereux, Paul. 1982. *Earth Lights: Towards an Understanding of the Unidentified Flying Objects Enigma*. Winnipeg: Turnstone Press.

Dolan, Richard. 2011. "A Breakaway Civilization: What It Is, and What It

Means for Us." At <afterdisclosure.com/2011/04/breakaway.html>. April.

Edwards, Frank. 1966. Flying Saucers: Serious Business. New York: Lyle Stuart.

Eldridge, Vic. 1967a. "Military Wants UFOs Reported." *Yarmouth Light Herald*, November 2.

———. 1967b. "Nothing Found In Search for Shag Harbor Mystery Object." *Yarmouth Vanguard*, October 12.

Fairfax, John. 1972. Britannia: Rowing Alone Across the Atlantic. New York: Simon & Schuster.

French, Richard. 2013. Citizen Hearing on Disclosure, April 29 to May 3, 2013. National Press Club in Washington, DC. At <citizenhearing.org>.

Good, Tim. 1998. Alien Base: Earth's Encounters with Extraterrestrials. London: Century Books.

Hind, Angela. 2005. "Abduction, Alienation and Reason." BBC Radio 4, June 8.

Huffington Post. 2013. "Richard French, Ex-Air Force Lt. Colonel, 'It Was A UFO And…There Were Aliens Aboard It.'" At <huffingtonpost.com/2013/05/13/alien-beings-repaired-und_n_3240437.html>.

Innis, Harold A. et al. (eds.). 1948. *Simeon Perkins*, vol. 3. Toronto: Champlain Society.

Jane's Defence Weekly. 1992. "Denial and Disinformation." *Jane's Defence Weekly* 18, 24/25, December 12.

Kuhn, Thomas. 1962. *The Structure of Scientific Revolutions*. Chicago: University of Chicago Press.

Lagarde, Ferdinand. 1968. Article in *Flying Saucer Review* 14(6).

LaViolette, Paul A. 2008. Secrets of Antigravity Propulsion: Tesla, UFOs, and Classified Aerospace. Rochester, VT: Inner Traditions / Bear & Co.

Ledger, Don. 2007. *Maritime UFO Files*. Halifax: Nimbus Publishing.

Ledger, Don and Chris Styles. 2001. *Dark Object*. New York: Dell Books.

Mack, John E. 1996. "Studying Intrusions from the Subtle Realm: How Can We Deepen Our Knowledge?" Paper presented at the MUFON Symposium, Greensborough, North Carolina.

———. 1994. *Abduction*. Bantam Books.

———. 1992. "The UFO Phenomenon: What Does It Mean for the Expansion of Human Consciousness?" Paper presented at the International Transpersonal Association Conference, Prague, Czechoslovakia, June.

REFERENCES

MacLeod, Ray. 1967. "Could Be Something Concrete in Shag Harbour UFO." *Halifax Chronicle-Herald*, October 7.

McClelland, Susan. "UFOs...Seriously." *Maclean's*. 2001. August 13.

McDonald, James. 1969. "Science in Default: Twenty-Two Years of Inadequate UFO Investigations." Paper presented at the Symposium of the American Association for the Advancement of Science, Tucson, Arizona.

Meares, John. 1967. Voyages Made in the Years 1788 and 1789, from China to the North West Coast of America. Orig. pub. 1790. New York: Da Capo Press.

Michalak, Stephen. 1967. *My Encounter with the UFO*. Winnipeg: Osnova Publications.

Mitchell, John. 1969. *The View Over Atlantis*. New York: HarperCollins.

Perl, M. 1956. "The Gravitic Situation." Technical report published by Gravity Rand Ltd., a division of Aviation Studies, London. December.

Persinger, Michael A. and John Derr. 1985. "Geophysical Variables and Behavior: Predicting Details of Visitor Experiences and the Personality of Experients." *Psychological Reports* 68, 55.

Persinger Michael A. and Gyslaine Lafreniere. 1977. *Space-time Transients and Unusual Events*. Chicago, IL: Nelson-Hall.

Pritchard, Andrea, David E. Pritchard, John E. Mack, Pam Kasey, and Claudia Yapp (eds.). 1994. *Alien Discussions: Proceedings of the Abduction Study Conference*. Cambridge, MA: North Cambridge Press.

Randle, Kevin. 2000. The Randle Report: UFOs in the '90s. New York: Evans & Company.

Randles, Jenny. 1983. *UFO Reality*. London: Robert Hale Ltd.

Robertson, Marianne. 1991. The Chestnut Pipe: Folklore of Shelburne County. Halifax: Nimbus Publishing.

Russian Today, July 21, 2009. "Russian Navy UFO recoreds say aliens love oceans". At <http://rt.com/news/russian-navy-ufo-records-say-aliens-love-oceans/>

Rutkowski, Chris A. and Geoff Dittman. 2006. The Canadian UFO Report: The Best Cases Revealed. Toronto: Dundurn.

Sanderson, Ivan. 1970. *Invisible Residents*. Cleveland: The World Pub. Co.

Smith, Wilbert. 1950. *Geomantics*. Ottawa: Department of Transport.

Styles, Chris. 2002. "UFOs & Reality Transformation." Paper presented at the MUFON International Symposium.

———. 1996. "Shag Harbour in Perspective." Paper presented at the MUFON International Symposium.

Talbert, E.A. 1955a. "New Air Dream-Planes Flying Outside Gravity." *New York Herald Tribune*, November 22.

———. 1955b. "Space Ship Marvel Seen if Gravity is Outwitted." *New York Herald Tribune*, November 21.

———. 1955c. "Conquest of Gravity Aim of Top Scientists in US." *New York Herald Tribune*, November 20.

Tonnies, Mac. 2010. The Cryptoterrestrials: A Meditation on Indigenous Humanoids and the Aliens Among Us. San Antonio, TX: Anomalist Books.

Vallee, Jacques. 1979. Messengers of Deception: UFO Contacts and Cults. San Francisco: Ronin Publishers.

———. 1975. The Invisible College: What a Group of Scientists Has Discovered About UFO Influences on the Human Race. Boston: E.P. Dutton.

———. 1969. Passport to Magonia: From Folklore to Flying Saucers. Chicago, IL: Publ. Henry Regnery Co.

Printed in Great Britain
by Amazon